I0748812

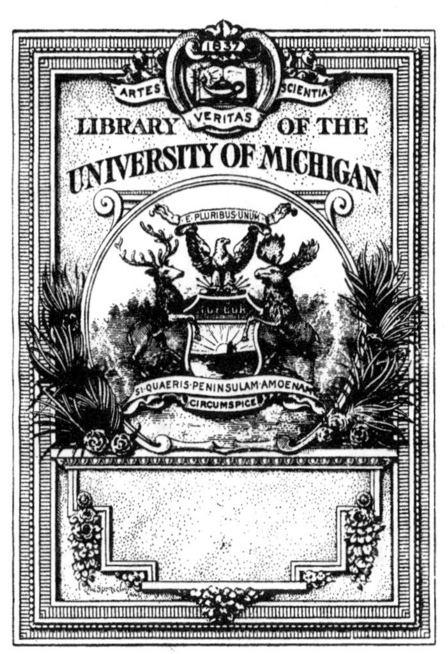
1837
ARTES
VERITAS
SCIENTIA
LIBRARY OF THE
UNIVERSITY OF MICHIGAN
E PLURIBUS UNUM
TUEBOR
SI QUAERIS PENINSULAM AMOENAM
CIRCUMSPICE

LETTERS

ON

CLERICAL MANNERS AND HABITS:

ADDRESSED TO

A STUDENT

IN THE

Theological Seminary,

AT PRINCETON, N. J.

BY SAMUEL MILLER, D. D.

A NEW EDITION, REVISED.

PHILADELPHIA:
PRESBYTERIAN BOARD OF PUBLICATION.

CONTENTS.

LETTER IV.

LETTER V.

LETTER VI.

LETTER VII.

LETTER VIII.

LETTERS

ON

CLERICAL MANNERS, &c.

LETTER I.

Thus saith the Lord of hosts, Consider your ways. — HAGGAI i. 5.

INTRODUCTORY.

MY DEAR YOUNG FRIEND:—You are soon, with the permission of Providence, to enter the pulpit, and to engage in the active duties of that profession, which, however undervalued by the worldly and the unbelieving, cannot fail of being regarded by every friend of Christ, as the most truly honourable and important under heaven. For this profession I trust you have the most essential of all qualifications; I mean unfeigned, vital piety. If I had any serious doubt as to this point, much as I respect your other endowments, and favourably as I augur of your capacity for the work of public instruction, I could not in conscience encourage you to take another step in your present pursuit.

But there is one qualification for the sacred office, in which, allow me with paternal freedom to say, you have always appeared to me to be defective. Whatever pleasure your friends may have felt in contemplating your respectable talents, your theological acquirements, and your laudable zeal for the advancement of the Redeemer's kingdom, they have been often pained to observe that, in what is called knowledge of the world, and in conformity to those habits of propriety and delicacy which are commonly established in cultivated society, you manifest a deficiency rather remarkable: — a deficiency which has often excited surprise in many who are acquainted with your good qualities; and which, if allowed to continue, will undoubtedly interfere in no small degree with your ministerial usefulness. Of this fact you are probably not sensible; for if you were, such is my impression of your conscientious desire to be useful, that I doubt not you would apply yourself with immediate and exemplary diligence to remedy the evil. Nay perhaps you may be unwilling to believe that the fact is so, even when assured of it. But let not self-flattery blind you to the truth, however mortifying. There is real need of your directing particular attention to this point. It is not a mere ideal deficiency of which I speak. What your most partial friends generally agree in noticing, must have some reality. Recollect, too, that this is a subject on which none but very intimate friends will ever venture to address you. If you were to make a blunder in conversation, as to a point of grammar, or of history, any common friend might be expected to give you some hint of your delinquency. But if you were every day to fall into some offence against the delicacy of polished manners, there is not one friend in a hundred that would take the liberty to intimate it to you. There is something so unpardonably offensive to most people in suggesting to them that they are deficient in good breeding, that very few will venture on the friendly office, even with their most intimate friends. It is no proof then that the imputation of which I speak is groundless, because you may not have heard it spoken of by those around you. If those who know you best, and love you most, are not respectfully listened to on such a subject, you cannot expect, from its very nature, to hear of it from any other quarter. I have known, in the course of my life, several excellent men, whose manners were, in various respects, so extremely faulty, and even disgusting, that they were objects of ridicule, and, in some instances, almost of scorn, wherever they went. Their good qualities, though many and striking, were absolutely lost sight of, on account of the prominence of two or three ridiculous foibles. By means of these their usefulness was not only impeded, but in a great measure destroyed. And all this, because they were unconscious of the evil themselves, or at least, of the extent of it: and their friends had not been faithful enough to apprize them of that which all who conversed with them saw and deplored, and which a little attention and resolution, especially if applied in early life, might have effectually corrected.

I am aware that many very worthy men entertain strong prejudices against all formal precepts or exhortations on the subject of manners, and are ready to consider them as worse than useless. These prejudices arise from various sources.

In some they are the result of ignorance. Many pious, conscientious men, and even some clergymen, are so totally ignorant of the world; so unacquainted with the most obvious and established proprieties of life; and so little aware how greatly a striking defect, as to this point, affects any man's acceptance and usefulness in society, that when they hear the subject introduced as a matter of serious discussion, they consider it as beneath their attention. Prejudices arising from such a source are, surely, unworthy of respect. As well might we allow the judgment of the profoundly illiterate man to weigh against learning. He despises or undervalues that of which he is not a competent judge; while those who are the best judges, that is, who themselves possess the accomplishment in question, and who have had the most ample opportunity of witnessing its influence and value, have always been found to estimate it most highly. I never met with a man of tolerable manners himself, who did not consider the subject as very important, and worthy of the diligent attention of every one who desired to be acceptable and useful to his fellow men.

The prejudices of others against every attempt to regulate and polish clerical manners, seem to arise from that eccentricity, or, as I would rather call it, that affectation of singularity, which prompts them to delight in those manners which are strange and peculiar, and to look with a sort of contempt on all rules of behaviour. There are persons, and even ministers of the gospel, who love to be singular; who take pleasure and pride in being thought above the ordinary laws of social intercourse: who, of course, violate those laws without ceremony; and make no scruple of indulging in what they know to be considered as rough, offensive manners. The miserable vanity of being thought independent, of setting at defiance public sentiment, makes them entirely undervalue, for themselves, every code of rules of which the object is to make them act like civilized people. And not content with this, they endeavour to pour ridicule on every attempt either to form or enforce such a system in regard to others. When weak or wicked men allow themselves to take this ground, it is little to be wondered at, and will probably do little mischief: but when good men permit themselves to assume so absurd a position, they know not what they do. The consequences cannot fail to be injurious, and sometimes to a deplorable extent.

But a still larger class, I suspect, are prejudiced against all such discussion as that to which I would request your attention, from an entire misapprehension of the object aimed at in such discussion. Many have seen so much of the affectation and folly of false pretensions to politeness; and heard so much of the hollow, insincere system of artificial manners inculcated by Lord Chesterfield, and others, of the same school, who have sometimes appeared willing to sacrifice every substantial quality at the shrine of "the graces;"—that they have conceived a disgust at every thing like rules or precepts on the subject of manners. And whenever they hear the subject mentioned, they take for granted that the object aimed at is that courtly polish, that graceful and punctilious adjustment of smiles, bows, dress, and minute attentions, which form so large a part of the Chesterfieldian code. Nothing, my dear young friend, is more remote from my purpose than the adoption of this exceptionable, and, in some of its parts, profligate system. For, although it certainly embraces many precepts and suggestions which are worthy of the attention of every man who wishes to be acceptable in well-bred society, it also embraces much, very much, which no Christian can regard but with unmingled abhorrence. It has been, indeed, not unjustly said, by some one, that the "Letters to his Son," of that far-famed nobleman, inculcate "the morals of a prostitute, and the manners of a dancing-master." This is all true; and no one reprobates the spirit, and many of the details, of those "Letters" more heartily than he who addresses you. Still, however, let us not indulge in prejudice against a whole subject, because it has been weakly or wickedly treated. Let us not imagine that it is unworthy of our serious regard, because perverted and corrupt views of it have been sometimes taken. No man in his senses considers the use of our daily food as improper or unnecessary, because the votaries of sensual indulgence have ransacked all the stores of ingenious refinement, to pamper the appetite, and gratify the palate, and have sometimes employed the most shameful means to accomplish their object.

Let me entreat you, then, to recollect, that when I earnestly recommend to you the cultivation of proper clerical manners, it is by no means my purpose to recommend those starched, artificial, formal manners, which display constant effort and constraint; or those ostentatious, splendid, and gracefully refined manners, which are formed upon mere worldly principles; which qualify their possessor to make a distinguished figure in a ball-room, or at the levee of a great man, and which manifest that he has studied Chesterfield more than his Bible. So far from this is my aim, that I am persuaded, many persons who pass for well-bred, and even highly bred, in such scenes, are among the most disgusting and troublesome, and, of course, among the worst-bred people in the world. But my object is to recommend those manners which become the Christian gentleman; which naturally flow from the meekness, gentleness, purity, and benevolence of our holy religion; and which both the precepts and examples of the Bible equally recommend.

There are others, who, whenever we speak of appropriate clerical manners, consider us as designing to recommend that habitual restraint and sanctimoniousness of demeanor, which approaches to a sort of professional dissimulation. They suppose that, in the formation of clerical character, there are certain glosses and concealments which clerical policy requires to be studied, and which are intended to deepen and extend their impression on the popular mind. And, therefore, whenever they hear of precepts and advices to candidates for the ministry, in relation to this subject, they regard them as making an attempt to initiate them into the *mysteries* of their profession, by which their reign over the minds of men may be more effectually maintained. This seems to be the prevailing opinion of infidels; and also of all those professed friends to the Christian ministry, who, being in a great measure regardless of spiritual living, and holy example themselves, are apt to refer to affectation, and even to hypocrisy, every thing which would establish a system of deportment more retiring, serious, and self-denied, than their own. Such artificial manners, it must be owned, have not been uncommon among ecclesiastics in certain parts and ages of the world. But they will be regarded with unmingled abhorrence by every honest man, to say nothing of Christian principle. I can only say, that I neither plead nor wish for any thing of this kind. My object is by no means to help you to weave a "professional cloak," for the purpose of covering mental imbecility, corrupt practice, or sinister design. It is not to recommend a buckram dress, for the purpose of repelling familiarity, or inspiring with awe. But, simply, to help you to *appear*, what you ought to *be*, — a pious, benevolent, amiable man; respectfully attentive to the welfare and comfort of all around you; and seeking, habitually and supremely, to promote the best interest of mankind.

By *good manners*, then, I beg you will understand me to mean those manners which Christian purity and benevolence recommend, and which, where those graces reign, they will ever be found substantially to produce. Dr. Witherspoon, in his "Letters on Education," while strongly urging the utility and importance of polished manners, remarks, that "true religion is not only consistent with, but necessary to, the perfection of true politeness;" and fortifies his opinion by "a noble sentiment," as he calls it, of the Prince of Conti, viz. that "worldly politeness is no more than an imitation or imperfect copy of Christian charity, being the pretence, or outward appearance, of that deference to the judgment, and attention to the interest of others, which a true Christian has as the rule of his life, and the disposition of his heart." And, truly, we have only need to see an example of that unaffected kindness, affability, respectfulness, gentleness, and attention to the feelings and comfort of all around us, which real religion at once demands and inspires, united with the gravity, dignity, and prudence becoming those who remember that for every word and action they must give an account; — we have only, I say, to see this happy union of qualities fairly exemplified in human deportment, to be convinced that nothing can be more nobly beautiful or attractive, in the view of every thinking beholder, than the undissembled expression of pure Christian feeling: and, of course, that to be an humble and assiduous imitator of Christ is the shortest way for a minister of the gospel, or any other man, to exhibit the most perfect manners of which our nature is capable.

So much for the general principle. Cultivate the Christian temper, and you will always, in precisely the same proportion, lay the best and the only true foundation for the manners which I recommend. But if you wish to reduce this great principle to practice, two things are to be remembered.

The first is, that, as the growth of Christian principle, in the individual heart, is a gradual process; as it is by no means a spontaneous affair, but requires the most assiduous and laborious culture; so the drawing out of that principle into all the practical duties of life is far from being an easy task. It requires unceasing self-denial, prayer, and watchfulness; and embraces a large class of duties, which cannot be expected to be developed, in all their relations and aspects, without being made the object of diligent and daily attention. Our pride, our vanity, our selfishness, our envy, our irascible feelings, our indolence, and indeed every corruption of our nature, are all so many obstacles to the faithful discharge of these duties. It happens, moreover, that the application of Christian principle to the various departments of social intercourse, in all their interesting and delicate details; in other words, the code of what may be called Christian morals, has been less happily illustrated and enforced by books than any other part of Christian truth or duty. In its leading outlines, indeed, it has been often and well exhibited: but the task of minutely filling up what the scriptures have so divinely sketched, has never yet, unless I greatly mistake, been satisfactorily performed. And yet, perhaps, there is no subject, which, on a variety of accounts, requires to be exhibited in more minute detail, or urged with more constant reiteration than this. Still no popular, adequate treatise on this subject, so far as I know, is to be found. And, of course, those who desire to attain excellence in this department of duty, have the greater need to study it carefully for themselves, and to embrace every opportunity of becoming more and more at home in its requisitions.

The second consideration which deserves our notice is, that many of those delicate proprieties of behaviour, which the laws of social intercourse demand, though founded, in general, on Christian principle, may be considered as, in part, the result of conventional agreement among well-bred people. Of course, to be adequately acquainted with them, requires no small knowledge of the world, as well as knowledge of the Bible, and of other good books. That young man will find himself egregiously deceived, who imagines that he can gain in his study all the information that is necessary on this subject. This would be just as unreasonable as to find any one expecting to attain eminence as a military commander, without ever seeing a field of battle. You must be acquainted with the actual world. You must see and study man as he is. You must become acquainted with the rules which regulate social intercourse, as exemplified in polished Christian society. You must even become acquainted with "the world which lieth in wickedness," and know something of the laws which govern the intercourse of those who make no profession of religion, that you may know how to understand and treat them; how to meet them on their own ground, and to adopt the best methods of conciliating and gaining them. You must not, for a moment, suppose that what is called a knowledge of the world, necessarily implies conformity to it. All that it implies, and all that I would recommend, is such an acquaintance with the assemblage of *facts* in relation to this subject, as will enable you to adopt them where they are good, or indifferent; to avoid them where they cannot be defended; and to make the whole subservient to the interest of your divine Master.

Do you ask me, how the "knowledge of the world," of which I speak, is to be obtained? I answer,—Not from books; they cannot teach it; though they may make useful suggestions, and may put you on the proper track for learning, which alone is the humble office I assign to this little volume. — Neither can parents always teach it; for frequently they possess it not themselves; and even when they do possess it, it is incomparably more difficult to be conveyed to others, than any species of book knowledge that can be named. Nor is it to be learned even by going continually into society, as many have done, who, nevertheless, were as ignorant of mankind at the end of a long life, as they were when they entered on their course. — But if you desire to learn it, you must, first of all, be in good earnest in paying close attention to the subject. You must feel its importance. While you study carefully the best examples left on record in the sacred scriptures, you must study, with no less care, the living and acting world around you. You must have an eye and an ear on the watch for instruction respecting it, every day that you live, and in every company that you enter. You must watch with especial vigilance, every part of the manners, deportment, and conversation of the wise, the virtuous and the polished with whom you may happen to associate from time to time. The true reason why so many are in the world, and even, sometimes, in the polite and great world, for threescore years together, without gaining a particle of what we call real "knowledge of the world," — no doubt is, that they have always passed along through society either with so much levity and inattention, or with so much hebetude of feeling, as to this particular point, that they have observed nothing, and, of course, learned nothing. They have, therefore, closed their career, in old age, just as ignorant, in this respect, as they were in the tenderest boyhood. In short, if men have not the knack of closely observing, and the faculty also of laying up their experience, and profiting by their observation, I know of no way in which they can hope to become tolerable adepts in the science of human nature, however ample and long continued the external advantages which they may enjoy.

Do you ask me, of what real importance, after all, well regulated and polished manners can be, to a man engaged in an employment so elevated and momentous as that of a minister of the gospel? Is it not a matter, perhaps you will inquire, rather too small to engage the attention of one, whose time and talents ought to be occupied about much more exalted things? That a clergyman ought not, and, consistently with his usefulness, cannot, have manners either glaringly ridiculous, or grossly offensive, you will say, you allow: but where is the great advantage of pushing the cultivation of the exterior beyond this negative character? I have often heard suggestions of this kind; but am deliberately of the opinion that they are founded in false and narrow views of human nature, and of human society.

For, in the first place, with respect to large numbers of those with whom clergymen, as well as others, are called to associate, they look quite as much, if not more, to manners than to solid worth. They are poor judges of talents, learning, prudence, and even piety; but of easy, mild, respectful, amiable manners, every one is a judge; and, of course, every one is capable of being favourably impressed by them. Can there be, then, a more obvious dictate both of policy and duty, than to cultivate that which to multitudes is more attractive than real merit; which secures to merit a hearing and an influence which it would not otherwise obtain; and which will be likely, in many cases, to open a door to usefulness, which, without it, would, in all probability, have continued impenetrably closed? In repeated instances, have I known men of weak minds, and of small information, but of remarkably fascinating manners, carry all before them, in circles of society, into which men of far higher qualifications, both intellectual and moral, but defective in the attractions of manner, were scarcely able to obtain admittance. A soft, insinuating address has, a thousand times, rendered its possessor triumphant, when, upon every principle of truth and justice, he ought to have failed.

But, in the second place, it is not only true that, in very large portions of society, a well regulated manner is every thing, atoning for the want both of virtue and knowledge, and frequently superseding the highest worth; but it has more influence, even with the most discerning and virtuous, than is commonly imagined. To every human being, that which is intrinsically excellent appears doubly attractive when presented in a pleasing manner. Truth, even to those who know it to be truth, finds a more cordial welcome; and duty, even among its most sincere and enlightened friends, commands a more ready obedience, when they are clothed in an attractive garb, and speak in alluring accents. That the very same words, which, when uttered by some, are intolerably offensive, when spoken in the mild respectful manner of others, are welcome and even delightful; that the very same action, which, performed by some, is censured, when performed by others, of perhaps less talent or virtue, is lauded to excess, are among the most notorious facts in human life; and that, not in the circles of the ignorant and unprincipled only, but also in those of the most estimable portions of mankind.

How is it possible, then, for a thinking man to consider the subject on which I address you as unworthy of his regard, or as even of small importance? To adopt this opinion is equally to oppose reason and experience, and to set at naught some of the most precious means of gaining access to the human heart.

Let me entreat you to remember, too, that those who bear the office to which you aspire, stand more peculiarly in need of the aid which polished and attractive manners furnish, than any other class of men. To them the use of "carnal weapons" is interdicted. They neither have, nor ought to have, as ministers, any other influence in society, than that which arises from the sacredness of their office, the excellence of their character, and the attraction of their manners. It is their great business to win men to the love of the truth and of duty by moral means, and among others, by exhibiting in their own temper and lives, the meek, lowly, amiable, and benevolent spirit of the religion which they inculcate. If they fail of doing this, they fail in one of the most important means of professional success. And yet it is plain that every minister must essentially fail here who does not succeed in setting forth, in his own person, a style of manners adapted to conciliate the respect and good will of all whom he approaches.

And when I recollect how extremely important

the first steps of a young minister are; at how early and inexperienced an age he frequently enters on his public work; how much depends on the character of his habits and manners when he is least sensible of the fact; and how completely he may prostrate his dignity, and foreclose his usefulness, by a few ridiculous foibles, or inadvertent habits, of the existence of which it would be sometimes difficult to convince him: — I say, when I recollect all these things, I am astonished that candidates for the ministry think so little of this matter, and are so little concerned to form a style of manners, which may be conducive, at once, to their comfort and usefulness.

Allow me further, my dear young friend, to remark, that if you wish to succeed in forming such manners as it is the object of these pages to recommend, you must begin early and labour patiently; otherwise, you will never make the attainment. As the discipline of the temper and feelings ought to be commenced with the earliest dawn of reason, and is the work of a lifetime; so the discipline of the manners, if the expression may be allowed, depending, as it does, for success on "ruling our spirits," should be begun as early as possible; the sooner the better. Say not, it is too soon for you to begin to "put on the clergyman," when you are only in the second year of your theological studies. Let me tell you, my friend, if you begin now, and labour in this species of culture with the utmost assiduity, I shall consider you as doing great things if you succeed in forming even tolerable clerical manners by the time you are ready to enter the pulpit. It is, as I have already said, a gradual work. In the conflict with your old habits, and your unhallowed feelings, you will have many a painful struggle, and will probably suffer many a discouraging defeat. It will be much if you ultimately gain the victory. If you are so happy, you will find it to be no easy conquest. But, when gained, it will be the most glorious and the most precious of all victories — *a victory over yourself.*

You will perceive that my counsel extends beyond the time that you propose to spend in the Theological Seminary, and, indeed, will apply, in some of its parts, to the whole of your clerical life, should it be ever so long. This was expressly intended. It occurred to me that a little manual, addressed to one of those who bear to me the relation of pupils, adapted to promote his benefit, not only while he continues in the institution of which I am an officer, but when he shall have taken his leave of it, nay, as long as he lives, might, at the same time, if given through the medium of the press, be of some use to others, to whom I have had, and may yet have, the honour and the pleasure to stand in the same relation; not merely in the beginning, but throughout the whole of their course. And if the following pages should be blessed, in the smallest degree, to your advantage, or that of any other individual, in preparing for a profession which I love, I shall consider myself as abundantly rewarded.

I will only add, that in preparing this little system of advices, I have by no means forgotten how small my title is to assume the office of teacher on such a subject. It is a maxim in physical science, that a stream can never, in ordinary circumstances, rise higher than its fountain. If I thought this maxim applied as rigidly to intellectual and moral culture, I should lay down my pen in despair: or rather, I should not have dared to take it up for the purpose of discussing a subject at once so delicate and difficult. But it does not. Nothing is more common than to see pupils rising far higher than their instructors in knowledge and practical wisdom. This thought comforts and animates me in the undertaking. My office having placed me in the way of perceiving how greatly a body of precepts and suggestions on this subject is needed—having never seen any thing which appeared to me to approach toward answering the purpose in view—knowing that all that many ingenuous youth need to put them on the right track, is a collection of hints, for setting their own minds at work—and hoping that what is "sown in weakness," may be "raised in power," I venture to make the attempt which the title of these letters announces. May our common Master accept and bless it!

LETTER II.

See that ye walk circumspectly, not as fools, but as wise. — EPH. v. 15.

GENERAL CHARACTERISTICS OF CLERICAL MANNERS.

MY DEAR YOUNG FRIEND: — In pursuing the subject introduced to your view in the preceding letter, a question presents itself, which seems to require some discussion, before we proceed to the details which are intended to occupy the following pages. The question is this — Is there any thing peculiar in the style of manners proper for a minister of the gospel? Ought the manners of a clergyman perceptibly to differ from those of a well-bred man of a secular profession? I think they ought. That is to say, I am clearly of the opinion that they ought to bear a stamp, in a variety of particulars, characteristic of the hallowed spirit and sacred office with which they are connected. All other professional men, indeed, would be the better for having the same sort of manners that I am about to recommend to ministers of the gospel; but with respect to the latter, they are so indispensably necessary to the complete attainment of all those advantages which manners can impart to their possessor, that they may be said, without impropriety, to be peculiarly clerical in their nature.

If I were to attempt to exhibit the peculiarity in question, I should say it may be expressed in six words — Dignity, Gentleness, Condescension, Affability, Reserve, and Uniformity.

1. *Dignity.* By this I mean that happy mixture of gravity and elevation in human deportment, which evinces a mind habitually thoughtful, serious, and set on high things. An air and manner opposed to levity; opposed to that propensity to jesting, which is so often manifested by some who bear the sacred office; opposed to what is grovelling; opposed, in short, to every species of lightness or volatility, which, however tolerated in young persons of secular professions, is barely tolerated, even in them, and certainly adds nothing to their respectability in the view of any one: but which, in ministers of the gospel, is peculiarly unseemly, and never fails to lower the estimation in which they are held by all discerning people. I have often thought, my young friend, that you were by far too ready to give way to your risible feelings. Every public man, and especially every clergyman, ought to cultivate that habitual sedateness, and command of his countenance, which will prevent his being the sport of every ludicrous occurrence, or merry-andrew, who may happen to be presented to his view.

The dignity of which I speak also requires its possessor to avoid those companies, in which language and scenes are likely to be exhibited, which ought not to be even witnessed by a minister of the gospel. If any thing of this kind be expected in a company before it assembles, a minister ought to decline making one of its number. And if, after he has joined it, there be any indication of the approach of such scenes, he ought to take an early opportunity of escaping before they actually make their appearance. Even dining or tea parties, in which any thing like the reign of levity, and especially of revelry, is anticipated, ought to be invariably shunned by an ambassador of Christ. That you will not allow yourself to be present at places in which cards or dancing are made a part of the professed and prominent entertainment, I take for granted. But I will go further. When you are invited even to what are called family parties, and you find either cards or dancing about to be introduced, though it be on the smallest scale, and in the most domestic way, make a point of withdrawing. It is, on all accounts, better to be absent. When a clergyman allows himself to be found in the midst of exhibitions of this nature, though he take no part in them, yet, if he have a proper sense of Christian and ministerial duty, he will be more or less embarrassed; and, if he attempt to be faithful in reproof or remonstrance, may, perhaps, do more harm than good. Many a minister of Christ, in these circumstances, has been involved in conflicts, in the course of which his feelings have been lacerated, his dignity lowered, and his comfort wounded in no small degree. Lay it down as a fixed principle, that you cannot possibly be in light, frivolous company, or where frivolous engagements are going on, even if there be no other mischief, without having your dignity impaired. If the gravity and respectability of your character do not prevent every thing unseemly, or approaching to it, from occurring, it is no place for you. How much better is it, with a wise caution, to avoid, as far as possible, all such embarrassing places and companies! "The prudent man foreseeth the evil, and hideth himself."

The dignity of which I speak should also prevent ministers, however youthful, from engaging in many of those recreations, which may not be unsuitable for others, but in which one, who is officially bound to be grave, ought not to indulge. If you happen to be thrown into young company, and any of the little plays, which are frequently resorted to by youth of both sexes, for passing away time, happen to be introduced, it will be by no means proper that you take any part in them. However admissible such plays may be for children, or for those who are just rising above the age of children, a minister, or a candidate for the holy ministry, ought to be more gravely and appropriately employed.

Again; the dignity of manner which I wish to inculcate, may be impaired by various little infelicities of deportment into which those who are not prudently and delicately on their guard, may be betrayed. I have known worthy men, who had so little knowledge of human nature, and so little sense of propriety, that they suffered themselves to be involved in angry contention with ostlers, with stage-drivers, with boatmen, and other coarse and vulgar men, with whom they were brought in contact. Carefully avoid every thing of this sort. Rather suffer wrong, than run the risk of a public conflict with those who are generally rude and foul-mouthed, and too often altogether lawless. It is unbecoming enough for any grave man to be involved in such controversies; but for a clergyman, it is peculiarly unbecoming. I might not always estimate his talents; but I should certainly always estimate his personal dignity by observing the degree of care and vigilance with which he avoided rencounters of this kind.

Further; when I speak of dignified manners in a minister of the gospel, I refer to that character of deportment which is opposed to littleness, not to say meanness, in his dealings. There is often found, in this respect, in some ministers, otherwise men of great excellence, a striking want of just taste and delicacy. They can higgle and chaffer about a cent, with almost as much pertinacity as might be expected from a beggar. They can resort to as many petty arts for gaining a favourable bargain, even in the smallest affair, as if dexterity in dealing were their trade. And, even with the poorest individuals with whom they deal, they are ready to contend about a trifle with the most determined obstinacy. In short, I have known men of the sacred profession, in whom the rage for little savings, in all their pecuniary transactions, appeared to be a besetting infirmity, and to follow them through their whole course, and on some occasions led them to exhibit themselves in a point of light altogether unworthy of their office. In making these remarks, I have no design to censure that habitual, and even rigid economy, which must, of necessity, and certainly ought to be practised, by those whose circumstances are narrow, and who have no means of enlarging them; and this is probably the case with a majority of those who devote themselves to the service of the church. In all such, a constant care to guard against unnecessary expenditure is not only allowable, but is, doubtless, a Christian duty. But there is a wide difference between this, and conducting pecuniary expenditures, when we resolve to incur them, in a pitiful manner; a manner which indicates a mind inordinately set on the most paltry gains and savings. I remember once to have received a very unfavourable impression of a clergyman, on observing that he employed a considerable portion of precious time, and expended no small share of ingenuity, in recovering from a particular friend five cents, when he had just received from that friend what was of more value than ten times that amount.

Again; the dignity which I recommend, is opposed to all those arts in social intercourse, which, though not really crooked or disingenuous, yet approach the confines of what is so, and may possibly be liable, with some, to that imputation. Make it a sacred point never to engage in any covert or questionable course of action. Let both your speech and your conduct be always so perfectly fair, candid and honourable, that the more they are scrutinized, the more perfectly correct and creditable they will appear. Never venture, in any case, or for the purpose of gratifying any person whatever, to do or say that which, if it should become fully known to the public, would place your character in an undesirable point of light. Even if the disclosure of it be very far from fixing the charge of dishonesty upon you; yet if it may expose you to the charge of littleness, of imprudence, of paltry management, or of undignified interference in the affairs of others, you will furnish matter of regret to every serious friend of clerical character.

I will only add, that another characteristic and advantage of dignity in manners, is, that, when properly exercised, it tends to repress the risings, and repel the approaches of impertinence. I have seen many men in whose presence it was impossible to take any improper liberty. Not because they were haughty, overbearing, or sanctimonious; but because there was such a mixture of gravity, respectfulness, and benevolence in their whole air and manner, that the impertinent, the frivolous, and, of course, the profane, were abashed in approaching them. "There is something defective," says the eloquent Wm. Jay, "especially in a minister, unless his character produces an atmosphere around him, which is felt as soon as entered. It is not enough for him to have courage to reprove certain things; he should have dignity enough to prevent them; and he will, if the Christian be commensurate with the preacher, and if he 'walk worthy of God, who hath called us into his kingdom and glory.'"*

2. *Gentleness.* By this you will readily perceive to be meant that habitual mildness of disposition, and softness of manner, which carefully guard against every thing, in speech or behaviour, adapted unnecessarily to offend or to give uneasiness. It is opposed to every kind of harshness or undue severity, and forms a deportment calculated to conciliate and attract all to whom it is manifested. You, doubtless, remember that this disposition, and the corresponding expressions of it, are represented in scripture as

* Life of Winter, p. 299.

among the fruits of the Spirit. "The wisdom that is from above," says the apostle James, "is gentle." And the apostle Paul, speaking particularly of ministers, says, "The servant of the Lord must not strive, but be gentle unto all men, patient, in meekness instructing those that oppose themselves."

I am aware, indeed, that gentleness has been confounded by many with something very different, and by no means laudable. It has been considered and despised, as that tame, passive spirit, which knows not how to deny the most unreasonable request, or to resist the most unjust encroachment. There cannot, however, be a greater mistake. Some of the firmest men in the maintenance of their own principles that I have ever seen, were remarkable for the mildness and gentleness of their manners. Perhaps it may even be said, that those who have been most distinguished for the exercise of courage, as a moral quality, have been, at the same time, the most signal examples of bland and accommodating deportment. "True gentleness," says one, "is to be carefully distinguished from the mean spirit of cowards, and the fawning assent of sycophants. It renounces no just right from fear; it gives up no important truth from flattery. It is, indeed, not only consistent with a firm mind, but it necessarily requires a manly spirit, and a fixed principle, in order to give it any real value. It stands opposed to harshness and severity, to pride and arrogance, to violence and oppression. It is properly the manifestation of that part of charity which makes us unwilling to give pain to any of our brethren. Compassion prompts us to relieve their wants: forbearance prevents us from retaliating their injuries: meekness restrains our angry passions: candour our severe judgments: but gentleness corrects whatever is offensive in our manners; and by a constant train of humane attentions, studies to alleviate the burden of human misery."

A conscientious man, who is habitually intent on doing good, will find occasion almost every hour that he spends in company, for the exercise of this invaluable spirit, and the deportment to which it prompts. The occasions are extremely few in the walks of social intercourse, in which a blunt, rough, or authoritative manner is either proper or profitable. Whereas, by a soft answer we may turn away wrath; by a mild, respectful address, we may at once reprove impertinence, disarm violence, and even put brutality to shame. By making a point of accosting all whom we approach with tones as well as expressions of a kindly and conciliatory character, we may often open a way for the reception of truth into minds which might have been otherwise invincibly closed against it. Learn, then, the happy art of conversing with gentleness, of giving your commands with gentleness, of arguing with gentleness, of contending with gentleness, of even reproving with gentleness, that is, of guarding against every thing harsh, passionate, or boisterous in your mode of administering reproof. Nay, do not think it strange if I go further still, and recommend that you cultivate gentleness in all your actions and movements; in walking; in changing your place in the parlour; in opening and shutting doors, and in all similar actions. There is more dignity in this mode of conducting our movements than in any other. There is also more safety; for a very large part of the casualties by which our persons are injured, are, doubtless, induced by the want of gentleness. Can it be considered as becoming to see a grave divine skipping about with the impetuosity of a boy; slamming doors as if in a passion; jerking chairs and other movables, which he may have occasion to handle, as if snatching them from robbers; or passing along the streets with that kind of military air and rapid step, which might be expected in one who was walking for a wager?

3. *Condescension.* If you live to be a minister, a large part of your social and professional intercourse will be with those who, according to popular language, are your inferiors. To the poor, the deserted, the friendless, the afflicted, if you possess the spirit of Christ, your attention will be incessant and unwearied. It is, therefore, of peculiar importance that you acquire the art of treating such persons in a manner best adapted to soothe their feelings, inspire their confidence, and win their affections. This can be done only by habits of condescension; that is, laying aside every thing like an air of haughtiness or superiority, and addressing them in the tones and language of benevolent respect. Guard against reminding them continually, by your looks and expressions, that you consider them as beneath you. Go to their dwellings as a friend and comforter. Listen with patient attention to their complaints and requests. Manifest, what you ought undoubtedly to feel, a readiness to serve them to the utmost of your power. Remember that your Master, while upon earth, was peculiarly attentive to the indigent and the miserable; and that the most tender

and condescending language that ever escaped from his lips, was addressed to such persons, or had a reference to them.

Let me entreat you not only to manifest quite as much alacrity in finding out the hovel of poverty, and the couch of suffering, as the mansion of the rich, and the table of feasting; but also, when you have found the abode of penury and affliction, to enter it in the kindliest manner; to accost every member of the humble circle with Christian respect and sympathy; to seat yourself by the bedside of the sick and dying with affectionate benevolence; to pour the light of instruction, and the oil of consolation into their minds with tenderness and patience; and to accommodate yourself, as your Master would have done, to all their wants, and ignorance, and darkness, and doubts, and trials. Receive their civilities with thanks. Accept of their homeliest fare with cordiality; and study to convince them, by every proper method, that you heartily wish them well, and are ready to do them good. Need I say that such things are grateful to them to a degree not easily expressed? One of the most excellent ministers I ever knew; a man of refinement and polish, as well as of ardent piety, exceeded most of my clerical acquaintance in his incessant attentions to the poor. He would go to the houses of the meanest and poorest, with an ease and freedom truly exemplary; would seat himself on a broken stool or block of wood, and appear to enjoy himself as if he were in the most convenient parlour; and would, with a singular felicity of manner, place those whom he addressed just as much at ease, as if they were conversing with an equal. It was in reference to him that a poor but eminently pious old woman said — "O, sir, you cannot think how kind and good he is. *He's not a bit of a gentleman.* He comes in, and sits down in my poor place here, just as if he had been used to being with the like of me all his days." Though I knew the venerable man to be a real and uncommonly well-bred gentleman, I was particularly struck with the old woman's significant language, "He's not a bit of a *gentleman;*" and thought it one of the highest compliments she could pay him. She had, no doubt, been accustomed to associate, in her own mind, that title with manners of the supercilious, revolting kind;—an association to which, I am sorry to say, the manners of many, who would be thought real gentlemen, give too much countenance.

4. *Affability.* This quality of manners is allied to the last mentioned characteristic, but still it is not the same. An affable man is one who may be approached and accosted without embarrassment or difficulty;—one who has the happy talent of conversing pleasantly and courteously, and of placing every one in conversation with him perfectly at his ease. The opposites of this quality are coldness, haughtiness, habits of taciturnity, arising from whatever cause, and, in short, every thing in manner that is adapted to repel, or to prevent freedom and comfort of approach. On the other hand, the dispositions which lead to affability of manner, are good-nature, benevolence, and that habitual kindness of feeling, which rejoices in the welfare of all, and especially of those who look to us for instruction, counsel, or any other benefit.

Now it is manifest that all classes of men, and especially of those who are commonly called professional men, would find great advantage in cultivating the affability of which I speak. In fact its advantages in conciliating public favour, and in facilitating social intercourse, are incalculable. But to the minister of the gospel, the importance of this social quality is peculiar. A physician or lawyer may be remarkably deficient in affability, and yet his professional reputation and even usefulness may sustain no material drawback on this account. But when a minister of the gospel is thus deficient, it may be maintained that his usefulness cannot fail of being, in all cases, proportionably diminished. He is not only called to visit "from house to house;" to address all classes of persons on the most important of all subjects; and to study to gain access to the minds of the high and the low, the rich and the poor, the learned and the ignorant; but all descriptions of persons are in the habit of resorting to him, in private as well as in public, for counsel and aid. The perplexed, the doubting, the timid, the feeble-minded, the tempted, the desponding, are all, it may be, in succession, seeking in him a counsellor and guide. How unhappy, when his personal manners are such as to repel and discourage! How unhappy, nay, in some cases, how fatal to the eternal interests of men, when instead of a manner which invites confidence, and inspires freedom of communication, the ambassador of Christ, by his repulsive mode of address, as it were "breaks the bruised reed," "quenches the smoking flax," or so completely chills and discourages the anxious inquirer, as to deter him from ever making a second visit! It is manifest, then, that by a remarkable deficiency in the quality under consideration, ministers will not only lose much in regard to public favour and acceptance; but what is infinitely more important, by this deficiency, they may be the means of repelling from the church of God many a soul who was on the road to salvation, and who, but for this cause, might, humanly speaking, have reached the blessed goal.

Say not that an affable man, like a poet, must be born, but cannot be made. That constitutional temperament has, in many cases, much to do with this thing, is not denied. But it is utterly denied that the faculty of which I speak is beyond the reach of successful cultivation. Only lay to heart the importance of the attainment, and strive and pray to be enabled to make it, and your labour will not be in vain. But there may be a mistake here. In attempting to be affable, be not fawning. In endeavouring to invite freedom and confidence, do not break down the barriers of the most perfect mutual respect. For, in order to form a complete finish in clerical manners, there must be a proper attention to that respect which is due to the man, and his office, as well as that which is due to those with whom he converses.

5. *Reserve.* By this I mean, not the opposite of frankness; but a manner standing opposed to excessive and unseasonable communicativeness. This is in no respect inconsistent with any thing which has been already recommended. The most attractive affability is not only quite reconcilable with a delicate and wise reserve; but really requires it, and

cannot be of the best character without it. There are many subjects on which a minister of the gospel ought not to allow himself, in ordinary cases, to talk with freedom, if at all; and, of course, concerning which, when they are introduced, he ought generally to exercise a strict reserve. Every wise man will see at once the reasons, and the importance of this counsel: especially in reference to one who bears so many interesting relations to those around him as a minister of religion. He ought certainly to be affable. But if by this he should understand to be meant, that he ought to talk freely, at all times, to all classes of people, and on all subjects, which the idle, the meddling, the impertinent, or the malignant may choose to introduce, he would soon find to his cost that he had totally misapprehended the matter. Affability is good, is important; but incessant and indiscriminate talkativeness will soon reduce in public esteem, and entangle in real difficulties, the official man who allows himself to indulge it.

There are many points concerning which every man who wishes to hold a respectable standing in society ought to exercise habitual reserve; but concerning which it is peculiarly important that ministers do so. A complete catalogue of them cannot be given; but good sense and prudence will enable you, for the most part, to see what ought to be considered as belonging to the list. You can be at no loss, however, to decide, that the private affairs of your neighbours; the characters, plans, and conduct of the absent; questions which implicate the principles and views of other religious denominations; the conflicts of party politicians; your own private concerns; the petty scandal of the neighbourhood; what others have communicated to you, in reference to delicate subjects, whether under the injunction of secrecy or not; your opinions concerning the passing events and persons of the day, unless in very clear and special cases; on all these and similar subjects, if you are wise you will exercise much reserve; nay you will seldom allow yourself to converse at all, even when all around you are chattering about them. You can seldom do any good by talking on such subjects. "Let the dead bury their dead." Your time and breath ought to be devoted to the discussion of subjects by which you will be likely to benefit yourself and others, and by which you will not be liable to be implicated in any difficulty hereafter.

It is the part of wisdom also to exercise much reserve as to the article of giving advice. It is not uncommon for your sanguine, precipitate men to give advice, even unasked; and to give it on all occasions, freely, when only slightly or indirectly solicited, and when, perhaps, they have a very imperfect, and altogether *ex-parte* knowledge of facts. This is never discreet. A truly benevolent man ought not to be, and will not be unwilling to incur the responsibility of giving advice, when he sees his way clear to do so, and when there is a probability of good being done by it. But to incur this responsibility, needlessly, with small information on the subject, and when there is but little hope of doing good, is both weak and rash. Many a man in a public station has greatly impaired his influence by a few instances of such indiscretion. In very many cases solicitations for advice, while they are kindly received, and respectfully treated, ought to be denied altogether. In many other cases, all that ought to be done is to state the *pros* and *cons* in the most impartial and luminous manner that we can, and having done so, to leave the individual to select his own course of conduct.

But it is not enough that a minister himself exercise this prudent reserve, both in private and public. If he have a family, it will be necessary to inculcate upon every member of it, as far as possible, the exercise of the same caution. My opinion is, that the wives and children of ministers ought seldom to allow themselves to speak of the opinions, plans and movements of their husbands or fathers. In a great majority of cases, perhaps, this may be done without the least ill consequence; but when they least apprehend evil from such communications, it may be most seriously the result. Nor can it ever be certainly known when such evil may arise. It is obvious, therefore, that, in this matter, reserve ought to be unceasing and vigilant.

6. *Uniformity.* The importance of this characteristic of clerical manners is much greater than would, at first view, appear. Few things have a more unfriendly influence on our acceptance in social intercourse than the opposite of what I now recommend. To be at one time pointedly respectful and affable, and, at another, to the same individual, so cold and ungracious as to surprise and repel; to treat an acquaintance to-day with a degree of attention and kindness bordering on excess, and little short of fawning; and to-morrow scarcely to recognize him at all, or to pass him with the most frigid indifference, is a style of deportment, which, though sometimes

seen in excellent men, is always unhappy, and often in no small degree mischievous in its influences on social comfort. This apparent caprice arises from various sources; sometimes from an actual defect of eyesight; at others from strange and fitful anomalies of memory, of which I have known many examples; perhaps still more frequently from those revolutions in feeling, which are occasioned by a nervous system liable to the alternate extremes of elevation and depression; from occasional fits of absence of mind; and, possibly now and then, from an affectation of eccentricity, which, however unworthy of a man of sense and piety, has actually been manifested by those who claimed to possess both.

Now, though several of these sources of apparently capricious manners may not at all times admit of a perfect remedy; yet more than one of them may be counteracted with entire success; and with respect to all of them much may be done to diminish their influence. The great secret of correction lies in one word — *attention.* — Try to learn the happy art of attending to each case as it arises, as being always of more or less importance, if not for its own sake, at least in reference to the formation of a suitable habit; and I have no doubt you will soon be surprised to perceive the degree of success that has attended your efforts.

But there is one method of obviating, to a certain extent, the evil under consideration, which, perhaps, may not so readily occur to every one, and especially not to every young man. I refer to that important point in the manners of all public men, viz. the wisdom of not being "over civil," or excessive in your polite attentions to any one. I have known ministers, as well as others, who have been really lavish in their civilities to a few individuals among their friends and neighbours, so much so as to attract particular notice; while others, equally, or perhaps more worthy, but less conspicuous, they have scarcely treated with common decorum. Their coldness to the latter, would not have been so observable, had it not contrasted with their extreme civility to the former. Diversities of this kind ought to be as much as possible avoided; and the correction ought to be applied to both extremes. It is never wise for a minister to be so excessively intimate, so inordinately friendly with any particular individual, or individuals, among his people, as to become a subject of remark, or to embarrass him in his intercourse with others. *Ne quid nimis* is an invaluable maxim, in its application to clerical intimacies and civilities, as well as to a thousand other things. Those which are carried to excess, seldom last long, or end well. The most truly judicious and generally acceptable public men I have ever known, were remarkable for not being extremely civil to any, even to those whom they were known most highly to value; but for that moderate, yet vigilant attention to all, which was by no means inconsistent with special friendships, but which indicated a desire to be truly useful to all classes of persons.

I hope you will not be disposed to say, that the foregoing counsels are adapted to form that cold, selfish, and calculating style of manners, which ought to be avoided, rather than cultivated. If it be so, I am egregiously deceived. Let me entreat you to go over every item again carefully, and see whether wisdom, prudence, and the word of God do not sanction them all. The idea that the manners of any one ought to be left to take care of themselves, is a miserable delusion. As long as we are bound, every hour, to "consider our ways," and, "whether we eat or drink, or whatever we do, to do all to the glory of God," it will be incumbent upon persons, of all ages and stations, to endeavour in all things, even the minutest, to "order their conversation aright." But for a minister of the gospel, who stands continually as a "watchman," and a "defender," on "the walls of Zion;" and who is acting every hour, not only for himself, but also for the church of God; — for him to doubt whether habitual care as to every word, and look, and action, is incumbent on him, is indeed strangely to misapprehend his obligations.

If you ask me, where you shall find a model of such clerical manners as I have endeavoured to describe, I answer, No where, in all its parts, in absolute perfection. This, however, is no more a reason why an attempt should not be made to portray and recommend such manners, than our inability to find a perfect pattern of the Christian temper, in any mere man, is a reason why that temper should never be described or inculcated. But I have been so happy as to meet with a few examples of manners nearly approximating to those which are recommended in this letter. One of the most venerable and excellent clergymen in the United States has remarked, that he thought some of the more polished and pious of the ministers belonging to the Moravians, or United Brethren, furnished specimens of manners as worthy of imitation as any he had ever seen. In this opinion I am inclined to concur. I have marked in a few of those worthy men, that happy though truly rare union of gravity, dignity, gentleness, and unaffected kindness of deportment, which it would be delightful to see copied by every minister of religion in the land.

LETTER III.

Giving no offence in any thing, that the ministry be not blamed.
2 Cor. vi. 3.

OFFENSIVE PERSONAL HABITS.

My dear young friend: — There are many personal habits, which all polished people concur in regarding as offensive; and which, of course, cannot be indulged in the presence of such persons, without giving them pain.—Sometimes, indeed, so much pain, that after a while, the society of those who habitually indulge in them, if not avoided altogether, will be in a degree unwelcome, wherever they go. These habits are painful to well-bred persons on various accounts. Some of them, because they are offences against personal cleanliness; others, because they make an uncomfortable impresssion, in other respects, on the senses of those with whom we converse; and a third class, because they indicate the absence of that respect and attention to those around us, which every man of correct deportment is expected to pay, and which he never omits to pay, without incurring a serious disadvantage.

I propose, in the present letter, to mention some of these personal habits. And let me entreat you not to consider me as unnecessarily minute or fastidious in my enumeration. Some of the particulars adverted to may excite a smile, and others a less comfortable emotion. You may rest assured, however, that I shall mention none but such as I know to be offensive; to many persons deeply so; and to have been remarked upon with great severity. This is enough for a delicate, conscientious man, who will consider no correction of an evil habit as beneath his notice, which will give him more ready access to all companies, and render, perhaps, many of his personal efforts to do good much more acceptable and useful.

1. Among these offensive habits, the first I shall mention, is that of spitting on the floors and carpets of the apartments in which you are seated. This is a habit with which Americans are constantly reproached by those Europeans who travel among us, or who have occasion to remark on our national manners. Nay, a late writer in one of their periodical works, pronounces, that "the Americans must give up all pretensions to good-breeding as long as they allow themselves to spit on floors and carpets in company, as is now common among them." I do not allow that this charge can be said by any means to be more commonly applicable to the better portion of Americans than of Englishmen. Still I do believe the habit in question is more common among the plainer classes of our citizens, than it is among the corresponding classes of any nation on earth, of equal culture, in other respects, with ourselves. And, truly, a habit so filthy, so peculiarly disgusting, and so calculated to give trouble to every neat housekeeper, may well be regarded as equally discreditable

5

to the breeding and the benevolence of those who allow themselves to practise it.

I have known some persons who, in consequence of their habitually chewing tobacco, or some other substance, or smoking, were under a necessity so constant and pressing of discharging saliva from their mouths, that they were really a trouble to themselves, as well as to every body else. They bespattered the clothes and persons of all who were sitting in their immediate vicinity; defiled the floor or carpet beyond endurance; and thus rendered themselves a nuisance in every house which they entered. Indeed, I have known a few tobacco-chewers, in whom this habit had reached such a degree of concentrated virulence, that they rendered their immediate neighbourhood intolerable; formed puddles of tobacco-spittle at their feet, in the parlour, or in the pew in church in which they were seated; and, in some instances, even compelled persons of delicate feelings, especially females, to leave the room, or the pew, and retire in haste, to avoid sickness of stomach.

To say that this filthiness is very indecent, is to speak but half its condemnation. It is unworthy of a gentleman and a Christian; and he who, after being warned, continues to indulge it, ought to be banished, without scruple, from all decent society.

If it be asked, how those who spit much shall manage, I answer, if possible, let them instantly discontinue all those practices which lead to the secretion of an excess of saliva. This is, in every point of view, the best and most effectual method of removing all difficulty. But if this be not possible, then let such persons, when they go into company, make interest with their kind entertainers to furnish them with spitting-boxes; or let them endeavour to sit near a window; or let them rise and withdraw from the apartment as often as it becomes necessary to discharge the contents of their mouths; or let them take care to have in their pockets extra handkerchiefs, which may be employed to receive the superfluous saliva; or, if none of these safeguards or auxiliaries can be had, let them even — stay at home, and thus be sure that they trespass on no premises excepting their own. Even there, indeed, they will annoy and disgust all who visit them: but then this will be a penalty incurred voluntarily, and endured only as long as each individual can find a sufficient inducement to sustain it. For I have certainly known at least one tobacco-chewing clergyman of whom a respectable professor of religion declared, that he would most cheerfully pay his board for a week or more, at a tavern, or at any other place, rather than endure his company at a single meal, or for one evening, in his own dwelling. How melancholy, that a minister of religion, instead of being a pattern of neatness and purity, and possessing such manners as to render his company attractive to all classes of people, should allow himself, by his personal habits, to drive all cleanly and delicate persons from his presence!

Imagine not, however, that it is merely against this miserable extreme of the filthy habit in question, that I protest. It is against every degree of it that I would warn you. Rather than once allow yourself, on any occasion, to spit on the floor in company, you ought to walk a hundred yards, or more, to find a door or window, or to submit to almost any ordinary inconvenience. In fact, to go to the root of the evil, the habit of spitting much at all, is a bad habit; and any thing which tends to the secreting, and, of course, to the necessity of discharging much saliva, ought to be, by all young persons, who are forming their manners, carefully avoided. And scarcely any thing, let me add, admits of being placed and kept more fully under the influence of the will, in ordinary circumstances, than this.

2. Another offensive habit, closely connected with the foregoing, against which I would warn you, is the excessive use of tobacco, in any form. I do not deny that chewing, smoking, and snuffing tobacco, within certain limits, may be considered as quite consistent with the habits of gentlemen; because many gentlemen practise them; and some who practise more than one, or all of them, even to a degree of excess, yet, from their great personal neatness, and constant attention to appearances, have still avoided becoming, in any considerable degree, offensive to those around them. Such instances, however, are rare. At any rate, nothing is more common than the reverse; and the cases are so numerous in which the consumers of this hateful weed become a source of inconvenience to all with whom they associate, that even the ordinary use of it ought to be regarded with apprehension, by those who would escape the excess to which others have become victims.

You ought to be aware, my young friend, that no class of persons are more apt to fall into excess in the use of tobacco, in every way, than students; and no class of students, perhaps, more remarkably than those who are devoted to the study of theology. Whether their sedentary habits, and especially their habits of stated composition, form the peculiar temptation by which so many of them are unhappily beguiled, I know not: but it has fallen to my lot to know a very large number of ministers, young and old, who by excessive smoking, chewing, or snuffing, have deranged the tone of their stomachs; have undermined their health; have seriously injured their voices; have had the fumes of tobacco so thoroughly inwrought in their persons and clothing, that it became impossible for many delicate people to sit near them with impunity; and have laid themselves, after a while, under so absolute a necessity of smoking, or chewing incessantly, that they have been obliged to withdraw from company, or from the most urgent business, and even to break off in the midst of a meal, and retire to smoke, or else run the risk of a severe affection of the stomach.

In vain do you remind such people, when they are young, and when their habits are forming, that the use of tobacco is, in most cases, unhealthful, and in many, extremely so; that if they use it at all, they are in danger of being betrayed into excess, in spite of every resolution to the contrary. — In vain do you remind them that many persons, of both sexes, cannot bear either the smoke or the perfume of tobacco, and, of course must be driven from the room, if not from the house, in which this offensive practice is going forward; that, like tippling, one degree of excess in this indulgence leads to another, until a sort of necessity of continuing it is incurred; that habits of smoking and chewing, especially the former, will render them intolerable inmates in many families; and that by the excessive use of tobacco, more particularly in the form of segars, thousands have been insensibly betrayed into habits of drinking, and have become confirmed sots, before they were aware of being in the least danger: — I say, in vain do you remind many young men, and even pious young men, who are commencing such habits, of these dangers. In vain do you hold up to their view particular cases, as examples of all that you say. They will not believe you. They are in no danger. Others may have insensibly fallen into excess, and become offensive; but they never will. Onward they go, with inflexible self-will, "as an ox goeth to the slaughter," resolving to follow appetite at all hazards, until some of them become themselves fearful examples of the evils against which they were warned!

I have already hinted at one of the dangers arising from the excessive use of tobacco, which very many, even after being put on their guard, cannot be persuaded to appreciate. I mean the tendency of the segar to generate a fondness for intemperate drinking. He whose mouth and fauces are frequently and strongly stimulated by the fumes of tobacco, is apt to be thirsty; and to such an one, simple water is insipid, and scarcely tolerable. Something stronger is, of course, sought after. And hence it so often happens, that habits of disgraceful, and finally of ruinous tippling, grow out of the excessive use of the segar.

The truth is, no man, especially no young man, ought ever to use tobacco in any shape, who can possibly avoid it; that is, who does not find himself reduced to the same necessity of taking it, as a medicine, that he is, now and then, of taking digitalis, opium or calomel; in which case, instead of allowing himself to contract a fondness for the article, and living upon it daily, a wise man will take it, as he would the most nauseous medicine, in as small quantities, and as seldom, as possible. I beseech you, my young friend, not to disregard this advice. Rely on it, if you are so happy as to escape the thraldom which the odious vegetable in question has imposed upon millions, you will rejoice in it as long as you live. But you probably will not escape, unless you renounce the use of the article entirely. If the most servile votary of the segar, the quid, or the snuff-box, could take even a cursory glance at the ruined health, the trembling nerves, the impaired mental faculties, the miserable tippling habits, the disgraceful slavery, and the revolting fúme, to which they have insensibly conducted many an unsuspecting devotee, he would fly with horror before even the possible approaches of the danger.

3. Another habit which every friend to the honour of religion, and to human happiness, ought to avoid with the utmost care, is, that of indulging in the use of intoxicating drinks.

The habit of which I now speak is not that of intemperate drinking. This is a sin so unquestionable and degrading, so destructive of health, of reputation, and of all that is good, that no argument can be necessary to convince a professing Christian, and especially a candidate for the holy ministry, that every approach to it ought to be regarded with abhorrence. And I have no doubt that every manifest and known approach to it, will be so regarded by every conscientious man. But there are approaches to this sin so remote and insensible, that thousands are drawn into them without the smallest apprehension of danger; and it is not, perhaps, until it is too late to apply any human remedy, that their fears begin to be excited. Happy is he who sees the evil afar off, and is wise enough to escape from every measure of its influence.

That intoxicating drinks, as a general fact, are injurious to all who are in health, I hold to be established by the soundest medical wisdom, and by the dictates of all sober experience. The use of them, as a beverage, tends to excite morbidly the nervous system; to impair digestion; to generate hepatic and other chronic and loathsome diseases; to interfere with the happy operation of medicines in cases of sickness, and, of course, to diminish the prospect of recovery; to shorten life; to weaken and derange the intellectual powers; to unfit men for the feeling and profitable hearing of the gospel, and for all the practical duties of life. Such are the daily and hourly effects of intoxicating drinks. They do more to generate crime, to destroy human life, and to prostrate domestic and social peace and happiness, than sword, famine, and pestilence, all combined.

Now to oppose the power of this destroyer; to discourage the use of this tremendous poison as a beverage, the pledge of total abstinence from all that can intoxicate, has been introduced and recommended by benevolent men. I cordially approve this pledge. I have taken it again and again. I have recommended it to my children, and to all, young and old, within my reach. I set no alcoholic or fermented liquor on my own table, and never offer it to any under my roof, or in my employment, unless its exhibition as a medicine becomes necessary. This is no painful self-denial to me. All my experience most decisively and unequivocally tells me that I am far more healthful and comfortable without stimulating drinks than with them. And I firmly believe that ninety-nine out of an hundred of all human beings in health are not benefited, but rather injured in their physical frame, by such drinks; to say nothing of all the dreadful intellectual, moral and social mischief which alcoholic beverages are daily producing in our world.

Under these deep impressions, I consider it as equally my duty and my privilege to lend all my influence and example, toward discouraging and diminishing the use of this dreadful destroyer. I cannot, indeed, concur with some of the *ultra* advocates of "total abstinence," who believe and teach that the word of God forbids the use of all intoxicating drinks, even in the most temperate degree. I cannot so interpret the language of Scripture on this subject. I must think that several passages in the New Testament, as well as the Old, teach that wine may sometimes be used without sin; and that old, mature wine is preferable to new. I know not how otherwise to understand John ii. 1—11; 1 Timothy v. 23; and Luke v. 39. But when the friends of temperance plead for "total abstinence" on the principle of expediency, on the ground which the inspired apostle assumes in Rom. xiv. and in 1 Cor. viii. 13, I am cordially with them, and sincerely wish that every friend of human happiness might give his countenance to the cause which they are banded to promote. When I see so many individuals and so many families ruined by intoxicating drinks, I cannot consider as excessive any zeal or any self-denial which has for its object, to discourage the use of this insidious poison. Every patriot, and every Christian, is bound to do all in his power, to save those around him from the vice of intemperance; but ministers and candidates for the sacred office are specially and professionally bound to be, in this as well as every other department of duty and happiness, labourers for the public good.

My firm persuasion is, that, in general, no one who is in health, ought ever, as a system, to drink any thing stronger than water. It is the most natural, the most salubrious, and, in all respects, the best drink. The cases of the most robust and ruddy health that I have ever seen, have been those of persons who drank nothing but water. Among the old Romans, in the purest and simplest periods of their republic, no man was allowed to drink any kind of strong drink, until he had attained the age of thirty years. And if I could prevail upon every young man to act rigidly upon this plan, putting every thing out of view excepting his bodily health, and his interest for the present life, I should consider myself as having gained a most desirable object.

He who drinks nothing but water, has but little temptation to drink at all more frequently than he ought. Yet it is very possible to take too frequently and too much, even of this simple beverage. I have known some individuals, chiefly students, who unhappily contracted the habit of requiring something to moisten their lips every half hour, or oftener; and even in the pulpit, they could never get through a discourse of ordinary length, without taking repeated sips of water. This is not only a habit troublesome to others, as well as ourselves, but it is multiplying our wants; it is rendering the lips and fauces more apt to become parched, on the slightest use of them; thus increasing the inconvenience which it is intended to remedy, and constantly spreading a snare before the individual, to crave something less innocent when water of a good quality is not to be procured.

I would say, then, to every one who is forming his habits in this respect, — let your plan be to drink but little of any thing. Even the excessive drinking of water may prove injurious, and has proved so to multitudes. The digestion of students is generally feeble at best; but taking much liquid of any kind into the stomach is calculated to render it still more feeble. Drink, therefore, as little as possible, without being incommoded by importunate thirst. Habituate yourself to as few wants, in this respect, as possible. Let not your first request, when you call at a friend's house, be, as the manner of some ever is, to be furnished with "something to drink." Such a request commonly leads to the offer of every tempting article of drink, that may be within reach of your entertainer, and may thus cause him to lay in your way a most serious, and it may be, a fatal snare. Of all men in the world, clergymen, who are very often in the houses of their friends or parishioners, and who are constantly in the way of receiving kind offers of refreshment, ought to be men of self-denial, especially with regard to all stimulating drinks. Without a large measure of this grace in habitual exercise they may be considered as constantly standing on the brink of a precipice.

My earnest advice, therefore, is, that, for the double purpose of guarding against personal temptation, and of setting a good example to others, you decline the use of ardent spirits altogether, however pressingly they may be urged upon you; and that you make as little use of any kind of stimulating drink as possible. Discountenance the use of such drinks among all with whom you associate. Let it be seen that you do so on principle. And let your practice testify that you believe and obey your own doctrine.

4. Closely connected with the foregoing particular, is another habit, against which a minister of the gospel ought to be especially on his guard. I mean that of manifesting or cherishing an excessive fondness for luxurious eating.

I shall probably say something hereafter on the mischiefs of intemperate eating, in reference to the bodily health. My design, at present, is merely to speak of those improprieties of manner which are apt to grow out of an undue estimate of this indulgence.

When worldly men show, without reserve, that they worship their palates; when in public houses, and in private families, they are continually manifesting their epicurean character; when they are disposed to give trouble for the gratification of their appetite wherever they may be; when they eagerly seize upon the best pieces of any article of food on the table, thereby showing that they prefer the indulgence of their own taste, to the gratification of any one else; — I say, when worldly men allow themselves to act thus, all correct judges know that they violate good manners; but as "they have their portion in this life," they are expected, when unrestrained, to feel and act with this supreme regard to appetite. And, even with respect to manners, luxurious men, in concerns of this nature, often have influence enough to make a sort of "law for themselves."

But, in ministers of the gospel, or candidates for the ministry, nothing of this kind ought ever to be seen, or so much as suspected to exist. Habits of the most marked simplicity and moderation, in eating as well as in drinking, ought ever to characterize them. Let none, then, ever have reason to accuse you of being particularly fond of gratifying your palate, or of being particularly nice in what is required for that purpose. Eat whatever is set before you, without a word of question or difficulty. And while many eat with a rapidity or a greediness which indicates a mind inordinately intent on the pleasure of eating, let every movement, on your part, indicate that moderation which becomes a minister of Christ. At a luxurious table exercise self-denial with peculiar vigilance. Let it be seen that you have no alliance with the character of a gourmand. Eat commonly but of one simple dish. Eat slowly; gently; without that smacking of the lips, and that noisy motion of the mouth, which are expressive either of extreme hunger, or vulgarity, or both. Eat and drink guardedly, too, lest some article passing the wrong way, should embarrass you before company, and which, in nine cases out of ten, results from haste, and want of care. And finally, eat without talking much about eating. Nothing is more common in company, than to hear much said respecting the pleasures of the table; the excellence of particular articles of food; the relish of certain kinds of cookery, &c. Let nothing of this kind ever engage your thoughts, or your tongue. Let nothing indicate that you are a man "given to appetite." Wherever you may be, or whatever may be the subjects of conversation with others; let every word and look, on your part, evince that you are seeking higher and better objects than those which "minister to the flesh." And, although it may seldom be proper or seasonable to administer a direct rebuke to those who are fond of such topics of conversation; yet it is always both seasonable and proper, by abstaining from any participation in them, to administer what may sometimes be a most powerful rebuke, to those around you. When at your own table, or the tables of others, think how your Master, or one of his inspired apostles, would act and converse in similar circumstances, and endeavour to make that the model of your own conduct.

5. Guard against loud or boisterous laughter in company. It is a mark of ill-breeding. Some persons, of manners otherwise correct, greatly offend in this particular. I have known a few ministers, of buoyant animal spirits, who were in the habit of laughing with as much unrestrained coarseness and noise as the boatswain of a man-of-war; insomuch that they were heard over a whole house, and even in the street. I need not add, that, until their worth became known by an intimate acquaintance, they excited surprise and suspicion in most who heard them. The laughter of a polished man, and especially of a

clergyman, however hearty, ought never to be obstreperous, and seldom audible.

6. It is the habit of many, almost as soon as they are seated in company, to take out a penknife, and to begin to pare their nails; or, if they have been sufficiently pared before, to scrape, or polish, or clean them. This is an indelicate practice, always carrying with it the idea of the want of cleanliness, and no less of a want of respect to those in whose presence we are seated. It is, indeed, important if we would appear decent, that our nails be kept properly pared, and carefully divested of the foul matter which is apt to accumulate at the ends of them. But let these operations always be performed in private. Why should they be performed before company any more than washing our hands and face, or cleaning our teeth? It is certain, that to some they are peculiarly offensive. I once heard a clergyman of great eminence, for both piety and talents, say that he "would be nearly as willing to see a person pull off his shoes and stockings, and fall to cutting his toe nails in company, as to see him constantly trimming and cleaning those of his hands."

7. Many persons who are aware of the impropriety of cutting or cleaning their nails before company, are apt, when sitting in the presence of others, either from embarrassment, or from having nothing to do, to be picking at the skin on their hands, as if they were picking off scales, or were incommoded by some cutaneous disease. This has an ill appearance. To many persons it is extremely revolting; and nothing is more natural than to associate with it the idea of something uncleanly or unwholesome.

8. The practice, by no means unfrequent, of combing the hair in company, is quite exceptionable. It is an offence against delicacy and cleanliness, and ought always to be performed in private. Yet I have known many candidates for the ministry, and even ministers, do this without reserve; and, what is more, wipe off what had accumulated on the comb in the course of the operation, and scatter it at their feet.

9. The practice of yawning in company, ought, as far as possible, to be avoided. It looks as if we were weary of our companions. And although it is often an involuntary act, yet there is no doubt, at the same time, that it may be encouraged, so as to occur far more frequently than is absolutely necessary, and even to be established as a habit. Avoid it as much as possible even in private; for if you desire to form good habits in company, you must endeavour to establish them in your most secret retirement. And when it does involuntarily occur in company, hide it as much as you can by the delicate use of your handkerchief.

10. The act of coughing in company is not always a voluntary act: yet nothing is more certain than that it may be restrained and mitigated to a great degree. Many persons, however, make no attempt at this restraint. They cough in the largest circles, with a frequency, a loudness, and an apparent straining of the chest, which cannot fail to give pain to all who witness it. Such persons ought, if consistent with duty, to remain at home: or if compelled to go into company, it ought to be their constant aim to restrain their cough. By this means, while they avoid giving pain to others, they will be benefited

themselves; for nothing is more certain than that the irritation of continual coughing is quite as injurious to the patient himself, as it is annoying to those around him. It will readily occur to every person of delicacy that peculiar caution in this respect ought to be exercised, while seated at table. The practice in which many vulgar people indulge, of coughing, yawning, and sneezing over the dishes placed in their immediate neighbourhood, is intolerable, and has driven many a delicate person from the table.

11. The practice of picking the teeth, while seated at table, is proscribed by all correct people. If you cannot avoid it without being very uncomfortable, cover your mouth with your handkerchief, and let the operation be as little conspicuous as possible. As to picking your teeth with the *fork* which you employ in eating, (which I have sometimes witnessed) I presume your own sense of propriety will instinctively revolt from it, as peculiarly offensive.

12. When sitting at table in company, guard against leaning with your elbows on the table. There is a slouching and disrespectful familiarity in this practice, which ought never to be indulged by any one who wishes to be considered as a man of correct manners. It is enough for incorrigible loungers to be leaning upon every thing which stands within their reach. Guard against any assimilation to their habits. You ought to be very much at home, indeed, where any thing of this kind is allowable. But the fact is, it ought not to be allowed, even at your own table, when strangers are present.

13. There are some personal habits so very offensive, that it is difficult to speak of them without ex-

citing, in many delicate minds, a state of feeling almost as painful as that which would be produced by witnessing the habits themselves. On this account, I cannot dwell upon them in minute detail: and yet to pass them altogether without notice, would be doing injustice to my design. I shall, therefore, simply name, in a cursory manner, a few of those which I have in view, and trust to your own discernment and good sense to supply the rest of the catalogue, as well as to suggest the reasons why they are prohibited in all polished society.

Among the habits alluded to, are those of audible and uncovered eructation; picking the nose, and the ears, not in a guarded and delicate manner, with the handkerchief, but with the finger, and with full exposure to view; blowing the nose in a loud and disgusting manner; looking into the handkerchief, after blowing the nose, as if apprehensive of finding some threatening appearance in the secretion inspected; sneezing frequently, without breaking either the force or the noise of the blast by the application of a handkerchief; holding the handkerchief at a distance from the mouth, and spitting into it, instead of silently and covertly wiping the saliva from the lips; snuffing up the nose with an offensive frequency; the habit of hemming, and clearing the throat very loudly and frequently, and in a disgusting manner, as if labouring under some organic obstruction; — these, and a number of other similar habits, ought carefully to be avoided by all who wish to attain decent and acceptable manners. It is no excuse for these habits to say, that some of the things alluded to are involuntary acts. This is, no doubt, true. But it may, nevertheless, be asserted, even of those which are most decisively of this class, that, by a little delicate attention, they may be very much controlled and mitigated, and by the discreet use of the handkerchief, they may be easily deprived of almost every thing offensive in their character.

14. The mode of sitting in company is a point concerning which no little indecorum is often indulged. The offences against propriety in this respect are numerous. Many, when seated, even in large and ceremonious companies, are in the habit of lifting up one or both of their feet, and placing them on a neighbouring chair. Others, if they can get a place on a sofa or settee, lay their bodies upon it at full length, in a horizontal posture; and thus either exclude all others from sharing in the seat, or subject them to the danger of encountering their soiled shoes. A third class, the moment they fix themselves upon any kind of seat, appear to be searching for something to lean or recline upon; and when such an article is found, are incessantly hanging and lounging upon it. While a fourth class, though they have only a single chair to occupy, thrust out their feet as far as possible, and throw their persons as near to the horizontal posture as they can, as if the object were to cover the largest practicable space on the floor, and to subject those who have occasion to pass before them to the risk, every moment, of stumbling over their feet. I have often wondered that persons of the least delicacy or reflection should be found indulging such habits. If you have any disease of the feet or legs, which requires them to be placed in a horizontal posture, mention

the circumstance to the company, and obtain permission to use the needed privilege, and all will be well. I have only to mention, under this head, the incivility of sitting with your back to any portion of the company with whom you may be seated. This is never proper, unless an apartment is so crowded that avoiding it is manifestly impossible.

15. The habit of tilting your chair back, while you are sitting upon it, so as to rest only on its two hinder legs, is, on several accounts, improper. It has proved the fruitful source of many ludicrous, and even dangerous falls backward, as most persons have had an opportunity of observing. And it almost necessarily leads to those awkward, constrained, or lounging postures of the body, which have been already mentioned as offences against that respectfulness of manner which every gentleman is bound habitually to maintain. This practice of tilting back the chair in company, has been considered and represented in Europe, as one of the peculiarities of American ill-breeding.

16. The fact is, we owe it to our bodily health, as well as to good manners, to learn the art of habitually sitting in an erect posture. Few things are more important to a student. If he allow himself, in the privacy of his own apartment, to sit in a leaning, lounging, half-bent posture, with his elbows on his knees, or with his feet stuck up on a chair, or against the side of the fire-place, higher than his head, or on a level with it; he will be much more apt to contract a pain in his breast, and to find his eye-sight and his general health affected by three hours' study, in such a posture, than by five or even

six in a more erect one. Let your habitual mode of sitting, even in your study, be perfectly erect, with the breast rather protruded than bent in; and, in short, very much in that self-supported and firm manner, in which you would wish to sit in the most ceremonious company. This may seem, at first view, to be too formal; but it will become, in a short time, what it is the object of this counsel to make it, the most natural posture; and will, without effort on your part, confer all those advantages on the score of health and manners which it is desirable to gain from it. Besides, if now, in your youth, you are constantly seeking, as many appear to be, something to recline upon; if you cannot sit ten minutes without throwing yourself into the recumbent, or semi-recumbent postures, to which we see the young and healthy constantly resorting, what will you do in the feebleness of old age? If you cannot sit otherwise than half-bent at twenty-five; how will you sit at three score and ten? Let the sunken, revolting figures of many aged persons give the answer.

17. Many persons, the moment they seat themselves in company, and especially when they become engaged in conversation, if there be a screw, knob, or small fixture of any kind within their reach, which admits of being turned or handled, are incessantly engaged in performing this operation, to the annoyance of the owner of the house, and often to the incurable injury of the article thus roughly treated. Try to learn the art of sitting still, while you are conversing, without pulling and tugging at the furniture around you; without playing with any part of your own dress or person; without incessantly

stretching and cracking the joints of your fingers; without pulling out your watch every half minute, and twirling the chain in every direction, &c. The truth is, that kind of nervous restlessness which leads to things of this kind, ought ever to be resisted. He who must have something to play with while he is conversing, ought to consider himself as called upon promptly and firmly to apply a remedy.

18. Finally; let me enjoin upon you to avoid all slovenly habits of whatsoever kind, in your person, in the implements you use, and in the apartments you occupy. The offences against this counsel are so numerous and diversified, that I cannot pretend to specify them. Good sense, attentive observation, and general habits of neatness, will, I trust, render minute details unnecessary.

It is recorded of the celebrated Mr. Whitefield, that he was characteristically neat in his person, and with respect to every thing about him. He was accustomed to say, that "a minister ought to be without *spot.*" He would not allow a paper to be out of its place, or to be put up irregularly. He would have every part of the furniture of his room in its appropriate station before he retired to rest; and remarked, that he could not be easy, if he thought so small an article as his gloves were out of the proper place. Such were the feelings of a man whose evangelical labours were abundant to a degree almost without parallel; and whose heart was peculiarly intent on the great duties of his office as an "ambassador of Christ."

Let every apartment which you occupy, either permanently or for a short time, bear the character of neatness. When you quit your bed in the morning, lay up the bed-clothes decently, so that no visitant need be offended by the appearance of things. When you wash yourself, especially in the house of a friend, do it with gentleness and neatness, without wetting the carpet or floor, without bespattering the wall or furniture in the immediate vicinity of the basin, that you may as much as possible diminish the labour of servants. A conscientious man, in these circumstances, ought ever to act on the principle of giving as little trouble as may be to those around him; and, for this purpose, in all cases whatsoever, whether at home or abroad, to leave as little to clean after him as possible.

On the subject of slovenly habits, and several other points noticed in this letter, I would recommend to your perusal the Rev. Dr. Adam Clarke's "Letter to a Methodist Preacher." You will perceive that the learned and venerable author, though belonging to an ecclesiastical body rather distinguished for the simplicity and plainness of its members, and certainly by no means excessive in its attention to external polish, considers a negligence of cleanliness in a minister of the gospel, as not only disgusting, but as very closely allied to moral delinquency.

LETTER IV.

A word spoken in due season, how good is it! — PROV. xv. 23.

CONVERSATION.

MY DEAR YOUNG FRIEND: — Those qualities which enable any man to appear well in conversation, are among the most precious that can be possessed. To every public man these qualities are peculiarly important. But to a minister of the gospel, they are above measure valuable. The business of his life is to benefit his fellow-men. A large portion of his time must be passed, and ought to be passed, in society; and he who is best qualified to make all his social intercourse at once pleasing and useful, is, of course, best qualified to promote the great ends for which the ministry was instituted.

But while this accomplishment is certainly valuable beyond all price, it evidently engages much less of the attention of candidates for the holy ministry than its importance demands. Instead of "coveting earnestly this gift;" instead of studying daily to attain it, and to make progress in it, as is done with regard to some other things of less value; this great concern is left, pretty much, to take care of itself, or, at best, to depend on the exigency of the moment, both for exercise and improvement.

Every man, indeed, is not qualified to excel in conversation; but every man may be inoffensive, if not agreeable: and, as Dean Swift has somewhere remarked, there are hundreds of men who might not only be agreeable, but really shine, who, on account of a few gross faults, which they might easily correct in half an hour, are, at present, not even tolerable. They pass through life not only without usefulness, but are considered as a nuisance wherever they appear.

As I propose to make Religious Conversation the subject of a separate letter, I shall confine myself, at present, to some general principles, which, it appears to me, ought to regulate all our social intercourse. Most of these principles, indeed, apply equally to all classes of persons. Some of them, however, are more especially worthy of the attention of those who seek or sustain the sacred office.

This subject is recommended to our attention, not only by common sense and experience, but also by the word of God. Holy Job exclaimed — "How forcible are right words!" "A word spoken in due season," says the wise man, "how good is it!" Prov. xv. 23. And again, "A word fitly spoken is like apples of gold in pictures of silver." Prov. xxv. 11. Again, the inspired apostle exhorts — "Let no corrupt communication proceed out of your mouth, but that which is good to the use of edifying, that it may minister grace unto the hearers." Ephes. iv. 29. And again, "Let your speech be always with grace seasoned with salt, that ye may know how to answer every man." Coloss. iv. 6.

Allow me, then, to put you on your guard against

some of the most common faults in conversation, and to recommend some of those excellencies, which appear to me particularly worthy of your attention.

1. In the first place, be upon your guard against talking too much in company. He who is very talkative incurs disadvantages of the most serious kind. He cheapens himself; tires his hearers; and, of course, renders what he has to say, however rich it may be in wisdom, much less likely to prove either acceptable or useful, than if he talked less. Speak seasonably, nay frequently, if you have opportunity, but never long. Contribute your equitable share to the conversation; but do not allow yourself to go beyond these limits. "Pay your own reckoning," as one has expressed it; "but do not undertake, at your own expense, to treat the whole company. This being one of the few cases in which people do not wish to be treated; every one being fully convinced that he has wherewithal to pay his own bill." This fault is particularly noticed and reproved in Scripture. "A fool's voice," says the wise man, "is known by the multitude of words." "In the multitude of words," says the same inspired teacher, "there wanteth not sin; but he that refraineth his lips is wise." And again, "He that hath knowledge, spareth his words." Eccles. iii. 3. Prov. x. 19. Prov. xvii. 27.

I have never known a great talker, however enlightened and instructive, who did not, at length, become wearisome to his company. Nor did I ever know one of this character, who, in the multitude of the remarks and opinions which he threw out, did not sometimes utter that which he had better have kept to himself; and which, in some instances, became the source of great subsequent trouble. It is very unwise in a man who bears such a relation to society as a clergyman does; who is set for the instruction and guidance of the people; who comes in contact with so many individuals in all classes of society; whose remarks and opinions are important, and if he be at all respected, likely to be remembered and quoted; nay, whose judgment on the current topics of the day may have no small influence on the minds of some, when he shall have passed off the stage of life;—surely it is unwise for such a man to be throwing out his opinions on all subjects, without due consideration. Surely it is unwise for him to speak hastily and rashly. And if he be "full of talk," he will seldom be, for an hour together, wholly free from rash and indiscreet speaking. Let every man, but especially every minister, be swift to hear, and slow to speak.

2. A fault, directly the reverse of that which was last mentioned, is the extreme of silence in company. I have known some from physical temperament; others from abstraction and absence of mind; and a third class, perhaps, from still more exceptionable causes, wrapping themselves up in a chilling reserve; never speaking but when addressed, and then answering as briefly as possible, and relapsing into silence again. This is certainly unhappy for one who ought to be, wherever he is, an instructor and benefactor. While you avoid garrulity, then, sink not down into silence. While you guard against monopolizing the conversation, by no means give it up altogether. And if you find yourself frequently at a loss

for topics of conversation, take pains to have something ready for the discharge of this, as well as every other duty, by previously meditating on what may be adapted to utility in the particular company to which you may be introduced.

3. Another practical maxim, of great importance in conversation, is, that you avoid a tale-bearing tattling spirit. I have known some clergymen, who were the greatest newsmongers in their neighbourhoods. They were among the first to circulate idle stories; to give currency to unconfirmed statements; to trumpet abroad charges of the most serious kind, without adequate evidence, and were often, very often, afterwards obliged to explain, apologize, and even retract. This is a shameful spirit for any professing Christian to indulge; but is peculiarly shameful for an ambassador of Christ, whose course ought ever to be marked by caution, dignity, tenderness for the reputation of others, and universal benevolence.

Be not ready to credit, and in your social hours to recognize as true, every ill report that malignity or folly may put in circulation. If you have heard of any *faux pas* in the neighbourhood, or even if you know it to be true, be among the last to speak of it, unless plainly called in duty to do so. Let others lend themselves to the ignoble work of tale-bearing, or be willing to connect their names with the repetition of ill-natured reports; but let not your name be ever mentioned in such unworthy associations. If authority for slander or for contemptible gossiping stories is to be demanded, let it not be traced to a minister of Christ, who ought to have something to do infinitely more worthy of his calling. I have known ministers who were rash, credulous, and withal a little fond of news, taking for granted that what were communicated to them as facts, were really so; freely speaking of them as facts, and, not only so, but proceeding to act on the strength of them; to administer severe reproofs to the individuals supposed to be guilty, and even carry the subject into the pulpit; when the whole stories which they believed, caught up, repeated, and acted upon, were entirely without foundation. It is almost incredible how little reliance can be placed on reports, circulated even by good people, and accompanied with all the minute circumstances of time and place; and how utterly unsafe it is, in many cases, even to investigate the truth of them: because, frequently, even an investigation cannot be conducted, without repeating the story, and thus giving it additional currency. There are busy and wicked tongues enough for this work. The general rule for a minister of the gospel is, to take no share in any such conversation, unless it be, as far as he can with a good conscience, to mollify and repress: and then only to allow himself to take it up, when it is no longer possible, consistently with duty, to maintain silence.

When others speak to you of the misconduct of absent persons, as far as possible, in most cases, discourage such communications; and when severe censures are pronounced, manifest a readiness, as far as you conscientiously can, to suggest palliatives, and modes of viewing the subject which may be consistent with the innocence of the party, or at least lessen his criminality; remembering that "charity hopeth all things."

4. Closely connected with the tattling spirit against which I have warned you, is that which loves to pry into the private circumstances, and even the secrets of families, and to make them the subject of conversation. There is a littleness and even meanness in this, which all people of elevated minds despise; and which I hope you will sacredly avoid. You will have quite business enough of your own, without meddling with the private affairs of other people. In truth, no wise man will ever desire to become possessed of the secrets of his neighbour. They will always be found a troublesome commodity to have in keeping; and even after they have been imparted to him, he will much more frequently regret than rejoice that they ever came to his knowledge. There are many things of which it is much more a privilege than a misfortune to be entirely ignorant.

5. In conformity with the foregoing remarks, let me recommend, that, in company, even with your most intimate friends, you avoid the discussion of personal character and conduct as much as possible: and that you prefer dwelling on those principles, doctrines, and facts, which are always, and to all classes in society, interesting and instructive, and the discussion of which, moreover, is always safe. It was a question often repeated by a late distinguished physician and philanthropist of Philadelphia, a man as remarkable for the soundness of his mind, and the extent of his learning, as for the benignity of his disposition:—"Why are you so constantly talking about *persons?* Why not rather talk about *things?*" The lesson conveyed by this question is replete with practical wisdom. If conversation were generally

modelled upon it, the consequences would be happy indeed.

6. Study the happy art of making all your conversation useful. Conversation which is not religious, may still be highly useful. It may inculcate excellent sentiments concerning life, manners, education, &c.; or it may convey instruction, as to facts of great value. Where you have an opportunity of selecting topics of conversation yourself, make a point of introducing such as shall be adapted to benefit, as well as gratify, those whom you address. And even where you are compelled or induced to accept of those which have been introduced by others, try to give them an instructive turn. Especially study the happy art of making your conversation useful to young people as often as you are thrown into their company. A clergyman, or a candidate for the ministry, who has an enlarged mind, and a good stock of information, need not, and ought not, to converse five minutes in any company without throwing out something calculated to be thought of afterwards with profit. Nay, if we had the spirit of our Master, we should endeavour to make every word we utter useful.

7. Do not disdain to prepare yourself to converse in an intelligent and profitable manner on whatever may be the popular topics of the day. Whenever any interesting occurrence renders a particular place, or a particular event in history, an object of general attention, if you are not already accurately informed concerning the place or event in question, make a point of obtaining correct information as speedily as you can. You may be publicly appealed to for information in the presence of those to whom you would

be unwilling to appear ignorant. And even if this should not be the case, you may lose many an opportunity of instructing and gratifying those with whom you converse. There is some danger, indeed, that he who has thus taken pains to inform himself in relation to popular topics, may be tempted by vanity to make a display of his knowledge; but this is no more an argument against his gaining the knowledge, and being ready to impart it in a proper manner, and on proper occasions, than the proneness of many to pedantry, is an argument against all endeavours to cultivate and store the mind.

8. One of the most important habits to be acquired in conversation is that of paying close attention to the individual with whom you are conversing. Nothing is more common than the violation of this plain dictate of propriety. Many are in the constant habit of either entirely withdrawing their attention, or, at least, bestowing a very small share of it, on the person who is speaking to them. In the midst of the most important remarks, which they are expected to understand and to answer, they plainly manifest, by the vacant countenance, by the averted eye, and sometimes, even by the indecency of humming a tune, in a half-smothered manner, that they are thinking of nothing less than the speaker or his discourse. This is a great breach of decorum, and as unwise as it is ill-bred. It is impossible to understand or answer that which we do not hear; and very often, by allowing ourselves to indulge this absence of mind, we lose many a wise and weighty observation; we suffer many an important link in a chain of argument to escape us, by which we might, had we secured it, have

been largely profited; and even if what is said to us be altogether erroneous, we can never refute, or dispose of it in any way, as we ought, if we do not attentively listen to it. If you think proper to take the time to sit down by a person, and to pretend to listen to him, make a point of listening to him really. When you think that the conversation ought to be broken off, break it off; but, while it continues, attend to what is said. Unless you do this, it is impossible to estimate its value, or to frame a proper reply, or to adopt the most wise and delicate method of bringing it to a close. Many a conversation has been prolonged to an hour, and, after all, has proved desultory and useless, when it might have terminated in ten minutes, and been mutually beneficial, had the parties only given to each other, for that short space of time, their undivided attention. I repeat it, then—if you would treat your friends with good manners; if you would profit by what they say; if you would gain the highest possible advantage from every conversation; if you would save time; if you would benevolently *impart* pleasure as well as *receive* it; if you would reply to what is said to you, in the wisest and most instructive manner; then pay strict and undivided attention to every word that is uttered, as long as you think proper to continue any conversation.

9. The foregoing remarks are intended to apply where another person is addressing you individually. The same general principle applies where an individual is addressing a company of which you form a part. In such case, as long as you continue to occupy your seat, attend to what is said. I have known many persons who, in such circumstances — in

the midst of an interesting series of remarks addressed to them equally with the rest of the company, turned aside their heads; began to whisper to the person who sat next to them on an entirely different subject; and thus diverted his attention as well as their own from the speaker. This is, undoubtedly, a gross offence against good manners. It is practically telling the speaker that you do not think him worth listening to, and is certainly calculated to embarrass, and even to interrupt him in his remarks. Surely those who are desirous of doing to others, as they would that others, in like circumstances, should do to them, will endeavour to avoid such a palpable indecorum.

10. Another radical maxim of good manners, in conversation, is to treat what is said by others respectfully. This maxim, as well as the last, is perpetually disregarded. To say nothing of the practice indulged by many, of habitually withdrawing their attention from those with whom they are conversing; there are others, who testify their want of respect for what is said to them in conversation, in a great variety of ways: by a smile of contempt; by a half-concealed sneer; by a manifest unwillingness to hear the speaker to the end; by interrupting him; by hints that his opinions are frivolous; in a word, by some look, tone, or gesture, not easily specified, or clothed in language, by which we may intimate to another that we regard what he is saying as unworthy of being seriously considered. In all these ways, do proud men, impatient men, obstinate, opinionated, vulgar men, treat with disrespect many remarks which are worthy of their notice, and wound the feelings of many a modest, timid speaker.

If you so far put yourself on a level with any one, as to converse with him at all, listen respectfully to what he has to say. It is very possible that when he has finished, and before he has finished, you may be constrained to think very little of his remarks. But do not wound his feelings, by giving him to understand, beforehand, that you expect very little from him to the purpose; or by any thing that shall indicate sneer or contempt. Do not practically tell him, that you have no respect for what he is saying. Not only listen to him, but give every thought and word which he may utter, its due weight. Treat him, in short, as you would wish and expect, in like circumstances, to be treated by him. In no other way will you be able, when he has done, to answer his remarks in such a manner as will be likely to be useful to him as well as worthy of yourself.

11. In conversation with an individual, look him in the face, and keep your eye generally fixed on his, as far as you can without staring, and looking him out of countenance. The power of the eye, in seconding and enforcing what is said, is incalculable. Besides, by talking to an acquaintance without looking him in the face, you forego a great advantage. You lose the opportunity of perceiving what impression your remarks make upon him; and of deciding, by his composure, or his sudden change of countenance, whether you are giving him pleasure or pain by your communication. Many a discerning speaker, by watching the countenance of him whom he addressed, has been warned, by its indications, of the delicate ground on which he was treading, and prevented from making further and perhaps very mischievous disclosures.

12. It is of great importance to a public character, and especially to a clergyman, to learn the art of opposing erroneous sentiments expressed in the course of conversation, with firmness, and, at the same time, without offence. No discerning individual can converse many minutes together, with almost any one, without hearing something with which he cannot entirely agree. Now, to oppose such erroneous opinions is, in most cases, a duty; and yet to perform this duty seasonably, delicately, and with a proper reference to time, place, and company, is one of those things which, more than most others, put in requisition our judgment, taste, good temper, and good breeding. Sometimes the best expression of your disapprobation will be by perfect silence. In other cases, this would be want of fidelity. When you find yourself constrained, however, to give utterance to your dissent, let it be done mildly, respectfully, and in a manner fitted to win, rather than to revolt, the errorist. For example; instead of saying, to one who has been delivering sentiments in which you cannot concur—"You seem to me to talk absurdly;"—or, "Such opinions are grossly erroneous and mischievous;"—or, "A person who can speak thus, must have either a weak head, or a bad heart;" rather say—"I cannot concur in that opinion, for the following reasons, &c.;" or, "You must pardon me for dissenting from that doctrine;"—or, "Perhaps you have not adverted to some of the consequences of the opinion which you have just expressed;" and so in other cases. We are never so likely to benefit those who broach erroneous opinions in our presence, as when we oppose them, without acrimony; with a mild benevolence of manner;

and with such an exhibition of our reasons, as is adapted to convince their judgment, without wounding their pride.

13. Avoid a haughty and authoritative manner in conversation. There are, undoubtedly, many clergymen who allow themselves to feel in the parlour, very much as they do in the pulpit; as if it were their prerogative to dictate their sentiments *ex cathedra;* and as if they expected to be heard, not as friends, but as superiors, and authorized instructors. Hence they have habitually, something in their manner in company, which banishes ease, which chills confidence, which represses free inquiry, and which causes them to be listened to rather with constraint and timidity, than with affection. Carefully shun every thing of this kind. When you are conversing with friends in a parlour, you meet them on terms of equality. You are to address them, not as a lordly dictator, but as a respectful friend: not as having authority over their consciences, but as a helper of their instruction and their innocent pleasure. Avoid, therefore, in such circumstances, all harsh, dogmatical expressions and tones. Do not think to convince by your *ipse dixit*, or to put down an opponent by your sovereign authority. This would be proud dictation, rather than conversing; and ought to be carefully avoided by one who wishes to succeed, by addressing and treating men as rational beings; by respecting the rights of conscience, and by convincing the understandings of those whom he desires to gain.

14. As far as you can, avoid controversy in conversation, especially in mixed companies. I say, as far as you can. It is not always possible to avoid it.

An impudent, rough, or vulgar attack, may compel you to take the stand and tone of a polemic, when you least desire it. When such a case occurs, it ought to be studiously met without heat or passion, and brought to a close as speedily as possible. But many good men love controversy; or, at any rate, are easily betrayed into it. They have so little knowledge of the world, and so little discretion, that they are always ready to give battle, whenever they see the banner of a party raised. And even if they be seated in large, mixed companies, and be in danger of having all eyes and ears turned to them; still they imagine that no disputable sentiment must be allowed to pass. This is a real infirmity. Watch and pray against it without ceasing. Never suffer the truth, if you can help it, to be trampled under feet in your presence. But there are many ways of interposing a mild, conciliatory word in its behalf, and doing it firmly, without allowing yourself to be drawn into a dispute. And in this case, the old medical maxim, *obsta principiis*, is of great value. Be on the watch to avoid controversy, from the first moment you perceive a discrepance of opinion. A slight effort may be sufficient, in the beginning, to avert the evil, which, after going a few steps forward, will be utterly unavailing. Before I take leave of this particular, allow me, with especial earnestness, to put you on your guard against being drawn into controversy, in company, with aged men and with females. Never dream that you will be able to convince, or by any means to effect an alteration in the opinions of a man who has passed the age of three score, or three score and ten. You do not dispute with such a one on equal terms. If his opinions be ever so erroneous, he is probably wedded to them by long habit, as well as by strong prejudice. He will naturally consider himself as your superior, and take for granted that you cannot instruct him. Of course, you will find it difficult to use the same freedom and scope of argument with him, that you would with one nearer to an equality with yourself in age. Many of the same considerations apply to females. In acuteness, wit, sprightliness, and delicate raillery, they often prove powerful opponents; while the hands of a male adversary are, in a great measure, tied, so that he cannot wield with unrestrained freedom many of those weapons which he might properly, and with great effect, employ against an adversary of his own sex.

15. Closely connected with this caution against sliding into unseasonable controversy in company, is another against losing your temper in controversy, when you happen to be either unavoidably dragged, or inadvertently betrayed, into it. Perhaps clergymen may be said to be peculiarly exposed to this temptation. For, besides the various other infirmities, which they share in common with all good men, they are, perhaps, peculiarly liable to feel deeply, when their profession or their opinions are attacked. Always set a double guard, therefore, at this point. Recollect not only the sin of all rash and unseasonable anger; but how much the exhibition of it lowers the dignity of a grave, official man; and also that, in controversy, according to an old maxim, he who first gets angry will generally be considered as having the weaker side of the argument.

16. Endeavour to cultivate an easy, attractive man-

ner in conversation. Not that I would have you put on the smiling, simpering countenance, which many affect, as giving them, what they think, a pleasant, social air. This is, to all discerning people, disgusting rather than attractive. But by the attractive manner which I would recommend, I mean that frank, courteous, unaffected, benign manner, which invites freedom of intercourse, and which is adapted to place all who approach us at their ease. Such a quality in a clergyman is peculiarly precious, and if properly cultivated and employed, may become a blessing to thousands. Of course, the attainment and exercise of it ought to be studied. And I know of no means of attaining it more effectual, than habitually cultivating that genuine Christian benevolence, which the spirit and the example of the blessed Saviour so powerfully recommended. A thousand rules on this subject, expressed with all the point and eloquence imaginable, and day by day treasured up in the memory, are of small value when compared with this successful culture of the moral feelings, and the heart.

17. While you cultivate habitual affability, good nature, and benevolence in conversation, be not too ready to make promises of service to those with whom you converse. The inexperienced and the sanguine, who have naturally an obliging temper, are extremely apt to be betrayed into this fault. They feel much disposed to oblige; and they hastily make promises, and excite expectations, which they cannot fulfil. Be not ready to promise, unless you are *sure* of your ability to perform. Be sacredly careful not to disappoint the just expectations which you have excited; and make a point, instead of doing less than you say,

to do more. I have known a number of men, and especially young men, in public stations, who were so ready to excite expectation of the great things they would do for individuals, or for public bodies, and so remarkably delinquent in accomplishing what they so hastily undertook, that, after a while, no confidence whatever was reposed in their undertakings.

18. It is of the utmost importance to one whose profession leads him much into society, that he be not ready to take offence at every trifle that occurs in the course of conversation. It is a real misfortune for any man, and especially for a clergyman, when his natural temper is jealous and suspicious, and when he is ever on the watch for some fancied design to offend him, or to wound his feelings. I have known men in the sacred office so extremely sensitive to every thing of this kind, that their best friends were obliged to converse with them with a degree of caution truly painful. The most innocent remark sometimes became matter of offence, and where no one else saw the remotest purpose of personal application, an unfortunate individual was made an offender for a word. Guard, I pray you, against this unhappy temper with the utmost vigilance. Never think of taking offence, until you are very certain offence was intended. Be sure to err rather on the side of forbearance and charity than of excessive suspicion. Nay, even if you have proof that there was an intention to wound your feelings, rather set it down to the score of temporary peevishness, than of settled malignity; and be ready to meet the offending individual, on the next occasion, with the same serenity and good will as ever.

19. Avoid becoming suddenly and excessively inti-

mate with strangers, at a first interview, and especially, committing yourself to them. This is a great mark of precipitancy and weakness. Be not ready to trust every body. Confidential friendship is a plant of slow growth. Many people appear extremely plausible, and even fascinating at first interview, who are utterly unworthy of your confidence, and will be speedily discovered to be so.

20. Never, if you can help it, put yourself in the power of any man. It is, indeed, a common maxim, that you ought never to put yourself in the power of any one but tried friends. I would go further; never do it in any case, unless it be absolutely necessary. For example, if it be impossible for you to proceed in a delicate and highly important matter, without making a confidant of some one, submit to the necessity. Make the best choice you can. But, on no account, let your communication go further. It can do no good, and may do much harm, in ways that you never thought of anticipating. The most prudent and useful public men I have ever known, were found among those who exercised the most impenetrable reserve respecting the delicate concerns of themselves and others;—who did not impart the knowledge of them even to their nearest relations.

21. When you are called to converse on a subject concerning which there is known to exist, or is likely to arise, a diversity of opinion, in your congregation or neighbourhood, do not be forward to deliver your opinion upon it, unless you feel imperiously called by a sense of duty to do so. And when you are called to give your opinion on such a subject, be careful to express it in a manner as little calculated as pos-

sible to mortify or irritate those who differ from you. Why should you intimate, that those who think otherwise are either "weak" or "wicked?" You will not be likely to do good by such language: and it may deeply wound, and even permanently alienate, many of your best friends.

22. Remember that a clergyman ought ever to maintain personal dignity in conversation. This is too often forgotten. Personal dignity, in this case, may be impaired, by levity, by buffoonery, by the recital of low, vulgar anecdotes, by any thing, in short, which evinces the want of that seriousness and self-respect, which can never be abandoned with impunity. Remember that, though it be not only lawful, but desirable, that clergymen should be affable and cheerful: yet that they can never manifest a spirit of habitual levity and jesting, without giving pain to all correct persons who observe it. Dr. Johnson was far from being a precisian, either in his feelings or manners; yet when he saw a couple of clergymen indulging in considerable mirth and jollity at a dinner table, he said with emotion, "This merriment of parsons is very disgusting." And, truly, when ministers of the gospel, who ought to set an example of dignity, as well as piety, undertake to exhibit themselves for the entertainment of company; to recite low, common-place stories; and not only to repeat, but also to *act* their narratives, with all the circumstances of comedy and farce which belong to them; it cannot fail of giving pain to every mind of correct Christian feeling, and of lowering the ministerial character.

23. Be not ready to join in noisy laughter against any one who has inadvertently committed a blunder,

either in speech or action. It gives pain; and is a mark of very coarse breeding. A dignified command of the countenance is a talent of great value to one in a public station, and adapted to save him from many an embarrassing and mortifying occurrence. It is a real infirmity, and, in a minister of the gospel, an unhappy one, to be ever ready to laugh, or to be noted as a great laugher.

24. It is a great offence against good breeding to be ever ready to turn the eyes of a company on a certain individual, to whom some remark, cursorily made, is supposed to be applicable, and thus, oftentimes, deeply to embarrass him. I have often seen this rule violated in the public assembly, as well as in the parlour. A remark is made, perhaps, which is levelled at the particular denomination or party to which an individual present belongs, or at some opinion which he holds, or some conduct with which he is known to be chargeable. In an instant, every eye is turned toward him; and perhaps some fairly turn round in their seats, to gaze with a smirk or a sneer at the supposed delinquent. There is something so indelicate in this, that a person of truly correct feeling will by no means allow himself to practise it.

25. I have long thought that the practice of retailing anecdotes was one by far too much indulged by many clergymen. To be able to tell a seasonable, appropriate, short and pointed anecdote, now and then, is certainly an accomplishment by no means to be despised, and very proper to be indulged by a clergyman, as well as by any other man. But to abound in them; to be continually resorting to them; to make the repetition of them a favourite amusement, and one

of our characteristics, is indeed unworthy of a Christian minister. I could name clergymen who have a set of anecdotes, which they are constantly retailing; some of them very vulgar; a large portion of them old and perfectly stale; not a few relating to ludicrous citations and expositions of Scripture, and, of course, calculated to make the Scriptures ridiculous in the view of many people; and these, perhaps, repeated the hundredth time, to the loathing of many who have heard them over and over again. A man must have a better memory, and a richer fund, than commonly fall to the lot of the retailers of anecdotes, who does not repeat the items in his list, many times over, to the same individuals. But this is not the worst. The persons in question, by the constant repetition of ludicrous stories, have insensibly cherished in their minds a habitual bias to levity, and have come at length to be expected to be the general jesters for their company.

26. This propensity to the incessant retailing of anecdotes becomes more highly exceptionable, when it leads, as it sometimes does, to the recital of those which include the repetition of profane or obscene language. It is in vain to say that he who only repeats the story, is not the author of the language, and by no means expresses his approbation of it. If the ear be polluted by the words of profaneness and obscenity, it matters little who first of all uttered them. The work of mischief is accumulating by every repetition; and the desire of every Christian ought to be that it never be heard again.

27. Nearly allied to the practice of constantly retailing common-place or unseemly anecdotes is that

of habitually repeating old and stale proverbs. These, from the circumstance of their having been repeated so many thousand times, have ceased to interest; and many of them are truly vulgar, so that to be continually repeating them would be really to subject yourself to the charge of habitual vulgarity. The truth is, making yourself remarkable for the frequent repetition of any particular form of speech, or proverbial expression, is alike contrary to all good taste, and good breeding.

28. And this leads me to lay it down as another fundamental principle of conversation, that nothing in the least degree bordering on the indelicate, or the coarse, ought ever to escape in conversation from the lips of a minister. If you wish to know how far I would carry this principle, I answer, if there be a thought or a word which the most delicate female would shrink from uttering in a public company; if there be an anecdote, which the most scrupulous matron would be unwilling to relate, if all the world were her hearers; then let no clergyman venture to give utterance, in mixed companies, either to the one or the other. His delicacy ought to be quite as scrupulous and pure as that of the most refined lady.

29. It is one of the most obvious dictates of good manners, not to interrupt another person when he is speaking; and yet how frequently is this plain rule of decorum violated! To interrupt one in conversation almost always carries with it an offensive character. It implies either that we are not instructed or interested by what he is saying; that we have not patience to hear him to the end, and are anxious that he should come to a more speedy close; or that we are

wiser than he, and more competent to give instruction on the subject on which he is speaking; neither of which is consistent with that respect and benevolence which we owe to those with whom we converse. But, while you sacredly guard against interrupting others in conversation, be not impatient of interruption yourself. Bear it with calmness, and without the least indication of irritated feeling. Set it down to the score of inadvertence, of nervous excitement, of irascible feeling, of constitutional impatience—in short, of any thing rather than a design to give offence, unless you are compelled by unquestionable testimony to adopt this unfavourable construction.

30. Never allow yourself flatly and offensively to contradict any one with whom you are conversing, provided you mean to remain on good terms with him. It is always a breach of good manners, and to many persons peculiarly painful and embarrassing. If you suspect, or even if you are certain, that a statement made is entirely incorrect, instead of saying bluntly, "that is false," or "that is not true;"—or, "the fact is not as you state it;"—how much more delicate and proper to say—"Do you not mistake?"—"Are you not misinformed?"—"I cannot help thinking that you are deceived with respect to that matter."—But, while you never allow yourself bluntly or harshly to contradict others in conversation, always make a point of bearing it patiently when you are contradicted yourself. Remember that it much oftener arises from coarseness of the mind, and ignorance of propriety, than from any intention to wound feelings; and, therefore, ought in common to be pitied, rather than resented or made matter of offence.

31. Guard against the indulgence of personal vanity in conversation. This is a foible, or rather a sin, which so frequently lowers the dignity, and interferes with the usefulness of men, otherwise of great excellence, that you cannot be too careful to fly from its approaches. In any man it is revolting; but in a minister of the gospel, or in a candidate for the ministry, it is peculiarly offensive and degrading. Let not the excessive love of praise get possession of your mind. Despise the petty and unworthy arts of those who are constantly seeking to draw it toward themselves. Beware of seeming to court observation or attention. Always remember that the larger your demands on others for their respect and admiration, the less they will be disposed to yield to you. No man is so likely to be both honoured and loved as he who appears never to think of soliciting or desiring either. Whereas he who insists on often dragging into view his own excellence, and who is continually blazoning his own talents, attainments and virtues, will generally be found to lose reputation just in proportion as he takes into his own hands the task of awarding it to himself.

32. Vanity, in general, is the parent of egotism in conversation;—another foible, against which I exhort you to guard. "Let not the idea of yourself appear to be always present to your imagination." Talk not of yourself, your plans, your doings, or your affairs in company, if you can easily avoid it. Do not embrace every opportunity of relating something to your own advantage, or that of your family or relatives. It can scarcely be done in any shape, however ingenious, without having an unpleasant appearance, and had, therefore, better be omitted altogether. Even speak-

ing of your own defects and weaknesses, will be considered by many as an indirect compliment to yourself; because it conveys the idea that you feel so secure in the acknowledged possession of higher and nobler qualities, that you can afford to be thought defective in those of minor importance.

33. Do not affect wit in conversation. Wit, like poetry, to be tolerable, must be very good. Now, very few persons are possessed of this commodity in its genuine, attractive character. The greater part of what is called wit, like most of the versifying in our world, is but an humble and vapid imitation of that which it wishes to be thought. Never attempt to force nature, then, in the one case, any more than you would in the other. Few things are more undignified and paltry, than to see a man impotently struggling with attempts at wit, when the only thing really ludicrous about the matter is, the utter failure of the effort. The probability is that you have not real wit. If you have, it will occasionally disclose itself in spite of your efforts to repress it. If you have not, affecting it, and trying to excite it, will only make you an object of ridicule. And, after all, it is not a very desirable accomplishment for a minister of the gospel. It has been commonly found to be a snare rather than a treasure to those who really possessed it.

34. Do not indulge pedantry in conversation. By this you will understand me to mean a formal and unseasonable ostentation of learning; a fault into which men of superficial knowledge, more particularly professional men, are extremely apt to fall, and with which some clergymen, and especially young clergymen, are frequently chargeable. If you have ever so much

learning, there is littleness in making a parade of it; and if you have but a small portion, there is something bordering on dishonesty in vaunting it as if you had much. The best rule in the world on this subject is, to get as much knowledge of every valuable kind as you can; and never to make any further display of it than the discharge of your duty necessarily demands. If you were to hear a physician or lawyer holding forth, in mixed company, on the technicalities and the recondite lore of his profession, would you not be disposed to smile? And ought you not to guard against exciting a smile in others by similar conduct on your own part?

35. Both the spirit and the language of flattery in conversation, are utterly unworthy an ambassador of Christ. In any man it is base; but in him who ought to be a pattern and a leader in all that is good, it is pre-eminently base. Yet there are clergymen who are by no means free from this charge. Their opinions of so many persons and things are either openly solicited, or indirectly required; and their temptations to gratify the feelings of many different classes of people, are so powerful, that they are not always able to resist them. I will not suppose any one who bears the sacred office, to be so unprincipled as to indulge in the habit of indiscriminate flattery, which, as it must defeat its own purpose, is as foolish and contemptible, as it is wicked. But what I warn you against is that delicate flattery, to which many good men are prone; which frequently disguises itself under the name of benevolence; and of which, perhaps, the poison is the more deleterious, because it is so delicately and sparingly administered. Never flatter any one. Never

make your praise cheap. It is not sinful, indeed, to commend another, where commendation is really deserved; but let it be bestowed at a proper time and place; and be conscientious in falling short of what is due, rather than going beyond it. Remember how inflammable a thing human vanity is; and guard against the risk of kindling it into a flame. "He that flattereth his neighbour," says the wise man, "spreadeth a net for his feet."

36. And as I would warn you against flattering others, so I would warn you, with no less solemnity, against inviting commendation and flattery from others to yourself. Nothing is more common, than what is most expressively called "fishing for praise." Sometimes it is almost extorted; and what is it then worth? Despise the littleness, as well as abhor the sin of this miserable beggary. I have known ministers who were in the constant habit, immediately after descending from the pulpit, if they fell in with a brother clergyman, of asking him his opinion of the sermon which he had just heard. Where such inquiries are confined to very intimate friends, they are, perhaps, not to be wholly blamed; although even then, they are in a greater or less degree, indications of vanity, and spread a snare for the honesty of our friends, and had better be omitted. But when addressed, as I have known them to be, to strangers as well as friends, there is a littleness about them truly contemptible. The same general remark may be applied to those cases in which, though there be not a direct solicitation to praise a discourse, there is evidently a door opened for that purpose. I once knew a clergyman, who, so far as I had an opportunity of observing, never failed of say-

ing, to every hearer whom he fell in with, for half an hour or an hour after the close of his own sermon, sabbath after sabbath, "We've had a very solemn subject to-day." This I have heard him repeat and repeat until it became perfectly nauseating; and have observed him to bow and smile with much complacency, when his own indirect compliment to his sermon, drew from one good-natured auditor after another, a dose of flattery.

37. Do not speak of your own performances at all, after they are brought to a close, if you can, consistently with duty, avoid it. If you appear satisfied with them, it will be thought vanity. If you profess yourself dissatisfied, it will be considered as an indirect method of inviting praise. If you merely make the general subject on which you have been discoursing, the subject of conversation in company afterwards, even with the purest motives, it will be apt to be misconstrued as an ingenious device to extort commendation for what you have done. Never boast, on the one hand, of the length of time, or the care which you have bestowed on your discourses; or, on the other, of the expedition and ease with which you prepare them. Never allow yourself to talk at all on such subjects, unless you are compelled to do it. A thousand other subjects, more likely in those circumstances to be useful, lie before you. If a discourse which you have delivered be commended in your presence, do not appear either to be too much gratified with the commendation, or to despise it. Receive the compliment either with respectful silence, with a slight bow, or with the shortest possible expression of thanks; and, as soon as is consistent with courtesy, change the subject.

38. Some persons, under the notion of avoiding formality and flattery, give way to a rude familiarity, which they call, indeed, by some favourable name; but which deserves to be severely reprobated. I have often known young preachers, when they had become a little familiar with their companions, in the habit when addressing them, of calling them by their Christian names only, or by their surnames only; and indulging habitually, not merely in the freedom, but also in all the coarseness of unbridled raillery. Rely upon it, this is, in general, not wise. Mutual dignity, and mutual respect, are indispensable to the continued existence of Christian friendship, in its most pure, delicate and profitable form. If you wish to maintain such friendship, be free and unconstrained; but never indulge in rude and coarse familiarity. Those who are worthy of your love, will certainly be repelled rather than attracted by it.

39. When I remind you of the importance of maintaining a constant regard to truth in conversation, you will consider me as enforcing a plain point in ethics, which no one can dispute. But I wish to go further than this language will be popularly considered as importing. I mean much more than that a minister of the gospel ought to avoid downright lying in company, whether the object of the lie be to flatter or to injure. It ought to be his object, in making every statement, in repeating the most trivial narrative, to guard as carefully against misrepresenting, or exaggerating any fact, as if he were on oath; to give no false colouring, no over-colouring, and not, even in jest, to misstate the smallest circumstance. I have had the happiness to be acquainted with a few men whose habits were

of this kind; and it was delightful to observe what weight it imparted to their word; and how completely they were delivered from all those troublesome explanations and retractions, to which the less scrupulous were constantly exposed.

40. Be strictly attentive to the circumstances of time, place, and company in conversation. Look round the room, before you introduce a particular new topic, and ask yourself, whether it is a suitable one for that company; or, whether there be any individuals present to whom it may be peculiarly unwelcome or embarrassing. There is an old French proverb, the import of which is—"Be careful never to mention a rope in the family of a man who has been hanged." It is a proverb full of good sense, and social delicacy. Yet nothing is more common than to see persons of absent or coarse minds, violating this rule. They introduce subjects, or indulge remarks, calculated to wound the feelings of some of the most estimable individuals present; and this, not for the laudable purpose of benefiting the individuals in question, or of bearing an honest testimony against vice; but from mere inadvertence or want of feeling. Think, therefore, before you speak, not only what you are about to say, but also to whom you are about to address it. It is said, that Bishop Burnet was so apt to wound the feelings of those with whom he was conversing, by an infraction of this rule, from mere absence of mind, that some of his best friends were afraid of introducing him to distinguished strangers, lest he should embarrass them as well as himself by an infirmity, which, if its effects had not been sometimes so painful, would have been often unspeakably ludicrous. Direct particular atten-

tion to this object; and it will soon become as much a fixed habit of your mind to advert to the persons addressed in every conversation, as to any other circumstance attending the communication.

41. When any persons impart to you a knowledge of facts in confidence, make a point of being delicately faithful to the trust committed to you. It not unfrequently happens that the sick and the dying; persons in difficulty and distress; and persons under anxiety of mind respecting their eternal state, make communications in confidence to ministers of the gospel; under the impression that they, of all men, may be most safely trusted. In every such case, preserve the most inviolable secrecy. But there are many other cases, in which, though no formal injunction of secrecy is expressed, still it ought by all means to be understood, by every delicately prudent mind. We all know how frequently, and with what strict honour, professional secrets are kept by lawyers and physicians; and I have long been of the opinion that habits of more strict reserve than have commonly been thought needful, ought to be maintained by clergymen, with regard to all communications made to them as such, whether formally confidential or not; and that even after an ordinary conversation on any delicate or important subject, it is always best to avoid repeating what has been communicated. No one can tell how many things may occur which may render it peculiarly important that he should have kept it to himself. You may publish your own secrets, if you choose to be weak enough to do so; but you have no right to publish those of others. In general, a public man ought to repeat very little of what is communicated to him. It

can do no harm, in common cases, to keep it secret, while the mischiefs of disclosing it may be endless.

42. It is the fault of many to be loud, and even boisterous in conversation. If the company be ever so large, the moment they become a little engaged and animated, they speak loud enough not only to be heard in every part of the room, but so as to attract and even force the attention of the whole company; and that, perhaps, when conversing on a subject which ought not to be a matter of such public proclamation. There is no little indelicacy in this. When you are publicly addressed across a room, in such a manner as plainly evinces a desire that the whole company should hear your answer, let your reply be audible, but not loud. Let mildness and dignity mark every word you utter.

43. Guard against the too frequent use of superlatives in your social intercourse. Persons of ardent, impetuous minds, and especially the young, are apt to manifest an undue fondness for the superlative degree in conversation. If they praise any person or thing, they seem to think of using no epithets but those which indicate the highest grade of excellence. If they commend any one's talents, they are sure to represent them as of "the highest order." If they would speak well of a sermon, they pronounce it "incomparably excellent." On the contrary, if they undertake to express an unfavourable opinion, the terms, "contemptible," "execrable," "detestable," are the softest which they think of employing. In short, the more high-wrought their figures, and the more intense and ardent their whole style of expression, the more interesting they suppose their conversation to be. Let me entreat you to guard against the habitual use of

this vehemence and intensity of language. It is seldom called for. Men of sense and good taste rarely permit themselves to employ it. A strict regard to truth generally forbids it. And with respect to those who are in the habit of employing it, both their praise and their blame soon become cheap, and, at length, worthless. He who wishes his approbation or his censure to go for much, must not be very lavish of either.

44. Seek all convenient opportunities of conversing with the eminently wise and good, and of listening to their conversation. Especially when you are engaged in investigating an important subject, endeavour, if possible, to enjoy the privilege of conversing on that subject with some individual, and even with more than one, of profound views, and extensive reading. You may often learn more in an hour, by conversing with such an one, than by the solitary reading or meditation of a month. Dr. Franklin once told a friend that some of his most original thoughts were suggested by the collision of conversation; and that, too, very often upon subjects foreign to those on which he was conversing. And Mr. Fox, the far-famed parliamentary orator, declared in the British House of Commons, that he had learned more from Mr. Burke's conversation than from all the books he had ever read in his life.*

45. Finally, be constantly and vigilantly observant of the habits in conversation of those persons who are considered as most pleasant and acceptable in this department of social intercourse. In every community there are those who are universally allowed to excel

* Rush's Introductory Lectures, p. 349.

in colloquial accomplishments. Now it will be very unwise to be humble imitators of such persons; but it will, undoubtedly, be the part of wisdom to take notice of the means by which they attain success; and to make use of what you see, as your own particular habits and character may render proper. I doubt whether any man ever acquired much excellence in this important art, without the happy talent of close observation, and, in this way as well as by his own good sense, making himself master of the proprieties and delicacies which become the social circle.

LETTER V.

Let your speech be always with grace seasoned with salt.
Col. iv. 6.

RELIGIOUS CONVERSATION.

My dear young friend:—To be able to introduce the great subject of religion, in an easy, seasonable, and acceptable manner, in the daily intercourse of society, is a most precious talent, the uses of which are more various, more rich, more numerous, and more important, than almost any that can be mentioned.

That this ability, when it exists in a high degree, is, in part, a natural talent, cannot be doubted. The physical temperament of some men is much more favourable to the ready and unconstrained performance of the duty in question, than that of many others. More stress, however, I apprehend, has been sometimes laid on this fact, than there ought to have been. Not a few allege that they have "no gift" of this kind, and, therefore, content themselves in the habitual neglect of the duty. At any rate, they rarely attempt it, and think that they cannot perform it, even tolerably. But it would be just as reasonable to plead, because an easy, pleasant, and attractive elocution is natural, in a peculiar degree, to some, that therefore others who cannot attain equal excellence in this respect, ought not to attempt to speak at all. The fact is, the power of introducing and maintaining religious conversation well, though to a certain extent a natural gift, is yet capable of great improvement, nay, it may be said, of unlimited improvement; and the true reason, no doubt, why some persons of plain talents, and with even striking disadvantages of physical temperament, yet excel in this happy art, is that they have taken pains to cultivate a talent so peculiarly precious to the pious mind, and so manifestly useful in all the intercourse of life. To what appear to me some of the best means of carrying on this cultivation, I shall advert before closing the present letter.

My first object shall be to point out some errors, in relation to this subject, which appear to me to be prevalent; and this will prepare the way for a few general counsels for conducting religious conversation, and also for cultivating a happy talent for the discharge of this part of Christian and ministerial duty.

1. It is an error to suppose that religious conversation must be introduced on all occasions, and in all companies, indiscriminately, whether the time, the character of the persons present, and the circumstances, favour it or not. No doubt many who have but little taste for such conversation, omit to introduce it, under the plea that there is "no good opportunity," when it is really otherwise. But there can be as little doubt, that there are many occasions, in which no suitable opening for it is presented. On such occasions, to drag forward the subject, in a formal manner, and, as it were, "by main force," is never judicious, and often very revolting. It frequently has the appearance of being done as a kind of official

task, which is never likely to do good. Be always on the watch for opportunities of saying something for the honour of your Master, and for the welfare of the souls of men; but do not think it your duty to compel people to listen to you on this most sacred, important and delicate of all subjects, when their character, their situation and their employment evidently close up every suitable avenue of approach.

2. It is an error to imagine that the same methods of introducing and maintaining religious conversation, are equally adapted to all persons, and all occasions. If I am not deceived, many adopt the notion that the very same plan of approach will answer in all cases, for the rich and the poor, the learned and the illiterate, the occupant of high office, and the most unpretending, obscure citizen. This is to set at nought all the principles of human nature, and to forget that the circumstances of men have much effect in modifying their feelings and character. If we open the Bible, we shall see ample warrant for addressing some persons on this subject unceremoniously and directly; and others in a more cautious and circuitous manner. In this sense, we ought, with the apostle, to "become all things to all men, that we may gain some;" not by flattering their prejudices, or countenancing their corruptions; but by endeavouring skilfully to adapt our instructions and exhortations to their several habits, attainments, circumstances, and tastes. Those who are most intelligent, and whose pride would be most apt to be offended by an abrupt address, might be approached, and perhaps won, in an indirect and gradual manner. There are thousands to whom I might safely say, "Pray, sir, do you cherish the hope

that you are a real Christian?" But there are many others, to whom if I were to address such a question, I should expect to be shut out from all opportunity of approaching or benefiting them afterwards. Yet the very same people might, by a little address, be insensibly drawn into a free conversation on the same subject, and to answer that very question without the least offence. This is one of the many cases in which some knowledge of human nature and of the world is essential to a wise discharge of duty. Nor is it a valid objection to this counsel to say, that, if we follow it, we may be tempted to defer too much to human rank, and corrupt refinement. There is, no doubt, danger on this quarter, against which we ought to guard. But the abuse of a thing is not a legitimate argument against its use. Counterfeits do not prove that there is no true money, but rather the reverse.

3. Another very common error in religious conversation, is to say too much. A man may be "too full of talk" on this, as well as on any other subject. That is, he may talk so much and so long, as to become "a weariness" even to his pious hearers, and much more to those who are not pious. This is far from being a rare occurrence; and it becomes especially an evil, when the pious sentiments uttered, are all of the most common-place sort; and, not only so, but dealt out in that common-place, task-like manner, which very seldom makes a favourable impression among discerning people. Guard, then, against excessive talkativeness, even here. Let what you say on this subject be a real "conversation." Let one object of your address be, to induce others to talk, and disclose their sentiments and feelings, that you may know how to

answer them. Let your part of the discussion be as lively, pointed, and short as you can make it. Never allow it to degenerate into formal, tedious preaching, or rather prosing.

4. Once more, it is the error of some to imagine that religious conversation is to be carried on with a tone of voice, and an aspect of countenance, peculiar to itself. Hence, while these persons converse on all other subjects in a simple, easy, natural manner, the moment they pass to the subject of religion, their whole manner is changed. It becomes formal and artificial; so that you would scarcely know them to be the same persons who had been a few minutes before conversing on ordinary subjects. This is a fault as unreasonable as it is repulsive. Why should men cease to speak naturally, when they come to speak on a subject the most interesting and delightful in the world? Shun this fault with the utmost care. Do not, indeed, allow yourself to fall into the opposite extreme; I mean talking on the subject of religion with levity. But, at the same time, let all grimace, all sanctimoniousness of manner, all affected solemnity, all lofty dictation, be carefully avoided. The more simple, affable, and entirely inartificial your manner, the more you will gratify all classes; nor is this all; the more easy will you always find it to slide insensibly into religious conversation, without alarming the fears of the most thoughtless; and the more easy to recur to it again, after a little interruption from other topics.

But, to guard against these errors, is not all that is incumbent upon you in privately conversing with men on their eternal interests. My next object, then, shall be to offer a few counsels, which I would fain hope may not be altogether useless. And,

1. My first counsel is, that you make a point of introducing religious conversation, whenever you have a good opportunity, and that you abound in it wherever you go.

It is melancholy to think how many hours ministers spend in company, without saying a word to recommend either the service or kingdom of their Master. Nay, some of these hours are spent in the company of the truly pious, with whom there is no obstacle to religious conversation; who expect it; who desire it; and who are disappointed at not finding it introduced. To be backward in introducing it in such company is unpardonable. But this is not all. In every company and in every situation, be on the watch for opportunities to speak a word for Christ. And when you do not find opportunities, by a little address, you may make them: and you will often do so, if you have as eager, and incessant desire to do good, as the miser has to turn everything into the channel of gain, and the ambitious man to gather laurels from all quarters. I have often been struck with that passage, in which the apostle Paul, when writing to the Hebrews concerning ministers, says — "They watch for souls." And, truly, the minister who acts on the principles of enlightened fidelity will thus "watch," not only in the pulpit, but daily, and in all the walks of private intercourse. Let me entreat you, then, to lose no good opportunity of conversing on the most precious of all subjects. Let your conversation continually be "with grace, seasoned with salt, that it may minister grace to the hearers." You may say a thousand useful things in private conversation, which you never could utter in the pulpit. You may answer questions, solve scruples, obviate objections, reprove faults, and communicate knowledge in the parlour, which could by no means be brought into the sanctuary. Above all, in many cases of private discourse you may come near to the heart and the conscience, and adapt your instructions to individual exigencies, in a way altogether impracticable in addressing a public assembly. It has, therefore, often occurred to me as a fact equally wonderful and humiliating, that Christian ministers are not commonly more vigilant in availing themselves of this advantage, and more unceasing in the use of it: that their minds are not found teeming with good thoughts, pious hints, and instructive, weighty sentiments, as well as direct addresses, wherever they go.

2. Cultivate the important art of introducing conversation on the subject of religion in an easy and happy manner. One of the greatest difficulties attending this whole subject is to begin well. A formal introduction of the subject; an introduction which, as it were, announces beforehand the intention of talking piously; and which, of course, excites the fears of those who have no taste for such conversation, ought certainly, in ordinary cases, to be avoided. No less undesirable is an abrupt commencement of this species of conversation, that is, suddenly entering upon it, when something very different had been, the instant before, the subject of discourse. But why should we ever do either of these? What subject can possibly be started, by any individual, or in any company, which a man of good sense, and whose heart is filled with pious and benevolent emotions, may not soon,

and without violence, convert into a medium of some useful suggestions on the subject of religion? The state of the weather; the prospects of the husbandman; the news of the day; an ordinary domestic occurrence; the return of spring; the approach of autumn; or an accident on the road;—these, or any analogous topics which may be hinted at, furnish ample occasions for the introduction of pious sentiments; insomuch that a social circle might, by a person of tolerable address, and of the proper spirit, be translated from the region of perfect levity, to the region of serious and devout reflection, before they were aware that the transition was intended. This is a happy art. All may learn it who will be vigilant enough, and take pains enough for the purpose. With a moderate knowledge of human nature; a tolerable address; a little attention to incidents as they arise; and a heart glowing with a desire to do good, the task is easy. "Covet earnestly this gift;" labour without ceasing to gain it; and you will not labour in vain.

3. Let your conversation be adapted to the character of the company into which you may happen to be thrown. If the company with which you are called to converse, be all professors of religion, there will, ordinarily, be little difficulty in adapting your discourse to them; for you may speak directly and pointedly on any topic which occurs as important. Especially, you may enter with freedom into all the refreshing richness of conversation on Christian experience. If, on the contrary, the company consist altogether of gay and worldly people, your utmost ingenuity will often be put to the test in leading them on to instructive and edifying, as well as pleasant

discourse. Yet even this may be done, if you take them by the right handle. When the circle in which you are seated, as will be apt more frequently to happen, is made up partly of professors of religion, and partly of those who are not so, a very happy use may be made of the former, as a medium of conveying instruction to the latter. As it is oftentimes one of the most effectual modes of addressing parents, to do it through the medium of their children; so we may frequently speak to the worldly and thoughtless most impressively through the medium of the pious, who are seated in their presence. In short, study diligently the different tastes and habits of the aged and the young, the polished and the rough, the learned and the illiterate, the fashionable and the plain, in whose society you may find yourself; and endeavour to have "a word in season," a set of topics, and a mode of treating them, adapted to their several characters.

4. Guard against giving your remarks on religion, in the social circle, an air of dictation and authority. This caution, which was mentioned before in reference to common conversation, is no less important in reference to the subject of religion. Ministers, from the circumstance of their being so much accustomed to speak with authority from the pulpit, are apt, spontaneously, and even insensibly, to fall into a similar manner of speaking in private; to be impatient of contradiction; and to feel, when their opinions are in any measure controverted, as if their official dignity were invaded. Let no spirit or feeling of this kind intrude into your social intercourse. The more entirely you can divest yourself of it, and sit down with your friends and associates on terms of perfect

equality, as a friend and brother, who claims no authority over their consciences, but is actuated supremely by a regard to their temporal and eternal interest, the more easy and affectionate will your conversation be, and the more likely will you be to make a favourable impression on their minds.

5. In conducting religious conversation, as much as possible avoid theological controversy. I before cautioned you against the habit of falling into controversy on any subject in company. But I would now warn you that religious controversy, when you are conversing with persons with a view to their spiritual benefit, is peculiarly undesirable, and ought to be avoided as much as possible. I say, as much as possible; for there are doubtless cases in which it is not possible to avoid it, without shrinking from the defence of the truth. You will sometimes fall in with persons, who, from a love of disputation, from ill manners, from enmity to the truth, or from a desire to put your ingenuity to the test, will compel you either to be silent, or to defend your opinions. When you meet with such persons, you must manage them in the best way you can. Do not, however, even with such, allow a dispute to be much protracted. Draw it to a close as soon as practicable. Carry it on, while it lasts, with all the "meekness and gentleness of Christ." And let them see that you take no personal offence at having your opinions questioned; but simply desire to defend what you deem truth, and to guard them from injurious error.

But in all cases in which controversy can properly be avoided, by all means decline engaging in it. Theological disputes, in the social circle, are seldom profitable, and often highly mischievous. They sour the temper; but commonly leave each party confirmed in his original opinion. In your ordinary religious conversation, then, keep as clear of what are called disputed points in theology, as possible, consistently with conveying sound and useful instruction in divine truth. When you are compelled to touch on them, let it be under a practical rather than a polemical aspect, and in terms as little adapted to give offence as possible. When you perceive the most distant symptom of approaching controversy, take measures to avert the impending storm. This may commonly be done by a few kind words, or by giving a practical turn to the argument. It may be easy to prevent the evil; but by no means so easy to cure it when we have once fallen under its power.

6. You will sometimes fall in company with infidels, who totally reject revelation. Conversation with them is always a delicate, and often a difficult task. Make a point of treating them respectfully, as long as they maintain decorum on their part; and even if they scoff and blaspheme, do not suffer yourself to be so far borne away by irascible feeling, as to address them in opprobrious language. As long as their deportment admits of your continuing to argue with them, do it in the spirit of meekness and benevolence. In addressing them, do not permit yourself to call them by hard names, or to impute to them base motives. Endeavour to convince them that you are actuated, not by a spirit of personal resentment, or wounded pride; but by a regard to the cause of God, and their own eternal welfare. In arguing with them, however, do not merely stand on the defensive; but show them,

on the plan of Butler's "Analogy," and similar books, that most of the objections which they urge against Revelation, lie with equal force against natural religion, which they commonly profess to believe. I have seldom seen an unbeliever who was able to stand five minutes before the *argumentum ad hominem* plan of treatment. Above all, in addressing them, while you appeal to their understandings, never fail, in a mild and respectful manner, to appeal to their consciences and their hearts. All my experience tells me that nothing is so likely to impress them as this.

7. In conversing with persons of a different religious denomination from your own, there is need of much vigilance both as to the matter and manner of your conversation. In all such conversations, guard against either manifesting or feeling a proselyting spirit. Be much more anxious to see them Christians, than to see them Presbyterians. Dwell, therefore, much more on the fundamental and precious points of our common Christianity, than on the peculiarities of either their or your church. While they see that you are deeply serious, and anxious to promote their eternal welfare, let them perceive that you are not anxious to win them to your party. Agree with them as far as you can. Treat them with pointed respect and attention; if they appear pious, with as much affection as if they belonged to your particular denomination; and even if they make overtures for joining your own church, do not be ready to catch at their proposal. Manifest no eagerness to receive them. On the contrary, rather show, in all their extent, the difficulties which lie in the way of transferring their religious connection. However unworthily, in relation to this

subject, persons of other sects may treat you or yours, never allow yourself to imitate their pernicious example.

8. The introduction of religious conversation among entire strangers, is often very desirable and important; and yet, frequently, requires no little address. I said that it is often very desirable and important; for more than once have I known a minister to be in company a whole afternoon, or longer, with a circle of strangers, several of whom, though unknown to him, were earnestly desirous of hearing him engage in religious conversation; and were not a little disappointed to find the interview at an end, without his having introduced it. Many a precious opportunity of instructing the ignorant, of directing the perplexed and inquiring, and of comforting the sorrowful, has been thus lost. Guard against all such omissions. Never allow yourself to be half an hour in company, even with the most perfect strangers, without endeavouring to ascertain whether any of them have a taste for serious conversation. There are many ways of ascertaining this, without intrusion or indelicacy. A cursory remark, or an apparently incidental inquiry, may, and probably will, elicit enough to solve your doubt. Many a precious conversation has resulted from such an exploring remark or inquiry. Like the discovery of a refreshing spring in a parched and dreary wilderness, not unfrequently has a minister of the gospel, as well as a private Christian, met with a spiritual feast himself, and been the means of imparting a feast to others, when he least of all expected such a pleasure; when, perhaps, he was ready to say within himself, "there is no fear of God in this place."

9. Introducing and conducting religious conversa-

tion with persons of wealth, and high station in society, is a peculiarly important, and, at the same time, a very delicate and difficult duty. Peculiarly important, because any good impression made on them, will be likely to extend itself more widely; and in many respects, delicate and difficult, because this class of persons are more in the habit of being approached with deference, and, for various reasons, more apt to be nice, and even fastidious in their feelings, than many others. At the same time, I have no doubt that the difficulties of this duty have been, by some, greatly overrated; and that plain, good sense, with a heart overflowing with piety and benevolence, will be found, humanly speaking, a safe and adequate guide, in all ordinary cases. My advice on this point shall be short. Never, on any account, court or affect the company of the wealthy and great. Never take pains to be much with them; and never boast of their acquaintance. When you are providentially thrown in their way, sacredly avoid every thing that approaches to a supple, sycophantic spirit of accommodation to their errors or vices. Never accost them with that timid, embarrassed diffidence, which may lead them to suppose that you have more veneration for them, than for your duty or your God. At the same time, let nothing of the unmannerly, the sullen, or the morose mark your deportment toward them. An old divine was accustomed to say, "Please all men in the truth; but wound not the truth to please any." Let them see that Christian duty is not inconsistent with the most perfect politeness. Introduce pious thoughts, and divine truth, to their view, in a gentle and sometimes in an indirect manner; and let them see that you are much more intent on doing them good, than gaining their favour. When you have occasion to oppose them, let it be done mildly and meekly, but firmly; with the air of one who dislikes to oppose, but feels constrained to "obey God rather than man." In a word, I believe that a minister of the gospel never appears to more advantage in the view of those who are considered as the great ones of this world, and is never more likely to make a deep impression upon them, than when he makes them to feel, not by ostentation, sanctimoniousness or austerity; not even by importunately soliciting their attention to his own views of truth and duty, but by exhibiting meek decision of spiritual character, that they are in the presence of a man, who regards the authority and favour of God above all things, and whose supreme and habitual object is to promote the everlasting welfare of his fellow-men.

10. Never imagine that it is your duty to violate good manners, either in introducing or continuing religious conversation. This is never proper, because never necessary. If you cannot persuade an individual, by a mild and respectful mode of address, to listen to you, it is better to forbear. An attempt to force what you have to say, on one who steadfastly or profanely resists you, is "casting pearls before swine." And violating the respect which is due to any person, under the notion of promoting, in this way, his spiritual interest, is, usually, of all delusions one of the greatest. If you watch for the *mollia tempora fandi*, you will have an opportunity of approaching him, if he be accessible at all. If you wait, with a proper temper, and with humble prayer, for a

door to be opened for doing him good, you will, probably, not wait in vain.

11. When you are called to converse with persons under religious impressions, address yourself to the duty with much seriousness and prayer. Remember that what you say, may influence their eternal condition; and, therefore, that every word is important; important to them, to yourself, and to the church of God. Remember, too, that the task of instructing and guiding those who are "asking the way to Zion," is as delicate and difficult as it is important. It requires much knowledge of the human heart, and of human nature, and much acquaintance with the gospel as a practical system. Study to qualify yourself for this interesting and momentous duty, by much converse with your own heart; by much intercourse with those whose ministry God has eminently blessed; by reading the best books which tend to throw light on Christian character and experience; and, above all, by humble importunate prayer for that wisdom which is adapted to "win souls," and to guide "them in the way of peace." He who allows himself to enter on this duty without much consideration, and humbly looking to heaven for aid; or to perform it in a slight and careless manner, must make a miserable estimate both of ministerial fidelity, and of the worth of immortal souls.

12. Before you enter on the duty of conversing with any one on this most important of all subjects, endeavour, if possible, to learn something of the peculiar character and temperament of the individual. There are peculiarities of this kind, which frequently exert an immediate and important influence on religious exercises. Some persons have a remarkably sanguine

temperament, and buoyant animal spirits, which are apt to impart ardour to their feelings on all subjects, and, of course, to confer on their religious impressions the appearance of more decision and intensity of character than they really possess. Others labour under a constitutional depression of mind, which is ever disposed to look on the dark side of things, and sometimes borders on melancholy, and even despondency; and which always prevents them from doing justice to the evidence in their own favour; while a third class are affected with some bodily disease, which not unfrequently benumbs or agitates the mind, and creates no small difficulty in judging of its real state. Now in conversing with an individual who is anxious respecting his eternal interest, it is of great importance to know whether he is under the special influence of any of these physical difficulties, or temperamental predispositions. For, by the result of this inquiry, the course to be pursued must be in some measure modified. The undue confidence of some ought to be firmly repressed; and the precipitancy of others restrained or cautioned. The backwardness of the timid should be stimulated, and the trembling apprehensions of the melancholy and desponding, if possible, removed, by affectionate encouragement. The wise physician of the body is always careful to inquire about the presence of disturbing forces in the mind, and prescribes accordingly. In like manner, the wise physician of the soul will endeavour to explore every physical idiosyncrasy which distinguishes the spiritual patient to whom he may be called, and address him in a corresponding manner. If you have not already a particular acquaintance with him, make such inquiries respecting his habits, life, temperament, and other peculiarities, as may put you in possession of all the requisite information. And instead of making your conversation, if such it may be called, to consist chiefly of continued address on your part, which is the favourite manner of some, resort much more to the plan of affable and affectionate interrogation, which will lead the individual, at every step, to disclose the state of his own mind, and thus furnish you with some of the best indications for adapting your addresses to his case.

13. Be careful to give clear doctrinal instruction concerning the plan of salvation to those who are anxious and inquiring. I have observed it to be the manner of some in conversing with such persons, to deal chiefly in tender and solemn exhortation; under the belief that the grand object aimed at ought to be to impress the conscience and the heart, rather than to impart doctrinal knowledge. But it ought to be remembered that neither the conscience nor the heart can ever be suitably impressed but through the medium of truth. It is only as far as gospel truth is apprehended, that any genuine scriptural exercises with regard to it can exist. Carefully study, then, to impart to every anxious mind clear views of the fundamental doctrines of the gospel. Not that, in conversing with such persons, you are ever to perplex them with the metaphysical refinements of theology, which ought ever to be, as far as possible, avoided. But the course which I deem of so much importance is, that you constantly endeavour to fill their minds with plain, simple, connected Bible truth; that you dwell on the scriptural character of God; the nature and requisitions of his

holy law; the pollution, guilt and danger of all men in their natural state; the divinity of the Saviour; the efficacy of his atoning sacrifice; the unsearchable riches and freeness of his grace; the work of the Holy Spirit in regenerating and sanctifying the heart; and the utter helplessness, and, at the same time, perfect responsibility and blameworthiness of man. Just as far as these great doctrines are fastened on the conscience, and impressed on the heart, and no further, may we hope to become the instruments of saving benefit to those whom we address.

14. Be not too ready to speak peace or to administer consolation to those who are in a serious, anxious state of mind. It is, undoubtedly, painful to see any one in distress; and the spiritual physician will be often strongly tempted by false benevolence, to encourage, and administer comfort, where he ought not. Beware of this. It is far better that an anxious inquirer after salvation should pass a few more weeks or months in a state of deep mental solicitude, and even anguish, than that he should be prematurely comforted, and led to repose in a false hope, from which he may never awake. Be not afraid, then, to be perfectly faithful: to lay open every wound to the very bottom, before you attempt to heal it. Be slow in administering comfort, while the least doubt remains with regard to the real state of the individual. Indeed I have often thought that it is very seldom proper for a minister, or any other pious man, in conversing with an anxious person, to be forward to pronounce a favourable judgment with respect to his state. You may be deceived in your opinion, and you may be the means of deceiving him fatally. It is, in general, much safer

and better for him to be brought to a favourable conclusion concerning himself, by that heavenly teaching, which cannot deceive; and which, though sometimes more tardy in exhibiting its results than earthly wisdom expects and desires, always furnishes the safest and best testimony.

15. Be not hasty in publishing the exercises or situation of those whom you know to be anxiously inquiring. It is deeply painful to observe the frequency and injudiciousness with which this rule is infringed. A person, perhaps, has scarcely become conscious to himself of deep solicitude respecting his spiritual interest, and given a hint of it to his minister, or to some pious friend, before it is blazed abroad; becomes matter of public speculation; and leads a number of persons immediately to crowd around him, and offer their services as his instructors and guides. The consequences of this method of proceeding are often extremely unhappy. Some are puffed up, by becoming objects of so much unexpected attention and conversation. Others are revolted, and, perhaps, deeply disgusted, at being addressed by so many on the subject of their exercises, and by some, it may be, very injudiciously. While a third class, whose impressions are slight and transient, are mortified at being held up to view as awakened persons, and afterwards lying under the odium of having gone back; and, possibly, in some cases so much mortified, as to withdraw from those individuals and opportunities, which might have been essentially useful. Besides all this, it has often happened, that the number of serious persons who have immediately clustered around an individual thus publicly announced as under religious

impressions, has been so great, and their talents, knowledge, experience, and capacity for giving sound instruction so extremely various, that they have perplexed, confounded, and most unhappily retarded, the object of their well-meant attention, instead of really helping him. With almost as much propriety might a physician of the body, when he found a patient ill of a dubious disease, throw open his apartment to every intruder, and invite every medical practitioner within twenty miles of him, however discordant their theories, to come in and prescribe at pleasure for the sufferer.

My advice is, that, when you ascertain that any one is becoming seriously thoughtful on the subject of religion, you keep it, for a short time, to yourself: indeed, that you thus keep the fact, until his exercises begin to assume a definite shape and character; being careful, in the meanwhile, to attend to the case with conscientious diligence yourself. When you judge the way to be open, communicate a knowledge of the situation of the individual to one or two of those persons in whose knowledge, piety and prudence you have most confidence, and whom you know to have the peculiar confidence of the individual in question. The case of the spiritual seed is a little like that of the natural. When we place a seed in the ground, we allow it a little time to vegetate under the concealment of the soil. He who should go every few hours to the spot, where it was deposited, and drag it forth, in order to see how the process of vegetation was going on, would be considered as a very unwise cultivator. So he who, in regard to seed of a much more important and delicate nature, will not give it time to shoot and grow a little, before it is forced on the public gaze, acts a part, I must think, by no means adapted to promote the best interests either of the individual immediately concerned, or of the church. If he would consent to wait a short time, the view taken would probably soon be found much more pleasant and edifying, or to assume a character which ought not to be made public at all.

16. Guard against conversing too much at one time, with those who are under serious impressions. I am deeply persuaded, that, in many cases, the minds of such persons, in consequence of being incessantly plied with conversation, even though of good quality, yet excessive as to quantity, have been kept in a state of agitation and conflict, longer than they would probably otherwise have been. And the evil has been, no doubt, increased, as I just hinted, when a number of individuals, of different degrees of knowledge, piety and judgment have undertaken to inculcate, each his peculiar views, on the persons in question. I am confident that although persons in this deeply interesting state of mind, ought to be frequently instructed and exhorted, by competent counsellors, yet few things are more injurious to them than to be annoyed by incessant, common-place conversation. It is an utter mistake to suppose that they are benefited by being always in society, even of the best kind. They need much time for retirement, self-examination and prayer, and ought to be referred much to the word of God, and the teaching of the Holy Spirit. A few thoughts at a time, from a pious friend, clear, seasonable, instructive, and to the point, will be most likely to be useful. After receiving these, at suitable intervals, they ought

to be left much in their closets, with their Bibles and their God; and to be frequently told to look rather to the Saviour than to man for help.

17. If, after becoming a pastor, you should be so happy as to know of any considerable number of individuals in your congregation who are beginning to think seriously on the subject of religion, it may become desirable to convene them weekly, or as often as convenient, for the subject of receiving instruction and exhortation together. This practice has been much recommended by experience, and is attended with several very important advantages. It enables a faithful pastor to accomplish more in the indispensable duty of conversing with the serious and anxious, in a single afternoon, or evening, than would be practicable in a week, in the ordinary method of visiting from house to house. The appointment of such a meeting, too, may induce many persons who are really in some degree serious, to come forward and put themselves in the way of conversation on the subject of experimental religion, who, if no such opportunity were presented, might conceal the state of their minds, and lose the advantage of being personally and pointedly addressed. I am also inclined to think that every pastor, even when there is not sufficient attention excited among his people to keep up such a weekly meeting of inquirers as I have described, ought to have a stated time, occurring as often, at least, as once a fortnight, and distinctly made known to his people, when he will make a point of being at home, and ready to attend to any, whether professors of religion or not, who may wish to converse with him on their spiritual state. A faithful pastor will rarely pass such an appointed time

without some visitors. And some will go, perhaps, and be happily led to the Saviour, who, but for such an appointment, would, humanly speaking, have lost their serious impressions, and hardened themselves in sin. Who does not know that, when the mind begins to be exercised on the subject of religion, the merest trifles will, in some cases, serve as excuses for concealing the fact? The inquirer will feel, it may be, that he ought to converse with his minister; but he cannot summon resolution to venture on the interview. He fears, perhaps, that he will not be at home; or that he will have company; or be otherwise engaged; or that it will be difficult to disclose to him his feelings. The consequence is he does not go; and his seriousness, after a short time, wears off. But if he knew that his minister, on a certain day, would be at home; that he would have no other engagement; that he would be hoping and desiring to see persons in his state of mind; and that his very appearance at the house of his pastor on that day would itself disclose the object of his visit, and furnish an introduction to a free conversation; his excuses would probably all vanish, and he would avail himself of the precious privilege.

If you should ever make such an appointment as I have last mentioned, and, if on the recurrence of the day, for several times, you should have no visitors, be not discouraged. Continue the appointment; and give public intimations, from time to time, in the manner that you may judge most suitable, that it is made in vain. No one can tell how far such intimations may serve to rouse up the pious, and excite them to prayer and exertion.

18. Be not too hasty in encouraging those of whose seriousness you have a favourable opinion, to go forward and make a profession of religion. This is undoubtedly often done with very undue precipitation. Persons of very tender age, and others, previously of very equivocal character, have been, literally, hurried to the Lord's table in less than a week after the commencement of their serious thoughtfulness; without allowing them time fully to "count the cost;" and before they were able to put their exercises to such a test as might be satisfactory to themselves or others. Hence many young persons, of both sexes, in a few months or even weeks, after making this solemn profession, have found themselves unexpectedly bereft of all comfortable hope; their evidences of Christian character gone; their interest in the subject in a great measure lost; and their minds filled with regret that they had been so hasty. It was now, however, difficult to retreat, and their whole lives, perhaps, have been spent in a heartless, and of course, a comfortless profession.

It is readily granted that neither scripture nor reason fixes any precise period, during which candidates for church communion are bound to wait, in order to put the stability of their religious character to the test. And it is equally evident, that extraordinary cases ought to prescribe rules for themselves. But, in general, it is evident that there ought to be a few months, at least, of serious and prayerful deliberation, before taking a step so solemn, so momentous, so irrevocable; a step likely to be followed with so many interesting consequences to those who take it, and to the sacred family with which they propose to become connected. Let no desire to see the rapid multiplication of professors, ever lead you to depart from this principle. I have more than once repented having given what afterwards appeared to be premature encouragement to come to a sacramental table; but never did I repent advising to a few months' deliberation and delay, when the preparation was doubtful.

19. In conversing on the subject of practical religion, especially with those who are not well informed on the subject, be sparing in the use of that technical language, which many continually employ. I refer to a number of phrases, of standing use in many pious circles, which, although the meaning intended to be conveyed by them is undoubtedly correct and important, are yet so remote from the language of ordinary social intercourse, that they sound strangely, not to say unintelligibly, out of the circles to which I allude. Many pious ministers and others are in the habit of using this language in a manner, and to an extent, which I know render their conversation not a little revolting to those who are unaccustomed to it, and frequently present a serious obstacle in the way of their acceptance and usefulness.

As it is desirable not to be misunderstood on a subject so important, I think it proper to give a specimen of the phrases to which I refer. Thus it is by no means uncommon to hear it stated, that "a great revival has broken out" in such a place; that there is "a great religious stir" in this or that congregation; that such an individual, or such a number of individuals, have been "struck under conviction;" that a particular person appears to be "in the pangs of the new birth;" that a person whose anxiety on the subject of religion is very great, "has been roughly handled, but is likely to be brought through;" that such another "has been happily brought through;" that so many, in a certain place, are "brought under conviction," and so many "have obtained hopes," &c. Now, although I am confident I need not assure you, that I am a warm friend to revivals of religion; although the ideas intended to be expressed by the phrases in question are, in my view, perfectly sound and scriptural, and infinitely momentous; and although any one who is capable of ridiculing these ideas, "knows nothing yet as he ought to know;" yet I cannot think that the use of these phrases, especially in mixed companies, is advisable. My objections to them are several. Some of them are, in a great measure, if not altogether, unintelligible to many to whom they are addressed. Others are derided as vulgar cant, as terms expressive of the appearance of a plague or pestilence, rather than of a rich blessing, and which rather repel, than instruct or conciliate. While a third class are regarded as a presumptuous invasion of the prerogative of Him who alone can know the heart, and tell the number of those who have become reconciled to him. Would it not be better to use language which all seriously disposed persons understand and approve? Would it not be quite as expressive, and more intelligible to many, if you were to say, that "a revival has commenced," or "a work of divine grace appears to have commenced," in such a place: that a particular individual is "under serious impressions," or is "deeply anxious on the subject of religion," or "appears to be convinced of sin," or is "in great distress of mind;" that "many appear to be awakened from a state of carelessness, and to be more or less anxious," and that others "appear, or profess, to enjoy the comfort of gospel hope?"

I presume, if you had occasion to interrogate an intelligent stranger, who you had reason to fear was destitute of piety, in relation to the state of his mind, on the subject of religion, you would hardly think it wise to begin by saying "Pray, sir, are you born again? or, are you yet carnal?" Yet, why not, as both the principal phrases in this question are taken from the Bible, and as you and I fully believe these phrases to be expressive of important realities? Your reason, I suppose, for not thinking it wise, would be, that this language is very imperfectly, if at all, understood by many who are well informed on other subjects; and that such persons, because they have frequently heard it bandied about by the ignorant and fanatical, and cannot enter into its precious meaning, are generally revolted by it.

I am far from agreeing with Mr. Foster, the pious and eloquent English essayist, in his proposal to discard what he calls, the "theological dialect," the "technical terms of evangelical religion." I am afraid that, if these terms were dismissed, the things intended by them would soon disappear also. I do not wish a single Bible phrase to be banished either from the pulpit or the parlour. Yet, I can easily conceive that there are even Bible phrases, which may be advantageously exchanged for others, more familiar to those who are ignorant of the Bible, and better adapted, until they become enlightened, to convey spiritual ideas to their minds. It is, evidently, on this principle that ministers, every Sabbath, in the pulpit, explain scripture, by using more common language, and that which is better understood, to express its heavenly doctrines. But the language which I advise you to avoid, is not, as commonly employed, Bible language at all. And I see no advantage, but rather the contrary, in the use of terms, against which many are strongly prejudiced; and which, if they do not deserve the name of cant, will certainly, by many, be considered as bearing that character. Let your general rule be, in conversing on the great and precious subjects of revivals of religion, and Christian experience, to employ terms which are warranted by scripture, and the most enlightened practical writers, and adapted to make the best impression on those whom we address.

20. Take pains to prepare yourself for conducting religious conversation in an easy and edifying manner. For this purpose, be familiar with practical books, and especially with the lives of eminently pious men. Take a few minutes to premeditate before you expect to go into the company of any person or persons on this important errand. Adjust in your own mind topics and thoughts for discourse, adapted to the cases of those whom you expect to meet. Study some variety in this matter. If you go over the same common-place, narrow, little round of remark, in all companies, for thirty or forty years together, you will soon entirely cease to interest any one, unless, perhaps, a stranger, who happened to hear it for the first time. Above all, let every attempt to perform the service in question, be preceded by humbly asking for divine help. Remember that God "will be inquired of" to grant us his aid; and that "he will not give his glory to another." Remember that he can render

the feeblest sentence that ever escaped the lips of simple piety, richly and eternally beneficial: while the most able and well conducted conversation, if administered without imploring a blessing upon it, may, and probably will, prove useless to all concerned.

21. If you desire to gain an easy, natural and attractive manner of introducing and maintaining religious conversation, let the foundation of all your efforts at improvement in this respect, be laid in the culture of the heart. Study daily to grow in vital piety. Perhaps there is nothing more indispensable to the happy discharge of the duty under consideration than that the heart continually prompt and speak; that heart-felt emotion and affection dictate every word, and tone, and look, while engaged in addressing a fellow-creature on the most important of all subjects. Truly, without active, fervent love to God, and to the souls of men, it will be vain to hope for the attainment of this happy art, in any considerable degree. But if your heart habitually glow with interest in this subject; if the "love of Christ constrain you;" if you daily cherish a tender concern for the salvation of your perishing fellow-mortals; if your mind be constantly teeming with desires and plans to do them good; then religious conversation will be as natural as to breathe. Then your lips will be opened seasonably, unaffectedly, and profitably to all around you. Then, instead of being at a loss what to say; or being timidly backward to say it; or saying it in an embarrassed, awkward, pompous, or unnatural manner; there will be a simplicity, a touching tenderness, a penetrating skill, a native gracefulness, an unction in your mode of conversing, which no spurious feelings

can successfully imitate. The true reason, I have no doubt, why religious conversation is so often what it ought not to be, and so often useless, is that it is so seldom the offspring of that unaffected, warm, spiritual feeling, which piety of an elevated characted alone can give.

22. Finally, it will be a stimulus to diligence, and an auxiliary to improvement, in the precious art of religious conversation, if you daily and faithfully call yourself to an account for the manner in which you have performed this duty. We stand in need of something of this kind to quicken us in every department of our Christian work; and in none more than those which consist in frequently recurring details, rather than in single great acts. Never retire from any company, then, without asking yourself, "What have I said for the honour of my Master, and for promoting the everlasting welfare of those with whom I conversed? What was the tenor of my conversation? What opportunity of recommending religion have I neglected to improve? From what motives did I speak, or keep silence? In what manner did I converse? With gentleness, modesty, humility, and yet with affectionate fidelity; or with harshness, with formality, with ostentation, with vanity, and from a desire to avoid censure, or to court popular applause?" Few things, I believe, would have a more powerful tendency to promote watchfulness, diligence, and unremitting perseverance in this important duty, than the constant inspection and trial of ourselves here recommended.

LETTER VI.

I taught you publicly, and from house to house.—Acts xx. 30.

VISITING.

My dear young friend: — Ministers are visitors by profession. It is a large and essential part of their official duty to teach and exhort "from house to house." Of course, every thing which tends to give this part of their work a better direction, and a more happy influence, is highly important to them, and to the cause of religion. Yet I have been constrained seriously to doubt, whether any thing, in the whole circle of ministerial, activity is, commonly, less appreciated, or worse managed. Accordingly, that which might be made a most powerful instrument for conciliating the good will, and promoting, in various ways, the best interests of those who are committed to their charge, many ministers are too apt, from indolence, or want of skill, so to conduct, as to make it of little value, as a source either of pleasure or profit. Allow me, then, with the same freedom with which I have offered you my counsel on other subjects, to suggest a few thoughts on this. My own experience convinces me that there is need of such suggestions, and that they may often do much good. For although I am conscious of not having accomplished, while I was a pastor, all that I might and ought to have done, in reference to this part of my duty; yet, if I had known as much at the commencement of my ministry, as I now do, of its importance, and of the means of conducting it, I should have pursued, if I do not deceive myself, a very different course.

I shall first speak of those visits which may be called pastoral; and secondly, of those which may be styled social.

I. By the pastoral visits of a clergyman, I mean those visits, of a formal character, which, in his clerical capacity, he pays to the families and individuals under his pastoral care. Of these visits, as distinguished from others, it is desirable that you should have just and appropriate views. In reference to such visits, I offer the following advices.

1. My first advice is, that you by no means neglect them; nay, that you be constant and diligent in making them. If you desire to gain the love and confidence of your people; if you wish to instruct and edify them in a great variety of ways which the nature of pulpit address does not admit; if you deem it important to be well acquainted with their situation, views, feelings, difficulties, and wants; then visit every family belonging to your congregation frequently, systematically, and faithfully. I say frequently. How often, must, of course, depend on the number of families belonging to your charge, and on the number of your avocations. But I should say, in the largest congregation, at least once a year; in one of medium size, at least twice; and, in all cases in which it is practicable, still more frequently. In short, the

oftener the better, provided your visits are conducted in a proper manner.

2. Attend to this duty systematically. Do not leave it to the caprice or the convenience of the moment. If you do, but little will be accomplished. Company, trifles, languor, procrastination, and a host of other obstacles, will incessantly stand in the way of performing what you really wish and resolve to perform. Have your fixed days in the week for visiting; and address yourself to it with the same fixedness of purpose, and the same inflexible perseverance, which you employ in preparation for the pulpit. In most situations a pastor may visit, on an average, from twelve to fifteen, or twenty families in a week; and, where the population is unusually dense, even more. If such an average, or anything like it, were carried through a year, what an interesting result would be obtained! The truth is, it is almost incredible what patient industry will accomplish. If any imagine that this is a drudgery to which a man of active mind can hardly submit, and that the time would be better employed in enriching and polishing discourses for the sacred desk, I can only say, all scripture is against them; all experience is against them; nay, all reason is against them. To say nothing of other considerations, one of the best auxiliaries in studying sermons, of which a minister can avail himself, is an intimate and deep acquaintance with the people of his charge. Rely on it, he who hopes to discharge the duties of the pulpit, ably, appropriately, seasonably, and to the greatest advantage of his flock, without being much among them, entertains a hope which is perfectly unreasonable, and will certainly be disappointed.

3. Let every official visit be preceded by prayer. If we believe in the doctrine of a particular Providence; if we believe that the Lord whom we serve, and in whose name we go forth, has all hearts, and all events, even the most minute, in his hands; is it not manifest that we ought to preface every attempt to do good to others, by humble, importunate prayer, that both they and we may be so enlightened, influenced, and guided, and that every thing may be so ordered, as that our effort may be crowned with a blessing? That minister who does not distinctly and earnestly ask for a blessing upon all his labours, has no reason to expect that he shall receive it.

4. With a rigorous adherence to system in performing this duty, unite habitual, persevering faithfulness. Let it be your study, in the fear of God, to render your visit, however short, as useful as possible to the individual, or the family, of which it is the object. For this purpose, consider, before you enter their dwelling, their situation, their character, their circumstances, their temptations, their wants: and look up to the Giver of all grace for wisdom and strength to perform your duty aright. As to the precise manner in which each interview shall be conducted, I apprehend that no uniform rule can be laid down, which will suit all cases equally well. I would only say, let a word be dropped in season to young and old; parents and children; masters and servants; those who are in the communion of the church, and those who are not. In short, let no time be voluntarily lost in vain conversation. Let there be as much of heavenly wisdom, of solid instruction, and of solemn impressive exhortation, as you can possibly crowd into the time

allowed you; and, in all cases in which circumstances allow of it, close with prayer. For the rest, your own piety and good sense must direct.

5. In attending to this duty, guard against a formal, task-like mode of performing it. Few things are more repulsive than to see a man going from house to house, running over a round of common-place expressions, however pious; not from feeling, but from habit; putting on a constrained, sanctimonious countenance and in a measured voice and manner, reciting, not what the company or the case before him demands; but what, from the frequency of its repetition, falls most readily from his lips. Never will the discharge of the duty in question, by any man, be either profitable to others or pleasant to himself, unless, with a feeling sense of its importance, and an anxious concern for the welfare of souls, he enters into the spirit of it, and applies his mind to each case as it arises, with a tender interest. The physician of the body, if he be called to fifty patients in a day, examines the symptoms of each, and inquires into his minutest sensations, with the most scrupulous exactness. If he fail to do this, his practice will be without success, and his character without confidence. Let the physician of the soul be at least as vigilant, and as anxious to adapt his ministrations to each particular case. Let him sit down with affectionate simplicity in the family or circle which he wishes to benefit; and, without erecting any of the barriers of official formality between himself and them, endeavour to learn the real character and wants of each, and to have "a word in season" for each. An appropriate word. A word uttered with a countenance, tone and general manner

expressive of that unaffected pious feeling, and deep interest, which ought ever to mark the minister of our meek and benevolent religion.

6. Be careful to extend the visits in question to the poor as well as the rich. Nay, if you make any difference, let it be in favour of the former, rather than of the latter. Your Master directed special attention to the poor. The gospel is peculiarly adapted to them. And they are more apt to receive evangelical attentions with gratitude than the rich. Of course, the probability is, that you will find more fruit of your labour among the poor. And, you may rely upon it, the rich themselves will never esteem or love you the less, for observing that you pay particular attention to the indigent and afflicted.

7. Study to make your visits as instructive and interesting as possible. Many excellent ministers manage their visits, and especially those in which religion makes a prominent figure, so unskilfully, that those who have not a pious taste, and more particularly the younger members of families, not unfrequently dislike to see them. This is a difficulty which it is certainly worth while to take some pains to overcome; and I know of no way of overcoming it, but by taking care that your deportment be conciliatory, and attractive to all classes of persons; and that your conversation so abound in instruction and entertainment, as to make your visits more welcome than those of almost any other person. I have known some ministers who had this happy talent in a remarkable degree. And it is far more within the reach of a man of ordinary powers of mind than would, at first view, be imagined. Never go to a house, without having, if possible,

something interesting to communicate; an appropriate little book, for more than one member of the family; an instructive pointed anecdote to repeat, from one of the periodicals of the preceding week; some popular, precious maxims to impress on the minds of the children and youth of the household; or a notice of some recent publication, of a valuable and pleasing character. The truth is, were ministers as intent on winning the hearts of all the domestic circles which they enter, as the active man of the world is to promote his object wherever he goes, they would enter no dwelling without being received with that smile of pleasure which indicates the most respectful and cordial welcome.

8. In all your visits be particularly attentive to children and young people. This is implied in the preceding particular; but it is so important as to demand separate and most pointed consideration. I have often wondered that a duty so obvious, and recommended by so many considerations, should be so much overlooked by discerning ministers.

Can any thinking man fail to remember, that children are the hope of the church? — that enlightened attention and labour bestowed on them, is more likely, humanly speaking, to be productive of the best fruits, than those which are bestowed upon persons of more advanced age? — that impressions made in the morning of life, are generally among the most permanent and ultimately beneficial? — that instructions then given, and sentiments then imbibed, though they may long lie dormant in the mind, often rise into life and fruitfulness, when he who gave them has gone to his eternal rest?

Can it be forgotten, also, that all experience testifies the importance to a minister himself, of paying particular attention to the youth of his charge? It forms a bond of union between him and them which time, instead of severing, will rather strengthen. We can scarcely conceive of a richer gratification in this life, than that likely to be enjoyed by a faithful minister, growing old in his work, when he sees rising around him a train of youthful members, whose parents he loved and edified; whom he baptized and blessed; whom, in their tender years, he watched over, catechized, instructed, entertained and encouraged; and who, in his declining age, gather round him, and honour him as their father in Christ. O, if ministers could fully anticipate the sweetness of this reward, a regard to their own happiness would unite with the purest benevolence, in impelling them to unwearied care in watching over the children of their charge, and in embracing every opportunity to enlighten their minds, and to win their hearts in favour of all that is good.

Nor is this all: Assiduous attentions to children are among the most direct and sure avenues to the hearts of parents. It often happens, indeed, that parents are more deeply gratified by kind efforts to promote the welfare of their children, and are more lastingly thankful for them, than for the same kindness bestowed on themselves. Nay, many parents who have no piety themselves, and who would not perhaps be willing to be very closely questioned on the subject in reference to their own hearts, will take it well, and even gratefully, to have their children carefully instructed, and pointedly questioned on the same subject, and that even in their own presence. And, let me add, that very striking instances have been known in which inquiries and exhortations addressed to children, in the presence of their parents, have been to all appearance blessed in the happiest manner to the benefit of those parents themselves. Indeed, I have sometimes doubted whether in many cases, ungodly parents might not be most easily and successfully approached through the medium of an address to their children, conducted in their presence. On the other hand, it frequently happens that children will lend a favourable ear to their minister, when their parents, though both pious and intelligent, have addressed them in vain.

On all these accounts, then, as well as others which might be mentioned, you ought, in all your pastoral visitation, to direct the most pointed regard to the children and young people of every family. Endeavour to gain their attention, to win their hearts, and to take every opportunity of putting in their way those notices, hints, books, and information of every valuable kind, which may tend to promote their best interest. Give them striking texts of scripture to commit to memory. Reward them, when they do well, with interesting tracts, of which every minister should always carry with him a small store. Take notice of them when you meet them in the street. Call them by their names with parental kindness. And to enable you to do this, keep a list, as far as you can, of the children and servants of every family; make a business of keeping up your acquaintance with them, and of recognizing and addressing them on all suitable occasions. There is no doubt that doing this, and especially doing it thoroughly, will require no little additional labour. But I hardly know of any species of ministerial labour more pleasant in itself, more promising, or more generally rewarded by the richest fruits.

9. What I have incidentally recommended with respect to children, I would recommend in general, as a concomitant of all your pastoral visitation; viz. that you carefully keep a record of persons and events, to aid your memory. The names, number, character, situation, and wants of many families, would utterly pass from your mind, if you did not secure to yourself the advantage of such a systematic series of memoranda as I have proposed. In this record, you ought to insert in a very brief form not only information as to the points which I have hinted at, but also to every other point important for a pastor to know concerning his people. The fact is, that the habit of keeping such a record will constrain a pastor to make inquiries in the course of his parochial visits, which might not otherwise occur to his recollection, but which ought never to be forgotten by one who is entrusted with the care of souls; such as, what members of each family are in full communion with the church; whether any who are not communicants cherish a hope of an interest in the Saviour; whether any, not of this character, are under serious impressions; whether any of them are unbaptized; whether they are all furnished with Bibles; whether they are all able to read; whether they are all punctual in going to the house of God; whether they make conscience of secret prayer; whether they are well supplied with orthodox and pious books, adapted to

promote their instruction and edification; &c. These, and various other matters, important to be remembered, ought to find a place in the record recommended; and the record, in order fully to answer its proper purpose, ought to be frequently reviewed, corrected, and modified, as new facts arise; and its contents ought to lead to daily and importunate prayer for divine direction in attending to them aright.

10. In some cases, several families may assemble together, at a house where you have appointed to be present. This may bring a larger number within the influence of the same visit, prayer and address; and it may tend also to nourish affectionate Christian feelings between the members of the same church. This is a plan of visiting especially convenient for young ministers, as it will enable them to accomplish more of this part of their work in a given time, and enable them to be more in their studies. There are, however, some disadvantages incurred by this mode of conducting parochial visits. A pastor cannot be so entirely unreserved where several families are together, as he may be in the bosom of a single family; nor will the persons present feel so perfectly free in their communications to him. The greatest advantage will be likely to result from the adoption of this plan, when the families brought together are not only acquainted, but intimate with each other.

11. In paying pastoral visits, it is very desirable, in many cases, to be accompanied by an Elder, and sometimes there may be an advantage in having with you more than one. This practice tends to make the Elders of the church better known to the private members; and also, at the same time, to render the

Elders themselves better informed concerning the state of the church over which they are called to preside, and to give them a deeper interest in its affairs. There can be no doubt, too, that the hands of a minister are, in many cases, strengthened by the presence of one or more of those who are appointed to "bear rule" with him in the church. And while it strengthens his hands, it is certainly adapted to make a deeper impression on the minds of those who are thus officially visited.

But I am persuaded, that in a large number of cases, it is better for a pastor to visit alone. Some families, and some individuals in other families, can be better approached without the presence of an Elder. To many conversations, which have for their object the removal of offences, it is essential to their prospect of success, that they be private and confidential. To call official witnesses to witness the rebuke and expostulation which it may become necessary to administer, would often be to rouse the feelings of wounded pride, and to harden the heart. Many persons have bowed with penitence and thanks to an admonition given in private, who would probably have received with rage, if not with violence, the very same admonition offered in public, or before even a single witness. Of the proper course of proceeding, therefore, in reference to this point, the conscientious and prudent minister must judge in each particular case.

12. It will be a very important part of your duty, when you become a minister, to visit the sick. Whether you are called to act as a pastor or a missionary, in either case this most important and delicate duty will frequently devolve upon you. That the

faculty of discharging it with faithfulness, and, at the same time, with prudence and tenderness, is of great value, is too evident to be doubted. Dr. Doddridge somewhere quotes Augustine, as expressing deep wonder and regret, that ministers should take so much pains to prepare their sermons, and bestow so little apparent thought on what they say to sick people, and on the best methods of conducting their visits. He who does not feel that the task of administering instruction and consolation to the sick and the dying, is one calculated to put in requisition all the wisdom, piety, benevolence, and knowledge of human nature which can be devoted to it, knows but little either of nature or of grace. It is, indeed, an office of awful responsibility to undertake to be, if I may so express it, the pilot of the soul, in passing "the valley of the shadow of death;" to awaken and alarm the unprepared; to counsel the perplexed and doubting; to calm the agitation of the timid believer; and to pour the oil of consolation into the wounded spirit.

Be always ready to visit the sick. Do not wait to be sent for. And visit them as frequently as your circumstances will admit. If they be numerous at any one time, keep a list of them, that none may be overlooked. Before each visit, lift a word of prayer to the throne of grace, that you may be directed and aided in the solemn interview. Sometimes the relatives of the sick are unwilling that they should be seen and conversed with by a clergyman. It is, obviously, no part of his duty to force his way into a patient's chamber. Yet he ought in general to bear testimony against a repugnance at once so heathenish and foolish.

If you do not previously know the character of the sick person whom you visit, make some inquiries on the subject, and as to his history, and opinions, and the state of his mind. But, besides this, commence your conversation with him, (after a few kind interrogatories respecting his bodily feelings, &c.) with queries and suggestions which may tend to draw from himself the degree of his knowledge, and his views, hopes, &c.

Let your manner of address by the bed-side of the sick be studiously mild and tender. Let nothing be said calculated to jar or agitate, excepting what fidelity to the soul renders necessary. Be plain, simple, and studiously faithful in your exhibitions of truth. That is not a time for any nice distinctions, or for extended reasoning. Neither is it a time for unfaithful soothing, or for saying, "peace, peace, when there is no peace." Where there is evidently no well-founded hope, guard against driving to despair; but guard, no less sacredly, against bolstering up a hope which will be likely to "make ashamed." Let your conversations and visits be short. The effort of even a few minutes in speaking, or in listening to a speaker, is often very oppressive to the sick. Do not, ordinarily, allow yourself to be seated by the bed-side of one who is really ill, longer than a quarter of an hour at any one time, unless the case be very peculiar, or you have very conclusive evidence that your presence is not burdensome.

Let your prayers in the apartment of the sick, be tender, sympathetic, appropriate from beginning to end; short, and as much calculated as possible to fix, calm, and enlighten the mind of the sufferer, and to direct his meditations. It is very injudicious to make prayers in a sick chamber, that are pointless, tedious, general, inapplicable in the greater part of their structure, or loud and harsh in their manner. Many topics proper for social prayer, on other occasions, ought to be left out here; and every tone should be adapted to the stillness and sympathy of a sick chamber.

In many cases it is desirable to converse with the sick alone. In this situation, they will sometimes be more free and confidential with you; and you will often feel at liberty to converse more faithfully and unreservedly with them. But every thing of this kind ought to be avoided in those cases in which you might be exposed to the charge of tampering with the mind of the patient, in reference to the disposition of his property, or with regard to any other worldly or delicate concern.

One of the most judicious and excellent clergymen that I ever knew, once informed me that he was accustomed to make a point of visiting the females of his congregation, as soon as propriety admitted, after the births of their children; and that he generally found them, on such occasions, in a state of greater tenderness of moral feeling, more ready to listen to serious remarks, and more deeply sensible of parental responsibility than usual.

Not only continue to visit the sick, as far as you may be able, during the whole course of their confinement; but if they recover, continue to visit them while convalescent, and afterwards. This may be the happy means of fastening on their minds serious impressions which might otherwise have vanished with their disease. If they die, visit their surviving relatives, with respectful attention, more than once afterward. The occasion may prove a favourable one for promoting their spiritual interest.

13. Be very attentive in visiting families, which, by the loss of friends or property, or by any other dispensation of Providence, are in depressed circumstances. Such families are very apt to be neglected by their former acquaintances; and they are no less apt to be very sensitive to such neglect, and deeply wounded by it. Instead of diminishing the frequency of your visits to families in this situation, rather increase it. And be especially careful to improve the opportunity which visits in such cases afford to recommend religion. The minds of men are seldom more open to religious impressions, than when humbled and softened by calamity.

II. But besides visits which are strictly official in their character, and in which ministers ought to abound; they will often find it advantageous, and indeed necessary, to pay some which are merely social and friendly. Let these by no means be neglected. Their uses are more numerous and valuable than can be recited in a short compass. Yet in reference to them also, there are some cautions and counsels which are worthy of your notice.

1. And, in the first place, let even your shortest social visits be made with prayer. One of the most eminent private Christians I ever knew, I had good reason to believe, never went out to make the slightest call on a friend, without spending, at least a minute or two, in prayer for a blessing on the visit. And why is not this always proper? He who controls and directs all things may, for aught we know, make the most common visit, from which we expected no special

result, productive of rich and permanent blessings, either to ourselves or to others. And is it not worth while to ask for such a blessing? To do this, in all cases, will, I know, by some be accounted drudgery; but it will not be so regarded by the spiritual man.

2. Do not make your social visits so numerous as to interfere with those which are more important. Pastoral visits are, in general, far more useful, and ought to occupy a large portion of the time which a minister can spare from his other official avocations. It would be unhappy, therefore, to allow mere social calls to be so multiplied as materially to interfere with those of a more serious and valuable kind, and especially to shut them out altogether. Let the latter, then, be the main object of your attention; but, at the same time, embrace every opportunity which the occurrences of each day may afford, to "drop in" at the house of one and another of your parishioners, if it be only for five minutes, for the purpose of mutual salutations and friendly inquiries. Visits of this transient and unceremonious kind may often be paid, when there is no time for those of a more formal and extended character; and they are adapted in various ways to attach your people to your person, and to extend your influence among them. They will be apt to consider your pastoral visits as an official matter; but your social calls, as a more immediate expression of friendly feeling, and, therefore, in this respect, peculiarly gratifying. If you could possibly find time enough to pay one pastoral, and one social visit every year, to each family in your congregation, you would execute a plan approaching as nearly what appears to me desirable in this respect, as one minister

in a hundred is likely to accomplish. Where a congregation is large and scattered, even this is beyond the power of many ministers.

3. Do not make your social calls too frequent in particular families. Nothing is more common than for ministers to select a few families in their respective charges, the society of which they find peculiarly agreeable, and in which, on this account, they visit very frequently. They are seen, perhaps, going to those houses ten or a dozen times, where they go to others once. This is not, in common, judicious. For, although ministers, like other men, will have, and ought to be allowed to have, their particular friends; yet, to a certain extent, they ought to deny themselves the gratification of this feeling, for the sake of promoting their usefulness among all classes of those committed to their care. And this remark will apply the more strongly, if the particular friends in question happen to be among the most wealthy and polished of their congregation. It has an ill aspect, which no preference or explanation can fully remove, when ministers are found every week, or oftener, in the houses of such individuals, while, perhaps, for a year together, they are not found in the dwellings of many others equally worthy, and, perhaps, far more devoted to the cause of Christ. But there is another consideration worthy of notice here. By visiting very frequently in particular families, rely on it, you will not raise yourself in the estimation even of those families themselves, but rather the reverse. There is such a thing as rendering your visits cheap by too frequent repetition. However they may love your company, they will venerate you the more, as a

gospel minister, for seeing you withdrawing your attention, in part, from themselves, to bestow it on others, especially on the poor, the afflicted, and the friendless. Besides, when a clergyman is seen lounging about almost daily, in particular families, it cannot fail of being considered as ominous of neglect in his study, as well as in other departments of official duty. Indeed, I hold it disreputable for a clergyman, at any time, and in any families, to be in the habit of making long and lounging visits. They exhibit him as an idle man;—a miserable character for one who has been set to "watch for souls as he who must give an account."

4. While you indulge, in a moderate and well-regulated manner, the feelings and habits of private friendship among the people of your charge, let it be manifest that, even in your social visits, you are quite as able to find the hovel of the poorest and meanest, as the mansion of the most wealthy. And if you make a social call at the latter more frequently than at the former, let it be seen that your object is, not to solicit favours for yourself, but to obtain aid for the indigent, the sick, and the forsaken. It has an ill aspect, indeed, when a minister of the gospel is found begging for his own emolument, or even indirectly endeavouring to attract presents to himself; but it is an honour rather than a discredit to him, when he often appears as a beggar for others; as the advocate of the poor, the almoner of the widow and the orphan.

5. The length of your visits is a point well worthy of notice. It may be readily granted, indeed, that in reference to this point no rules either absolute or universal can be laid down. Long and short are

relative terms; and are often understood very differently in the country, and in large towns. But this is one of the cases in which it is better to err on the side of excessive brevity than excessive length. It appears to me, then, that, on ordinary occasions, instead of spending four or five hours in one visit, it is preferable to divide that time into four, five, or even more visits, especially if they be merely of the social kind; — and in populous places, several visits of the social kind may be easily despatched within an hour. Here, as in preaching, it is better to rise and take your leave, while all are interested, and wishing you to stay longer, than to hang on until conversation flags; until some members of the circle become impatient at their detention; and, perhaps, all begin to wish you gone.

Nor ought you to suppose that this is a matter which will claim your attention only by and by, when you become a minister. It is worthy of your attention now. While you are a student, you should aim to form such habits, in reference to this, as well as other subjects, as will be suitable to go with you through life. Let me say then that now, and at all times, if you wish your visits to be welcome, you should make them short. He who sits several hours in a single visit, ought not only to be very much at leisure himself; but he ought also to be very sure that those whose time he is occupying, have nothing to do. Young and inexperienced persons are apt to feel as if they were the only visitors in the circles to which they resort. They forget to calculate what the consequence must be to the order and employments going on in those circles respectively, when perhaps the same encroachments on their time are made by other visitors five or six times every week. More than this, endeavour early to learn the art of discovering, by the appearance of things, at a glance, whether the members of the family in which you visit, are at leisure to attend upon you, or very busy, and desirous of being occupied. If you have reason to suppose that the latter is the case; if you know that they have been called from some urgent employment to receive you; or, if you perceive, that, by coming in, you have interfered with a projected walk or ride, it is always better immediately to withdraw.

Let this principle more especially guide you in your visits abroad, as well as at home, to clergymen, and other professional men, who, from their occupying public stations, are less masters of their own time than most others; and more incommoded, of course, by frequent and tedious intrusions on their time. There is indeed an old French proverb, which says, "that it is never any interruption for one literary man to visit another." I protest against the unqualified application of this proverb, as a dreadful nuisance. Lord Bacon was accustomed, with emphasis, to say, "*Temporis fures amici.*" Cotton Mather, and after him Dr. Watts, caused to be inscribed in large letters over his study door, these words, "BE SHORT." When an acquaintance, who was rather prone to be tedious, called once on the the venerable Dr. Doddridge, and said, after seating himself, "I hope, sir, I do not interrupt you,"—that excellent and laborious divine replied with characteristic frankness, "To be sure you do." Clergymen, if those of no other station do so, ought to sympathize with one another on this point. And I will add, if no others venture to adopt so candid a practice, they ought to learn and adopt the important art of hinting when they are particularly busy, and thus abridging interviews which are not likely to be very useful. This appears to me a matter in which the conscience of a good man must be deeply engaged. He whose time is much occupied in visiting the sick and the dying, in instructing the ignorant, counselling the anxious, and preparing for the pulpit those discourses with which the welfare of multitudes may be connected, surely cannot feel at liberty frequently to waste, or to allow others to waste for him, hours, or even moments, in the mere chit-chat of ceremonious visits.

A strict attention to this point will be of great importance to you during your connection with the Theological Seminary. Where a hundred young men are assembled for the purpose of Biblical and Theological study, the greater part of them under the same roof, if there be any intercourse between them at all, the utmost vigilance on all hands will be requisite to prevent it from degenerating into an inconvenience, and a burden. Those who are not habitual and systematic students themselves, can hardly ever be made to appreciate the importance of allowing others to be so. Hence no small portion of their time is spent in unnecessary, and often perfectly useless calls at the rooms of others; thus committing the double sin of squandering their own time, and encroaching on that of their neighbours, which, but for them, might be very profitably spent.

Set yourself mildly and delicately, but firmly, in opposition to these encroachments. Cause it to be distinctly understood, that you wish to enjoy certain definite hours for unbroken study; and if there be any with whom this understanding is not sufficient, I would deliberately advise that you lock your door, and utterly disregard all knocks, until the portion of time devoted to study shall have closed. Nor ought any to complain of your resorting to such means. You may thereby incommode or disappoint an individual now and then; but the sum of evil will be greatly diminished.

6. Be careful, in visiting private families, not to make your calls at unseasonable hours. The law of custom has proscribed certain hours for visiting as unseasonable; and the law of domestic convenience entirely coincides with that of custom. In all well-regulated families, there are certain hours set apart for particular family duties and arrangements. To these objects are commonly devoted three or four hours immediately following breakfast, and the same number immediately following dinner. To call, during these hours, (I refer now to populous towns, rather than to retired country places,) especially on the female members of a family, is generally agreed, by a sort of conventional understanding, to be an impropriety unless in special cases, or among intimate friends. This is so extensively known, that it might seem unnecessary to mention it, did not some liberally educated young men, as well as others, so frequently appear to lose sight of it. Make the case your own; suppose any one to call on your family at three o'clock in the afternoon, and to sit until nine or ten in the evening, and to require all this time to be attended by one or more individuals of the family circle, what

would be the consequence? You have only to imagine calls of this kind made frequently, and to what pass would domestic order and arrangements be brought? It would be utterly wrong, indeed, on the one hand, to apply a principle of this kind so rigidly as to preclude the performance of an obvious duty. But, on the other hand, it would be, to say the least, quite as improper to subject a family, from time to time, to a very great inconvenience, for the purpose of averting from yourself a small one. Endeavour then, as far as possible, to make your calls at those seasons which are commonly set apart, in orderly families, to social purposes; by which all understand to be meant the latter part of the forenoon, and the evening. You will be at such seasons a far more welcome visitant, and your visits will, of course, be much more likely to be pleasant to yourself, and useful to others.

7. If your lot should be cast in a populous town, you will have frequent invitations to attend dining parties. In some large cities, invitations of this kind are received, if not for every day, at least several times in each week. Let me advise you to be very sparing in your attendance on such parties. The tendency of frequent luxurious feasting is to injure the health; to dissipate the mind; to indispose for theological study; to undermine all spirituality; to lower the tone of ministerial fidelity and influence; and in various ways to ensnare those who indulge in it. I have seldom known any minister who abounded in this practice without incurring serious disadvantage in consequence of it; and in some cases the results have been of the most deplorable kind. If I were to lay down a rule on this subject, I would say, however

numerous the invitations which you may receive, never, as a habit, accept of more than one in a fortnight, or even three weeks. By this means your health will be better; your head clearer; your feelings more in harmony with your profession; and the impression left on the minds of those who invite you, more respectful and salutary.

8. Be careful, also, that your conversation and deportment at dining parties, be exemplary and even edifying. It would be on many occasions, indeed, quite unseasonable to make at the dinner table a formal address on any point of theology or of practical religion. How far, or in what cases, the subject may be directly introduced at all, where the company is mixed, must be decided by good sense, and a knowledge of the world, under the guidance of a prevailing taste for spiritual things. I have known quite as much mischief arise, on some occasions, from an ill-judged and ill-managed introduction of this subject, as, on other occasions, from a palpable and improper neglect of it. Wisdom is profitable to direct. Humbly seek direction in each case, and you will be led, substantially, in the right way. But there are some rules which a minister of the gospel, when seated with a dining party, may and ought to observe, in all cases, and which can never give the smallest offence, when the company is, as we may reasonably take for granted it always will be when he is present, a decent one. Allow me to hint at a few of them. Some of those which I shall mention, have been partly brought into view before; but I choose to present them in a group in this place.

Never indulge, at the dining table, in loud talking

or boisterous mirth. This is, in most cases, a mark of vulgarity, or of something worse. And if it occur toward the close of dinner, it may excite a suspicion in those who have not observed your strictly temperate drinking, that you are animated by wine.

Do not allow yourself to talk much of the excellence of particular articles of food or kinds of cookery, or of the qualities of different wines. It is unworthy of a minister of the gospel to manifest, or to feel, a disposition to attend to matters of this kind. Do not even praise, in a pointed or conspicuous way, any article before you on the table. Give no occasion to any one to remark, as has often been sarcastically done, that "the parson is very fond of good eating and drinking." If you enjoy an article of food or drink, do it pretty much in silence; or if a strong commendation of what you are eating, be pointedly addressed to you by another, assent to it moderately, if you can consistently with candour; but not with that warmth and repetition which evince particular engagement of mind.

While you forbear to converse in a style which savours of the epicure and the wine-bibber, be careful to embrace every opportunity to throw out good sentiments and pious hints. If you see no favourable opening to speak directly on the most precious of all subjects, there are many others, which you may introduce to all companies, without offence, and with much utility. Such, for example, as literature, edu cation, new books, humane and benevolent institutions, plans of usefulness, striking anecdotes, adapted tc impress good and seasonable sentiments, in short, any thing which may tend to benefit those around you and to show that your own mind is running on something better than mere animal indulgence.

Do not harangue at dinner tables. It is unpleasant to hear a minister of the gospel, especially a young one, address those around a convivial board, in a preaching, authoritative manner. It is unsuitable to a festive occasion, and revolting to delicate minds. Converse in a low, modest, respectful tone, with those who are seated near you, and seldom elevate your voice so as to be heard by the whole company, unless you are questioned, or otherwise addressed, by some one at a remote end of the table; and, even then, let your manner be studiously mild, unostentatious, and remote from dogmatism.

Avoid with special care all controversy, especially religious controversy, on such occasions. It is peculiarly inappropriate at convivial meetings. You must be very hard pushed indeed, not to be able, with a very small measure of address and delicacy, to put aside every thing of this kind, without giving offence.

Instead of eating more than usual at a table where there is a great variety of delicacies, rather eat less. Eating, even a little, of various attractive dishes, is more burdensome to most stomachs than an equal quantity of a single plain dish. A person of studious habits can rarely go far in indulgences of this kind with impunity, and ought, of course, where there is much temptation, to set a double guard on his appetite. Besides, it has a much better appearance for one who is known, in common, to live plainly (as most clergymen do, and as all ought to do) to manifest no particular disposition for extra indulgence when many delicacies are before him.

Be careful always, at dining parties, to set an example of abstinence from all intoxicating drinks. I sincerely hope you will be disposed, after what has been said in a former letter, to enlist, without hesitation, among the pledged advocates of "total abstinence from all that can intoxicate." But, even if you do not deem it your duty to go thus far; even if you allow yourself to "take a little wine" (which, if you do, in these days of temperance movement, I shall regret), set a double guard on this point at the convivial table. Never allow yourself, on any occasion, to take more than a single glass, that you may bear pointed testimony against every approach to excess. When I have heard ministers of the gospel at dining parties, join with emphasis in the praises of "exquisite wine," and have seen them swallow a number of successive glasses with apparently peculiar relish, I have been filled with regret at a scene adapted to depreciate the ministerial character, even in the estimation of worldly men.

Never sit long at the dinner table, after the cloth is removed; not only because a clergyman is to be supposed not to have time to waste in this manner; but also for the purpose of bearing a practical testimony against the habit of "tarrying long at the wine" after dinner.

9. In all your visits, as far as possible, avoid giving trouble. Against this rule perhaps none are more apt to offend than inexperienced young men, who have no families of their own, and whose attention has never been practically drawn to the different ways

and degrees in which a single troublesome visitor may break in on the order, and impair the comfort, of a family.

While you consult your own comfort, then, to a reasonable extent, wherever you go, remember that the comfort of others is to be quite as carefully consulted. This is to be done by making as few demands on their time and attention as may be; by encroaching as little as you can on the ordinary routine of their movements; by having as few wants and peculiarities as possible; by never calling upon them, unless in case of necessity, to prepare a meal for you at an unseasonable time, and after their own is completed; by eating and drinking whatever is set before you, without exciting the suspicion that you are not suited; and by endeavouring, in every variety of method, incapable of being specified, to accommodate yourself to the habits and comforts of those whom you visit.

Every one knows that, when he goes to a tavern, the more good things he calls for, and the more fully he puts in requisition all the luxuries, resources and servants of the house, the more pleasure he gives. But you will never, I trust, feel yourself at liberty to act upon this principle, even in a tavern, much less when you avail yourself of the hospitality of your friends.

When you are an inmate, then, in a friend's family for a single day or longer, be careful, as far as possible, to conform, in every minute particular, to the stated order of the family. Allow no part of it to be set aside for your sake. Ascertain the usual hours for taking their several meals, and never detain them a single moment, if you can possibly avoid it. Make a point of being within at an early hour in the evening, so as not to interfere with the usual time for dometic worship and retiring to rest. Employ the servants as little as possible in waiting upon you, and in going on errands for your accommodation. In short, study to accommodate all your movements to the ordinary habits and convenience of the family to which you are indebted for its hospitality. Christian benevolence demands that you pursue this course. It is only doing to others as you would that they should do unto you. A regard to your own interest also demands it of you. For it cannot be doubted that those who find you a very troublesome guest, will be glad of your departure, and not very anxious that you should repeat your visit.

10. Be careful in receiving, as well as in paying visits. When you have a house of your own, be hospitable. Your duty as a Christian, and as a minister, will demand it. Receive and treat your friends with unaffected benevolence and kindness. Entertain them comfortably, but always plainly. "Be not forgetful to entertain strangers, for thereby some have entertained angels unawares." But remember that what is called hospitality may be carried too far. When a minister of the gospel, under the notion of complying with this duty, "keeps open house," and allows his dwelling to be made a tavern, he does injustice to his family, and criminally consumes his own time. For to every guest some time must be devoted, and to some much time. I have known some clergymen in populous towns, a large portion of whose time was employed in this manner, to the utter destruction of

their studies; and whose households were thereby kept in a course of constant toil and confusion. As to the question how far you ought to go, in this respect, I can lay down no general rule. Christian wisdom must direct you.

11. When you visit large towns, do not calculate on going to lodge at the house of the minister with whom you may happen to be acquainted. Peculiar intimacy may indeed render this strictly proper; but never do it, without being decisively, and even pressingly invited. Your case, it is true, is but one; yet if two or three such cases occur every week, it is easy to see what the consequence must be to those ministers who live in populous places. A little reflection will show how you ought to act.

12. My last counsel on this subject is, that you never enter any house to pay the shortest visit without leaving some testimony in favour of religion. Even where there is no time or good opening for direct address, or even inquiry concerning the spiritual interests of those whom you address, you may still speak a word for your Master, and leave a hint, if it be but a hint, to his honour behind you. A single sentence expressive of trust in God, or some other pious sentiment; a reference to his all-governing Providence, and the dependence of all creatures on his power; a suggestion respecting the uncertainty of all worldly possessions, the stability and infinite value of heavenly treasures, and the blessedness of those who have a well-founded hope in Christ; an allusion to the superior importance of spiritual health, where disease of body is complained of; a mild and friendly check of anxiety, where an inordinate share

of it is expressed, by directing the thoughts of the anxious to the adorable government of God; a sentence or two of this kind, uttered, not with formality, but with mild and affectionate simplicity, may be "a word in season," a means of incalculable benefit to those to whom it is addressed. Many a time has a short sentence, spoken in the fear of God, and from a tender love to souls, though perhaps soon forgotten by the speaker, proved an instrument of eternal benefit to some individual or family, where such a result was least expected.

LETTER VII.

And let us consider one another, to provoke unto love, and to good works. — HEB. x. 24.

HABITS IN THE SEMINARY GENERALLY.

MY DEAR YOUNG FRIEND: — You are no longer a school-boy, nor even a college student. Having become a man, you will be expected to "put away childish things." Having taken your place in a theological seminary, as a candidate for the holy ministry, you thereby give a solemn pledge that every thing weak, irregular and disorderly, every thing calculated to retard your own progress, or to offend others, shall be carefully avoided. Many indeed carry this idea so far as to imagine that, in a theological institution, there can be no need for regulation or discipline at all. They imagine that all candidates for the sacred office will, of course, have so much gravity, prudence, sense of decorum, and fixed religious principle, as to render all specific measures for maintaining order altogether unnecessary. And hence it is, that such persons consider a system of rules, intended to control the personal deportment of such students, as altogether superfluous, if not an unworthy reflection on their character.

Such persons, however, take a hasty and narrow view of the subject. Their impressions are not derived from experience. They forget that the greater part of an associated band of theological students have just left college; and that there they have been accustomed to a certain set of habits appropriate to institutions in which the regular and the disorderly are mingled together, and in which puerility, and as much disregard of rule as can be ventured upon, are apt to be indulged by many. There students who profess to be pious, are, as a matter of course, subjected to the same regulations which bind the most licentious and unruly. Accordingly, they become habituated to that constant pressure of college authority, which, being found necessary for others, is extended to them.

With these habits they enter a theological seminary; in which the same rigour of inspection, and the same strictness of regulation, in detail, are considered as unnecessary, and even as improper. In such circumstances, no wonder that their first impressions are those of unlimited liberty. No wonder, that, in a few instances, they are found to need a monitor to remind them, that, although their personal habits, and their application to study, ought now to be left more to their own sense of duty than formerly, rule and order are still indispensable. And some are evidently more slow than others in accommodating their habits to the new system under which they are placed.

But, truly, if among young men from twenty to twenty-five years of age, all professors of religion, all considered, in a judgment of charity, as pious, all candidates for the holy ministry, and all supposed to be under the influence of those pure principles and elevated views which correspond with that sacred office, there be any individuals who stand in need of that minute inspection and regulation which are necessary in colleges; a theological seminary is no place for them, nor the gospel ministry an office which they ought ever to seek. The longer I have the opportunity of observing and reflecting on this matter, the more fully I am persuaded, that the petty details of academic or collegiate control cannot be considered as applicable to theological seminaries; and that the theological student, who, while in the enjoyment of health, needs to be frequently reminded of any prominent delinquency, in reference to the mild rules under which he has voluntarily placed himself, and which he has solemnly promised to obey, ought to be dismissed from the institution. He shows either a want of principle, or a want of consideration and circumspection, which affords a melancholy prognostic of usefulness as a minister. If there be a society on earth, the character of which may be supposed to supersede the necessity of a very extended code of personal regulation, surely it is a band of the sons of the church, assembled to put themselves under training for the ministry of reconciliation.

But still, a degree of regulation is indispensable. The fact is, that if a hundred clergymen of the maturest age, and of the most eminent piety and wisdom, could be supposed to be brought together, and placed in the situation in which you and your companions are placed, they would not only need a system of rules, but also a system of measures for enforcing them. The best men differ in their natural temper, in their tastes, habits, and general casts of character. What one feels to be no inconvenience to him is intolerable to another. What an individual might do without sin or mischief, if done by half a dozen, or a dozen, might be extensively mischievous. A strict attention to some rules, then, even in the society of the most pious and exemplary, is altogether necessary. I should not, therefore, consider my system of advices by any means complete, as to its parts, if I did not offer you a few counsels in reference to your general deportment in the seminary. And in this, as in other cases, it is pleasing to reflect, that every good habit which you form here, will be likely to exert a favourable influence on your character as long as you live.

1. Ponder often and deeply in your mind the advantages which may be derived from such an institution. Many members of this, and of other theological seminaries, I have no doubt, entirely fail of receiving much of the benefit which they might receive, and certainly ought to receive, from their not taking just and adequate views of the advantages within their reach; and, of course, not habitually aiming to improve them to the utmost. No one will be likely to attain that which he does not contemplate or seek. It is certain that the General Assembly of the Presbyterian Church, in founding the seminary of which you are a member, formed large expectations of the benefits likely to result from it to their rising ministry, and, through them, to the Church over which they preside. In bringing together large numbers of theological students, under the same roof, and the same teachers, and placing them in circumstances calculated

to awaken every intellectual power, to kindle into a flame every holy affection, and to bind every one to his fellows by indissoluble ties, they fully expected to see a race of ministers rising up superior, as a body, to those who had not enjoyed the same advantages—men of more profound, extensive and accurate knowledge, of more ardent piety, of more united views and plans, and prepared to act together in promoting the Redeemer's kingdom, with more harmony, zeal and efficiency, than those who had not been placed in a similar relation to each other. And, truly, when we contemplate what the society of such an institution might be, and ought to be; what pure and exalted friendships might be expected to reign among a hundred candidates for the sacred office, all engaged together in the pursuit of the best species of knowledge; what holy emulation in study; what mutual and delightful aid in the investigation of truth; what a bright and steady flame of piety; what unceasing stimulants to love and good works; what preparation to go forth as a band of brethren, united in every effort, and carrying light and blessing wherever they go; we shall readily conclude that the venerable Assembly did not expect more than was reasonable. And, certainly, so far as any have failed of attaining these rich advantages, and realizing all these expectations, it has been their own fault. For I can scarcely conceive of a society better adapted to promote the richest growth in knowledge, to nurture the most elevated piety, and to cement the firmest and most sanctified union of hearts, than that which is assembled at a theological seminary. And one great reason, I have no doubt, why it has proved to many who have been connected with it, both less pleasant, and less beneficial than it ought to have been, is, that they have neither duly appreciated the advantages which were within their reach, nor aimed, with suitable diligence, or with a proper spirit, to avail themselves of these advantages. In vain are the richest treasures strewed around us, if we have neither the skill nor the disposition to make them our own.

If, then, you wish to gain the whole benefit which you ought to gain, from your connection with this institution, take large views of the advantages which may justly be sought and expected in such a society, and with a steady aim, and indefatigable perseverance, pursue the attainment of them. The opportunity which you have of contemplating different grades of talent, among your companions in study — some of them above, and others below your own, ought to teach you equally to avoid arrogance and despondency; and to operate as a constant stimulus to diligence. From all the varieties of taste, temper, and habits, displayed among your associates, you ought to be constantly endeavouring to draw lessons of practical wisdom. In such an interesting society, your knowledge of the world, and of the human heart, ought to be every hour increasing. From daily intercourse with companions from almost every part of the United States, you ought to aim at deriving, while stationary, some of the advantages of extensive travelling. By witnessing different grades and species of eloquence in others, you ought to be daily gaining materials for exciting, correcting and improving your own. By the gentle and Christian attrition of mind against mind, both light and heat, of the most salutary kind, ought to be continually stricken out. In social study, you enjoy the means of awakening and stimulating your powers to their best efforts, and of correcting and extending all your knowledge. Here the choicest bosom friendships ought to be formed, to cheer, aid and bless the whole of your subsequent life. Here, every one, by observing the foibles and mistakes of others, ought to learn to correct his own. And here the flame of piety, kindling from heart to heart, ought to burn with a brighter and purer flame from day to day.

Now, resolve, in the Lord's name and strength, that you will endeavour to keep all these advantages habitually in your own view, and to pursue them with undeviating aim, and unwearied diligence; and that you will constantly endeavour also to hold them up to the view of others, by all proper methods, but especially by the lustre of your example. Resolve, if you stand alone in the resolution, among all your brethren, that you will never cease your efforts, in your proper sphere, to promote, to the utmost, faithful study; profound and impartial discussion; Christian regularity and order; the mutual correction of errors; deep, lively piety; gentle, benign, fraternal deportment; and fervent brotherly love among all with whom you are connected;—that you will labour without ceasing, and sacrifice every subordinate interest for the sake of attaining these great objects. A single student, in good earnest in adopting such a resolution; habitually animated with a corresponding spirit; and making all who approach him to feel, continually, the purity of his motives, and the elevation of his aims, might diffuse an influence over a whole institution, of which no one could estimate the value. Try to be such an individual, and your companions in study will have reason to remember you with gratitude as long as they live, and the future generations of the seminary will rise up and call you blessed.

2. Let me advise you to pay constant and strict attention to the laws of the seminary. You are bound, as an honest man, to do this: for when you entered it, you formally and "solemnly promised, in a reliance on divine grace, that you would faithfully and diligently attend on all the instructions of the seminary; that you would conscientiously and vigilantly observe all the rules and regulations specified in the plan for its instruction and government, so far as the same relate to the students; and that you would obey all the lawful requisitions, and readily yield to all the wholesome admonitions of the professors and directors of the seminary, while you should continue a member of it."

Now, it cannot be doubted, that this promise, or rather oath (for it partakes more of the latter character than of the former), lays you under solemn obligations, not only to make yourself acquainted, in minute detail, with all the laws and regulations of the seminary, but also to conform to them with a scrupulous exactness. These laws, as you know, are all publicly read before the assembled students, twice in the year. But the whole number of students are never actually present on these occasions; and some of those who are absent, perhaps, may forget or neglect to attend to the subject afterwards. I would advise you to keep a copy of all the laws and rules in question, in your room; to review them more than once in the course of each session; and to examine in the fear of God, how far your habits have been in all respects in conformity with them. For, be assured, your punctual obedience to every one of them, in every tittle, is not only expected and required, but is important to the best interests of the institution. You cannot infringe the least of them, without more or less injury to yourself, or the seminary, or both. Never ask, then, "Where will be the harm of a single infraction, on my part, of this or that law?"—But rather ask, when you are tempted to such infraction—"What would be the consequence if not only I, but all my fellow-students, were to take the same course?" This is the test to which every student of delicate moral feeling will bring such a question.

3. Cultivate the habit of passing from one part to another of the public edifice with gentleness, and without noise. All the movements of a theological student should be grave, sedate, and manly. No running, noisy walking, whistling, singing, loud talking, or boisterous laughter, should ever be heard in passing to and from the different rooms. That which would excite no attention, and produce no inconvenience, when indulged by three or four persons under one roof, becomes an intolerable nuisance, when practised without restraint, in the same edifice, by three or four score. There is a strong propensity in young men of buoyant spirits, however excellent their intentions, to forget themselves in reference to this point, and to infringe that dignity which they, no doubt, mean to observe. Hence the importance of beginning early in life, to check this propensity, and to form that habit of gravity and gentleness in all your move

ments, which will diffuse a charm over your manners in every situation.

4. Cherish a spirit of perfect order in all your engagements, as a member of the seminary. As you are bound to meet several different professors in the course of each week, and have different studies assigned for every day, some degree of system in study becomes absolutely necessary. You cannot possibly proceed without it. But it is manifest that some are much more successful than others in reducing their minds to that rigidly systematic and orderly character, at which he who is preparing for public life ought always to aim. My object is to prevail on you to pay particular attention to this point; and to endeavour here to form habits in this respect, which may exert a happy influence on your whole life. You cannot too early begin to be a man of perfect system. Let the strictest order pervade all your engagements and habits. Have a time and place, as far as possible, for every thing; and let every thing be done in its proper time and place. Let regular hours be assigned for devotion, for study, for exercise, for visiting, for sleep, and for miscellaneous avocations; and let no ordinary occurrence break in on those hours. Habits of this kind will be of greater advantage than you can easily anticipate. You will be able to accomplish far more by this method, than you possibly could otherwise. You will not be subjected to that incessant hurry and distraction which are generally observable in those who act without system. You will be delivered in a great measure from those moments of listlessness, which are apt to arise when we have not made up our minds what to begin next. In fact, if the plan of a

theological seminary should produce no other advantage to a diligent and wise student, it will undoubtedly tend to beget the habit of which I speak. And I will add, that he who cannot bring his mind to submit to such a plan, who frequently yields to the infraction of it, or who flies from it for relief, has great reason to fear, either that he labours under a constitutional infirmity of mind, which demands his immediate and decisive attention; or that he is giving way to the eccentricities of waywardness or caprice, under the delusive idea that they are the workings of genius. He who disdains to submit to perfect system in his pursuits, may succeed very tolerably as an occasional writer of poetical trifles, for a monthly journal; but as a profound, diligent and faithful minister of the gospel, he can never succeed.

5. Be particularly punctual in attending on all the devotional exercises of the seminary. On this point it would seem scarcely possible, that, among a band of candidates for the ministry, there should be room for counsel; and especially that the regular morning and evening prayers in the public edifice, should ever fail to be attended by any individual of the theological brotherhood who had health and strength enough to allow him to be present. Such impressions, however, will not always be found to be correct. Some occasionally absent themselves from morning prayers, because feelings of languor and debility, arising from late study, or some other cause, prevent their rising sufficiently early. Others are sometimes absent from evening prayers, because, owing to the want of strict order in their affairs, they are, perhaps, reduced to the necessity of attending to some business elsewhere,

in haste, at that hour, which might and ought to have been despatched before. While a third class, (I hope and believe it has always been a very small one,) it is to be feared, allow obstacles by no means insurmountable, to make them frequent delinquents, because their enjoyment of such exercises is less than it ought to be, and, perhaps, less than it once was.

Let me earnestly enjoin upon you to guard against every approach to negligence in this duty. The more you pray with your fellow-students the more you will love them, and the more delightful will it be to work with them, in digging in the mines of knowledge. If you ever, when in tolerable health, feel it a burden to meet your brethren, when they assemble at the throne of grace, it is an awful symptom of coldness and backsliding. Nay, if you are not willing to make some sacrifice for the sake of attending, and to take pains beforehand to adjust your affairs for that purpose, you have great reason to fear that your spiritual health is not prospering. I am always distressed when I see a candidate for the ministry abundant in his attendance on public prayer meetings, but frequently absent from those of a private or domestic nature, which he is under, perhaps, stronger obligations to attend; but which, at the same time, present little attraction, excepting to the mind which delights in communion with God. What inference are we almost compelled to draw from such a fact? Charity herself cannot fail to recognize it.

6. Guard against frequent or long continued absences from any of the exercises of the institution. There is a very remarkable difference between students as to this point. Those who love study and have no

desire to cheat themselves into indolence, are always found at their posts; and contrive, whenever it is practicable, to postpone until some season of recess, every business at a distance from the seminary which demands their attention. They steadfastly resist all proposals to take needless excursions, and appear to regret every occurrence which detaches them a moment, either from the study or the lecture-room. The studies of these are solid and unbroken; and they generally disclose the happy result when the day of examination arrives. Their knowledge is connected, systematic, and accurate, and their minds daily make progress in maturity. But there is another class of students, a few of whom have been found in this, and, I suppose, in every similar institution, who seem to be ever ready to yield to the slightest solicitation to quit their books, and go in pursuit of some object, either trivial in itself, or which might just as well be accomplished at another time. If their minds be active, it is only to teem with plans which draw them in a different direction from that in which their appropriate employment lies. It is not their design to neglect or slight their studies. On the contrary, they often conscientiously intend and promise to make up for every absence by extra diligence in time to come. But the season for such diligence never arrives. The next week or month brings with it a similar temptation, and they fall before it in a similar manner. Thus they spend the larger portion of their three years in the seminary, in a series of impotent struggles with irresolution and interruption; and when the period comes to an end, whether they perceive it or not, others perceive, that all their gains are small, ill-assorted, and of little practical value. They are nearly as far from being prepared to enter on their public work as when they commenced the course.

My dear young friend, fly from this miserable habit as you would from a pestilence. It is not only destructive of all solid intellectual improvement, but it indicates a mental character of the most unpromising kind. Cultivate habits of steady, unremitting diligence. If your health be good, let nothing take you away an hour, much less a day, from your appropriate work, unless it be a very distinct call of Providence. And you are not to consider as such a call, every simple opportunity of attempting to do good. For if you did, as such opportunities occur every hour, you would never study at all. Remember, that while you have a place in the seminary, its studies ought to form your constant and main business; and that every day that you unnecessarily withdraw from them, you do injustice to yourself, to the institution, and to the church of God.

7. Take pains to cultivate special friendships with such of your fellow-students as may appear most likely to be peculiarly useful and pleasant to you. You will, of course, love and honour all your fellow-students; but the idea of being equally attached to every individual, of a hundred companions, and equally intimate with every individual, would be at once unreasonable, and destructive of all valuable intimacy with any one. Special friendships are warranted by the example of the Saviour, and demanded by some of the best feelings of human nature. Nay, it seems to me not impossible that they may exist in heaven. While, therefore, you treat every brother with whom you are

associated in study with uniform respect, and with every manifestation of brotherly kindness; you ought to be allowed the privilege, and to avail yourself of the privilege, of having, among them, peculiarly beloved and intimate companions. This choice will, of course, be made with a special view to the promotion of your own personal enjoyment and edification. Make the choice with care, with deliberation, and with prayer. Let there be a little circle of three, four or five of these intimate friends. Frequently meet them, at convenient seasons, for conversation on your studies, and especially on experimental religion; and let every interview be hallowed by prayer. Be inviolably faithful to these friends. Let one of the objects of your intimacy be to correct each other's faults. For this purpose be affectionately unreserved with each other. If these peculiar connections are properly managed, they will be the happy means of nurturing a spirit of piety; of making your studies more useful; and of preparing for after life some of the richest pleasures of Christian and ministerial friendship.

8. Make a point of cultivating toward all your companions in study, a spirit and a style of manners calculated to conciliate their regard. Any man who becomes one of a circle of four or five score of theological students, will, of course, find some of them less suited to his taste than others. The manners of one may not entirely please him. The natural temper of another may be occasionally revolting. The captious, cavilling spirit of a third, may render him somewhat undesirable as a companion. And it may be wished that the piety of a fourth were more ardent and undoubted. But, though you may not feel pre-

pared to be equally intimate with all as chosen companions, you may treat, and ought to treat all, with respect and kindness, as brethren in Christ, into whose society, in the providence of God, you have been cast, and with whom it is your duty to live as amicably and pleasantly as possible. You are, obviously, not bound to entertain a high opinion of all. You are not even bound to be confident that all are, of course, truly pious. But you are bound, as long as you are united with them in study, and they continue in good and regular standing, as members of the seminary, to treat them all with uniform civility and kindness. Never allow the least approach to a contemptuous expression or look to escape you. Never permit a sneer, sarcasm, ridicule, or even chilling coldness, to mark your treatment of any. Cultivate a spirit of true benevolence toward every one. And if there be any individuals by whom you feel yourself more peculiarly repelled, set a double guard over your spirit and deportment toward them. Frequently pray for them. And endeavour, in the spirit of the gospel, to contrive something for their benefit. In short, whatever others may do, let it be your constant aim to render the society of the seminary as harmonious, friendly, and delightful as possible.

9. Be not too much in society with your fellow-students. There is such a thing as persons making themselves cheap even to their friends. This is always done, when they obtrude themselves into their society with undue frequency, unseasonably, and too long at a time. I have known many intimacies, once uncommonly close, first cooled, and, after a while, broken off, from causes of this kind. Rely on it, that

social connection which is not mutually pleasant, and mutually convenient, cannot last long. Carefully guard, then, against being too much in the society of even your best friends. Both you and they need much retirement, and ought to be left, at proper seasons, to enjoy it. Let your calls be seasonable, and such as you have good reason to think will not interfere with their arrangements. Indulge no undue liberties in your intercourse with them. Those friendships are most likely to be pleasant and most lasting, in which Christian dignity and respectfulness mark the intercourse on both sides.

10. Be much in the habit of conversing with your fellow-students respecting your studies. Those who take exercise in company with each other, or who are frequently brought together by any cause, are sometimes at a loss for conversation. But why should they ever be, when, not to mention other topics, of still more importance, their studies perpetually furnish matter for unlimited conversation? Half an hour's discussion, with an intelligent companion, may sometimes do more to enlarge and correct your views of a particular subject, than many hours, or even days of solitary study. There are many minds which are never excited to their most vigorous and productive action, but by conversation. Perhaps yours is of this cast. However this may be, you may meet with some which are; and it will be to your advantage to avail yourself of the fact wherever it is found to exist. It will readily occur, that you ought to seek the conversation of which I speak, as far as convenient, with those who are best informed, and most expert on the subjects which you wish to discuss. Indeed, that

man alone is wise, who, in all cases whatsoever, when he desires instruction, resorts to the society of those who are the most competent to confer the benefit.

11. Study to exercise peculiar delicacy and respect in conversation with those of your fellow-students with whom you may differ in opinion. It often happens in a seminary so largely attended, and so liberal in its constitution as ours, that students of several different religious denominations are associated together in its classes. These, of course, differ from the students of our own church on a variety of points; not to say that even the latter will often have minor points of difference among themselves. Now young men, whose knowledge of the world is small; who have not yet known much by experience of the evils of controversy; and who, in the ardour of their youthful feelings, imagine they can soon convince or silence an opponent, are extremely apt to bring up these points of difference unseasonably, to dwell upon them unduly, and, when they suppose that an advantage is gained, to indulge in language bordering on rude exultation. This is a practice not only inconsistent with good breeding and Christian delicacy, but it also ministers to evil in a variety of ways. It often leads to strife, instead of profitable discussion. Such continual attrition also chafes and alienates the minds of some whom it were desirable to win, and not unfrequently confirms them in error, or drives them still further from the truth. And, moreover, all experience proves, that when such a spirit finds its way into a circle of theological students, both the ardour and the comfort of vital piety seldom fail to decline. In conversing, therefore, with a fellow-student, between whom and yourself there

are points of difference in theological opinion, do not be for ever dragging them forward, and dwelling upon them. Never obtrude them upon him. When they are brought up, always treat them gravely and respectfully. Never ridicule either them or their advocate. Never impute to him either a weak head or a corrupt heart. Never indulge in language approaching to acerbity. And whenever you find that the discussion affects him unpleasantly, let it be instantly dropped, and not soon revived.

12. Be especially on your guard against all those unhallowed tempers and habits which interfere with fraternal intercourse, and which are hostile to brotherly love. Many tempers and feelings are apt to creep in among companions in study, and even among theological students, which cannot fail to exert an influence deeply hostile to that fraternal affection which ought ever to reign among them. In this revolting list, pride, vanity, selfishness, egotism, envy, unhallowed emulation, jealousy, and suspicion, hold a prominent place. Where any one or more of these reign, like the "dead flies in the apothecary's ointment," they are apt to cause the whole mass to send forth an evil "savour." Set a solemn guard over your spirit, with respect to these tempers. If you yield to the power of pride, vanity, or jealousy, in your intercourse with your companions, you will, assuredly, repel and alienate them. If you allow yourself to envy the superior talents or popularity of any brother, and to sicken at his success; there is, of course, an end of all fraternal feeling toward him. If you permit carnal emulation to reign in your breast, or dark suspicion to gain the ascendency in your mind, on the

ground of some equivocal word or action, you may bid adieu to all comfortable intercourse with the objects of such feelings. If any of your fellow-students be manifestly superior to yourself in any attainment or excellence, depend on it, the indulgence of fretfulness and envy at the view of it, and giving vent to corresponding expressions, will only serve to diminish your own comfort, and to render your inferiority more glaring. O how destructive of peace, as well as wicked, are all these tempers! How deeply are they capable of poisoning the social intercourse even of the pious! How uncomfortable to those who indulge them! And how humiliating their aspect, in the view of the wise and good, when they become visible! My dear young friend, abhor such tempers. Strive to subdue and banish them. Whether you regard your own enjoyment, or that of others, put them far away. Rejoice in the gifts and accomplishments of your brethren. Be always ready to put the most favourable construction on their words and actions. If you are tempted at any time to suppose, that they do not honour you as much as they ought, recollect that they are much more likely than yourself to have an impartial opinion on this point; and, especially, that the most fruitless of all methods of gaining honour, among the wise and the good, is to make an angry, or even a querulous demand of it. Be kind, respectful, and truly benevolent to every brother. Be ever disposed to give honour where it is due, without stint or grudging. Study to "please every one for his good to edification;" and you may safely leave your own standing among your companions to "Him who judgeth righteously."

13. Be careful to improve the excellent opportunity

which you enjoy in the seminary, for ascertaining and correcting your own foibles, as well as those of others. Solitude is a situation by no means favourable for detecting our foibles. In fact, many of them are not developed, until we go into society, and put our social feelings and propensities to the test. Many a serious young man, who, in early youth, and in retirement, appeared to be a pattern of all that was gentle, frank, generous and amiable, has been unexpectedly found, when brought more extensively into society, to disclose very different characteristics. If, on the one hand, he succeeded in gaining distinction among his companions, he became perhaps proud, supercilious, dictatorial, and, it may be, insufferably arrogant. If, on the other hand, he found his standing with his fellows less elevated than he was led to anticipate, he became sour, envious, jealous, full of suspicion, ready to misconstrue every word and action, and to consider the most innocent remark to have a hostile aim. Or perhaps his infirmity of character took the course of succumbing to his new circumstances, and appearing the flattering, creeping sycophant. Now, as society has a wonderful power in exciting these peccant humours into action, and bringing them into view; so the best society, such as that in a theological seminary ought to be, seems to present one of the best means of correcting them. Surely a circle in which cultivated knowledge, pious principles, and mutual and fraternal inspection reign, is one of the most favourable on earth for mollifying those asperities, rubbing or pruning off those excrescences, and applying a remedy for all the acidities and obliquities, which are so unfriendly to social and Christian enjoyment.

Whatever others may do, then, let me earnestly advise you to avail yourself of this advantage. You will never enjoy such another. Carefully watch the workings of your own mind, both toward those above you, and those below you, on the scale of talents and influence. And so far as you discover either pride or sycophancy; arrogance or despondency; envy, or a disposition meanly to flatter; never rest till you root them out, and banish them from your bosom. Entreat your intimate friends to tell you your faults with perfect candour, and reciprocate the favour with them. Watch over one another with affectionate fidelity. And when any of your defects, infirmities, or mistakes, are disclosed to your view by a brother, receive the communication with meek and humble thankfulness. As far as my experience extends, I would say, few things afford a worse prognostic of the spirit and destiny of a young man, than his resenting such a painful and self-denying effort to promote his benefit. In short, study daily to make your intercourse with your brethren a means of correcting, as far as possible, every moral and intellectual fault, and of promoting every amiable grace and virtue, both in yourself and in your associates.

14. Let me advise you to be punctual and devoted in your attendance on the theological society, which is connected with the seminary. It has not a little surprised me that the meetings of this association should be often so thinly attended, and so frequently marked with languor and want of interest. Surely a band of theological students might be expected highly to prize a society formed for the perfectly free and unshackled discussion of truth, and which might be

made every thing that the learning, zeal, enterprise, eloquence, and piety of its members chose to make it. That there is enough of all these among them to render it highly interesting and profitable, no one who is acquainted with their character can doubt. Why, then, one is tempted to ask, is there not more, much more interest actually infused, from week to week, into its discussions? I have no doubt the true answer is, partly from indolence, or the want of that enterprise and decision of character which are so indispensable to the accomplishment of much in any pursuit: and partly because the mass of the students do not take any thing like adequate views of what the society in question might be made, and of the immense contributions to their improvement which might be drawn from it. It surely might and ought to be made a source of the richest advantage to all its members. Let me urge you to contribute, as much as in you lies, to the attainment of this advantage. Be inflexibly punctual in your attendance upon it. When you are appointed to introduce the debate, prepare for the duty, and endeavour to perform it in an able and interesting manner. Surely when such a service occurs only once or twice a year, you can afford to take some pains to perform it well; especially when you consider that every effort of this kind which you make, entirely coincides with your main pursuit. Let it be seen that you always take a deep interest in the discussions, by participating in them on proper occasions; by taking pains to bring forward suitable questions for consideration; and by labouring to give such a direction to every thing, as will render it at once attractive and profitable to your brethren. A small portion of such a spirit conscientiously kept up, would be far more efficacious than any system of fines and penalties, which can answer little other purpose than to tease and alienate.

15. Prize every opportunity of speaking in the presence of your professors and fellow-students, and always, with avidity, avail yourself of it. That some of your companions in study should consider the rule of the seminary which obliges them to speak in public, at stated times, as imposing a burden, rather than offering a privilege, is a fact not difficult to be accounted for. The want of that energy, and diligence, which fit young men for high aims, and indefatigable efforts; and the want of that steady fixedness of purpose, which resolutely prepares in time for every prescribed task, are certainly among the principal reasons why so many fail of performing this service as well as they are really able to do it; and, of course, why they are so reluctant to perform it at all. There are those, indeed, who are almost ready to deride the performance of this duty, as if they supposed it impossible, in the nature of things, to speak well in such circumstances. This, however, I take it, is an utter delusion. It is often dictated by laziness, rather than by enlightened judgment. That much practice, even though it be on a small scale, is greatly conducive to the discipline of the voice, and to the attainment of self-possession in public speaking, all good judges are agreed. And, if I am not deceived, all that is necessary to the production of many excellent specimens of eloquence in our oratory, is, that due preparation be made, and due pains taken at the time, for the purpose. Let me entreat you no longer to suffer the

performance of this duty to languish in your hands. Never allow your name to appear among the delinquents; and address yourself to the work with the decision and diligence of one who highly appreciates its value. Let that which you speak be always perfectly committed to memory. The importance of this discipline of the memory may not now be seen in all its extent; but will be found to be great hereafter.

16. When called upon to criticise the speaking of your brethren, always do it with respectfulness, delicacy, and fraternal kindness. In regard to this matter, there are two extremes. The one is, habitually to deal in the language of excessive and indiscriminate praise, in other words, of flattery. The other is, as generally, to employ the language of satire, sarcasm, or harsh, unmerited censure; to endeavour to place every thing commented on, in a ludicrous light; and not unfrequently to turn the person, as well as the discourse of the speaker, into ridicule. I hope I need not put you on your guard against either of these extremes. They are both unworthy of a gentleman; especially of a gentleman who also lays claims to the benevolence and magnanimity of a Christian. Let all your criticisms be marked by a truly respectful and fraternal spirit. Be candid and faithful; but at the same time, benign and delicate. In short, with an unfeigned spirit of brotherly kindness, let your aim be, not to gratify either spleen or mirth, but to promote the real benefit and honour of him who is the object of your remarks.

17. Whether your place of boarding be in the public edifice, or in a private family, be careful of your deportment at your meals, as well as at other times. It

has been observed, that little things frequently afford as decisive an indication of character as greater; especially when it is considered that, with respect to the latter, we are apt to be on our guard; while, in reference to the former, we daily act without thought. Allow me to witness a man's deportment, for a single week, at his meals, and in his boarding-house, and I will tell you with almost unerring certainty, what kind of a man he is:—whether he knows any thing about the refinement and dignity of a Christian gentleman; or whether he labours under that coarseness, vulgarity, or levity of character, which cannot fail of making an unfavourable impression on the mind of every spectator. Let me entreat you to set a sacred guard over your tongue, and over your whole deportment, in the situation to which I allude. Let your mode of conversing, eating, &c., be all such as become a person of a serious and cultivated mind. Let no one ever have occasion, from your deportment, to remark, that theological students are not more grave, or more refined, than others. I once heard of a gentleman, who had made his will, and left in it a handsome legacy to our seminary. Soon afterwards meeting with one of our students, at a public house, where he stopped to dine—a student who, it must be acknowledged, was never in very good odour among his companions in study, the gentleman was so disgusted with his levity, coarseness, and epicurean feeding at the dinner-table, that he remarked, "If this be a specimen of the students of that seminary, I cannot, in conscience, encourage it;" and on his return home, he altered his will. It is thus that a single student (and, truly, the one in question stood almost alone in his "bad eminence,") may not only disgrace himself, but, what is much more important, dishonour religion, and the institution of which he is a pupil! Happy, indeed, would it be for the seminary, if all its pupils duly recollected how much its honour is involved in their daily deportment!

18. Carefully guard against injuring the books which you take out of the public libraries. It has been with me a constant matter of wonder, that some students, who, aside from their delinquency in this respect, appear to be young men of strictly honourable feeling and pious principle, should be capable of treating books, books not their own, books the property of the church, books purchased at great expense for their gratuitous accommodation, in so careless a manner as I have sometimes known them to do. There must, surely, be in some, either a want of thought, or a want of conscience, as to this point. It is of great importance that a student acquire good habits in reference to his treatment of books as early as possible. Pay particular attention to this matter. I would say, it is your duty to learn to treat all books which you take into your hands, with neatness and care; but it is especially your duty thus to treat all books obtained on loan, either from public or private libraries; to keep them clean; to guard against turning down their leaves, holding them over the fire, defacing, or otherwise injuring them; and to return them seasonably and carefully. I am deliberately of the opinion, that whenever a student has evinced habitual or frequent carelessness on any of these points, he ought to be considered as a person unfit to be intrusted with

books, and to have the shelves of a library closed against him.

19. Carefully avoid defacing or injuring any part of the public edifice or its furniture. There appears to be a physical temperament in some young men, which continually impels them to be cutting, scratching, or, in some other way, committing spoliations on every wainscot, table, chair, or other fixture, within their reach. Now, that this should be done by silly or unprincipled college boys, we no longer wonder, because, after all the "pledges of their truth and honour," that they will abstain from such things, we so frequently see it exemplified. But we are not prepared to see any thing of this kind done by theological students, and, happily, we very seldom do see it. Yet I have certainly known such a phenomenon in some rare cases to exist, at least in one theological seminary. Give no countenance, I pray you, to such a practice. Consider the seminary, and every thing belonging to it, as the property of the church. Be as careful to preserve every part of it from the smallest injury as if it were your own. Nay, methinks, a mind of rigid Christian delicacy will consider such property as far more sacred than his own; and will be careful to repair, to the least tittle, every injury which it may through him have sustained.

20. Finally, at the close of every day, and especially of every week, call yourself to a solemn account for the manner in which you have spent that day or week. We are so apt to become listless and indolent with respect to details so continually recurring, that we need a frequent, nay, a stated memento of

what is incumbent upon us. At the close of every day and week, then, let me advise you, in the solitude of your apartment, to ask yourself, How have I spent this day or week? How have I fulfilled my duty, my engagements, the plan of the institution in which the Head of the church has placed me? Have I violated any rule, either in its letter or spirit? Have I been diligent in study, punctual, to a moment, in my attendance on every prescribed task, and duly attentive to the feelings of all my brethren? And if you occupy a room in company with another student, let these inquiries be made an object of joint attention. You may, by adopting this plan, be the means of refreshing each other's memory, and stimulating each other's conscience; and thus doubling the benefit, both to yourselves and the institution of which you are members.

LETTER VIII.

Give attendance to reading.—1 Tim. iv. 13.

HABITS IN THE STUDY.

My dear young friend:—When a young man enters a theological seminary, he may be supposed to be already familiar with study. He must necessarily have made some decent acquisitions in the Greek and Latin languages, and in the branches of physical and moral science commonly taught in our colleges. Of course he may be presumed to have some acquaintance with mental exertion and discipline. Yet many, in these circumstances, have been so imperfectly directed, or so negligent of direction, in the earlier parts of their course, that they need to be put on a new track; and all, perhaps, may be benefited by an occasional suggestion and stimulus, in their future efforts.

The following counsels, you may rest assured, whatever may have been hitherto your habits, are worthy of your serious consideration.

1. One of the most indispensable preliminaries to your engaging in profitable study, is that you cherish a deep sense of the great extent and the infinite importance of theological science. No man will summon

his whole strength to any work, and put in requisition all his diligence and zeal in pursuing it, unless he act under the deep impression that it is both arduous and worthy of his best powers; that it will require his utmost efforts to accomplish what he ought to aim at; and that the advantages of making the attainment will be richly worthy of the labour. Accordingly, I have no doubt that one principal reason why so many candidates for the ministry pursue the study of theology in a languid, perfunctory manner, is that they take narrow and altogether inadequate views of the compass, depth, and value of this branch of knowledge. They hastily adopt the degrading notion, that a careful perusal of the Bible, together with some approved system of divinity, and twenty or thirty other volumes, will be sufficient to prepare them for the pulpit. No wonder that, with this sentiment, their studies are lazy and superficial upon principle. No wonder that they study but little, and that to that little they bring scarcely any real intellectual effort. It is impossible seriously to undertake the correction of such an unworthy and childish estimate of the subject as this. He who can, with any intelligence, glance over the list of studies prescribed for the regular course in this seminary; or he who can peruse such a book as Calvin's Institutes, Edwards on the Will, Butler's Analogy, Warburton's Divine Legation of Moses, or Magee on Atonement and Sacrifice, without receiving a deep impression that such a knowledge of theology, in its various departments and relations, as will qualify a man, in any tolerable degree, to be a teacher of thousands, requires profound, patient, and laborious study; must have either a very weak or a very perverted understanding. To gain knowledge enough to be what some call a "pretty preacher," (a hateful and degrading epithet for an ambassador of Christ) is not difficult; but to be a sound thorough divine, you may rest assured, is neither a common nor an easy attainment.

Sit down, then, to your studies every day, under the deep impression that what you have to do demands your best powers, and your utmost diligence. Take large views of theology and the auxiliary branches of knowledge. Cherish an ardent thirst for knowledge. Aim high, not on the scale of honour; but in the attainment of furniture with which to serve your Master. Resolve, if Providence permit, to be "a workman that shall not need to be ashamed." Account no labour too great that may be necessary for gaining your object. Then, and only then, can you hope to study to much purpose.

2. You will never study theology to advantage, unless you cherish a peculiar and devoted attachment to the office which you seek. You profess to have chosen the profession of a minister of the gospel, because you deliberately prefer it to every other. And in this profession I hope you are sincere. But this is not enough. You ought not only deliberately to prefer it, but to cultivate for it, habitually, an ardent love, a ruling passion, an attachment of the fondest and most heartfelt kind. If there be a profession in the world which is worthy of drawing forth, every hour, all the strongest and most elevated affections of the soul, the ministry of reconciliation is surely that profession. On this subject I cannot forbear to transcribe a short passage from a sermon by the eloquent Robert Hall.

"How high and awful a function is that which proposes to establish in the soul an interior dominion; to illuminate its powers by a celestial light; and introduce it to an intimate, ineffable and unchanging alliance with the Father of spirits! The moment we permit ourselves to think lightly of the Christian ministry, our right arm is withered; nothing but imbecility and relaxation remains. For no man ever excelled in a profession to which he did not feel an attachment bordering on enthusiasm: though what in other professions is enthusiasm, is, in ours, the dictate of sobriety and truth."*

If you have not learned, my young friend, the precious art of pursuing your professional studies, not only with a deep sense of their importance, but, as the Italians say, *con amore;* if they do not form the pursuit in which your heart delights, for its own sake, and more especially for the sake of its blessed end; your attainments will be tardy and imperfect. Be it your care, then, daily to nurture in your soul this attachment, this ardent delight; to enter more and more into the sweetness of that knowledge which is to be so nobly employed; into the preciousness of that profession, the object of which is the highest in the universe. Let men in secular professions toil for "the dust of wealth," or the "vapour of fame." The profession for which you are preparing, carries with it, more than any other on this side of heaven, its own reward. While it promotes the real welfare of men, and the glory of God, it purifies, enriches, and elevates the labourer himself, making him twice blest;

* Sermon on the Discouragements and Supports of the Christian Ministry.

blest in giving, and blest in receiving. Methinks, if you have a particle of the spirit of Christ in your bosom, it will be more or less kindled into a flame of holy pleasure in sitting down to studies of such a character.

3. Strive to acquire the habit of close and fixed attention in study. I know not a more fatal defect in a student, than the want of this habit. He who has not learned the art of fastening his mind on a subject, and of holding that subject strictly and firmly before it, will never look deeply into any thing; will never accomplish any thing which deserves the name of investigation. It is generally known, that, to the possession of this power, Sir Isaac Newton ascribed all his attainments in science. If you do not already possess the precious faculty in question, try to attain it. If you fail at one time, be not discouraged. Try again and again. It is richly worth all the agony of effort that you can possibly make for its acquirement. Make incessant efforts, then, until you succeed, to summon your powers to concentrated action; to shut out, at pleasure, all extraneous objects; to go from step to step without interruption; and to keep fast hold of the thread which you first seize until you trace it to the end. From the moment that you open a book, or take your pen in hand, give undivided attention to what you are about, until you close the one, or lay down the other.

4. Endeavour habitually to study with a devout spirit. By this I mean that you endeavour always to study under the deep impression, that the subjects which you are engaged in examining, are sacred subjects, and the knowledge which you are labouring

to acquire, is consecrated knowlede; that the great, and the only proper end of all, is practical usefulness, in promoting the glory of God, and the welfare of men; and that for all your privileges and opportunities, you are hastening to a solemn account. The motto of an old Spanish Catholic divine—*Oculus ad scopum*—ought to be continually fixed in your mind. Such impressions will give you a deeper interest in your studies; will promote diligence in them; will serve to fix that which you acquire more firmly in your mind; and will prevent your wasting your time in frivolous pursuits. O my young friend, if every hour spent in your study were spent under the practical recollection that you are not your own; that the eye of your Master is upon you; and that every mental effort may be considered as a seed of eternity, both with regard to yourself and others;—with what fixedness and solemnity of spirit would your studies be conducted!

5. Constantly implore the aid of the Holy Spirit in study. The duty of humbly and importunately asking the blessed Spirit's influence, to sanctify our affections, and to aid us in cultivating all the graces and virtues of the Christian life, will not, I suppose, be disputed by any one who has the smallest tincture of piety. But I fear it is not so universally recognized, even by pious students, that the same gracious aid ought to be solicited and expected, in all intellectual culture, and in all investigation of truth. Is it either unreasonable or unscriptural to believe, that the Spirit of God can, and often does, enlarge and invigorate the intellectual faculties, extend the scope of their vision, and give them deeper and clearer

views than without this aid they could have taken? It were, it seems to me, a species of atheism to doubt it. "Think with yourself how easily and how insensibly, by one turn of thought, the Father of lights can lead you into a large scene of useful ideas. He can teach you to lay hold on a clew which may guide your thoughts with safety and ease through all the difficulties of an intricate subject. By his secret and supreme government, he can draw you to read such a treatise, or converse with such a person, who may give you more light into some deep subject in an hour, than you could obtain by a month of your own solitary labour."* You remember, I presume, that Milton, in preparing to enter on the composition of the "Paradise Lost," recognized, in the most explicit manner, his desire and expectation of the divine help of which I speak. "This is not to be obtained," says he, "but by devout prayer to that Eternal Spirit that can enrich with all utterance and knowledge, and sends out his seraphim with the hallowed fire of his altar, to touch and purify the lips of whom he pleases." Did the poet speak thus of his work? And shall the divine, or the candidate for the sacred office, hesitate to adopt similar language concerning his infinitely momentous inquiries and employments? Nay, did not even heathen poets frequently begin their composition by invoking the aid of their fancied deities; and shall Christian ministers, who know that they have an omniscient and omnipresent God, who is "able and ready to help," neglect to apply day by day, for that help? If you wish, then, to investigate

* Watts's Improvement of the Mind, Chap. I.

profoundly and profitably; if you desire to avoid the deplorable delusions into which others have fallen, and to be preserved from that pride and presumption of intellect which have ensnared some of the greatest men that ever lived; "pray without ceasing," that the Spirit of all grace may enlighten your mind; may strengthen all its powers; may inspire you with wisdom and discernment; and may deliver you, in your search after truth, from the influence of that pride, vanity, prejudice, bigotry, and passion, which are so apt to blind the perceptive faculties, and control the judgments, even of good men. Especially do this, with more than usual care and solemnity, when you are entering on a new study, or engaging in the perusal of a new book. Does every Christian implore the blessing of God when he sits down to a social meal? And can a Christian student sit down to an intellectual feast or effort, without importunately asking of Him who gave him his mind, and supports it every moment in exercise, to preside over all its operations, and to crown them with his abundant blessing?

6. Never imagine that any valuable amount of knowledge, and especially of accurate knowledge, is to be obtained without labour,—and much labour. I do not forget that you have a mind, to a very respectable degree, vigorous and active. But, notwithstanding this, rely upon it, if you will not consent to apply yourself to the acquisition of knowledge, laboriously, patiently and indefatigably, you will never attain much. I have directed close attention to this subject, ever since my connection with the seminary; and the result, without one solitary exception, is, that I never knew an individual gain any considerable mass of

really digested and valuable knowledge, without unwearied industry. The maxim, Μελετη το παν, of Periander, the old Grecian sage, is worth its weight in gold. Patient application is literally every thing. Without it, you may have a number of half-formed ideas floating in your mind; but deep, connected, large and consistent views of any subject, you will never gain.

But in relation to this point, I suspect there is a very prevalent error. It is, that these deep views of particular subjects are to be obtained by one or a few mighty efforts. Be assured, whatever may be the case with a rare genius now and then, it is, commonly, not so. The old French proverb, "*Pas à pas on va bien loin*," i. e. "Step by step one goes very far," affords the real clew to the proper course. A mountain is not to be passed at a single leap, nor a deep and rich mine to be explored by a single stroke of the spade. But a sufficient number of slow, cautious, patient efforts, will accomplish the enterprise. So it is in study. Impatient haste is the bane of deep intellectual work. A little, thoroughly done, every day, will make no contemptible figure at the end of the year. If I could be sure of your entering completely into the spirit of this principle, I should have no doubt of your accomplishing much.

7. Closely connected with this counsel is another, viz: That you leave nothing till you have done it well. Skimming over the surface of any subject is of very little use. Passing on to something else, before that which precedes is half understood, is really oftentimes worse than useless, because it deceives with the name of knowledge; and because it deposits in the memory,

if there be a deposit made there at all, mere abortions, instead of mature births. The instances in which young men, and even candidates for the holy ministry, cheat themselves by indulging in this practice, by running over a task, as eye-servants are wont to do, without performing any part of it well, are as numerous as they are melancholy. My dear friend, be not thus unjust to yourself. It is your own interest for which I plead. If you are studying a language, be careful to sift to the bottom the grammatical character, as well as the strict meaning of every word, before you proceed to another. If you have occasion to ascertain the time or place of any particular event, be sure to examine instantly and thoroughly, and endeavour to form some plan for fixing it firmly in your mind. If you are investigating any important doctrine, be not ready to leave it. Come to it again and again, seeking light from every quarter; and perusing with attention the best books, until you have entered, as far as you are capable, into its profoundest merits. And if compelled, by any circumstance, to leave the subject before you have reached this point, hold it in reserve for another and more satisfactory examination. In short, let your motto, and, as far as practicable, your habit, be, to leave nothing till you have thoroughly mastered it. And by mastering a subject, I mean investigating it to the bottom, until you come to a clear view of the fundamental principles on which it rests. For, until you do this, you cannot really be said to understand any subject. On this point, Mr. Locke, in his "Conduct of the Understanding," (§ 43) makes a remark which I think worth transcribing. "There are fundamental truths which lie at the bottom, the basis upon which a great many others rest, and in which they have their consistency. These are teeming truths, rich in store, with which they furnish the mind, and, like the lights of heaven, are not only beautiful and entertaining in themselves, but give light and evidence to other things, that without them could not be seen or known. These, and such as these, are the truths we should endeavour to find out, and store our minds with.

8. With respect to all important subjects, I would advise you to bring your acquaintance with them to the test of writing. It is wonderful how far the crudeness and inadequacy of a man's knowledge on a given subject, may be hidden from his own mind, until he attempts to express what he knows on paper. He then finds himself at a loss at every step, and cannot proceed without much extension, and no less correction, of his former attainments. Nay, sometimes he finds that he must begin again, from the very foundation, and that he has not really mastered any part of the subject. Now to obviate this difficulty, from the outset, in studying every subject in which it is practicable, make a liberal use of your pen. I believe, indeed, that one of the best methods of becoming accurately and familiarly acquainted with any subject, is to write upon it. It was said of one of the most voluminous writers of the eighteenth century, that, whenever he wished to make himself well acquainted with any branch of knowledge, he wrote and published a book upon it. In writing, he was undoubtedly wise: in publishing, it may be questioned whether he treated the republic of letters with as much respect as he ought. It was, in fact, palming upon it the immature

productions of a tyro, rather than those of a master workman. But, without giving the least countenance to the thought of imposing your juvenile lucubrations on the public, I would earnestly advise you to employ writing, as far as may be consistent with your health, and other engagements, as a constant medium of investigation. I would say, with the learned and pious Dr. Adam Clarke, in his "Letter to a Methodist Preacher," before quoted, "Have always some essay or dissertation upon the anvil." And, I will add, if no other eye than your own ever see it, the labour bestowed upon it will certainly be more than repaid by its benefit to yourself.

9. In investigating the fundamental doctrines of theology, let the testimony of scripture hold the first place. With many, the order of proceeding is entirely different. The first thing they study is the systematic work of some favourite author. Having done this, they resort to the scriptures rather to confirm his statements, than to bring them to the test of the only infallible standard. Their minds are made up before they come to what ought to be the most decisive point of the inquiry. I hope you will never allow this to be your course of proceeding. When you are about to examine the correctness of a particular doctrine, approach it rather as a detached subject, to be scrutinized from the very foundation, than as a settled article of orthodox belief. First of all, collect, arrange, and weigh the principal passages of scripture which appear to bear on the doctrine in question. Having done this, as thoroughly and impartially as you are able, let your next step be to read with care the best works which have been written on the subject,

both for and against what is deemed the orthodox opinion. It is not only the duty of a theological student, as an humble and sincere inquirer after truth, to do full justice to all the reasonings of its opponents; but it is no less his policy, as a teacher of others, to endeavour to go to the bottom of the most powerful arguments which are brought against his own creed, that he may be able effectually to expose their error, and to establish the truth as it is in Jesus. He who has studied only one side of any question, even though that be the right side, is by no means qualified to meet and vanquish the enemies of his Master.

10. Carefully maintain order in study. He who does not study upon a plan, will never pursue his studies to much advantage. In our seminary, indeed, order is absolutely indispensable, if you would do any thing; for there is an order in all the public exercises, to which every student is bound to adhere, and without a substantial adherence to which, he had better be absent from the institution. Have a fixed time, then, for every study; and, as far as practicable, adhere to it inflexibly. I say, as far as practicable; for there is such a thing as a student's making himself the slave of his plan, instead of using it as an auxiliary. He may erect it into an end, instead of employing it as a means. His plans were made for him, and not he for his plans. Let your plan of study, therefore, be at all times judicious, practicable, and adapted to your situation; such as you will not be compelled frequently to violate. Do not be perpetually altering it; and yet accommodate it, from time to time, to your situation. If you either alter it, or depart from it very frequently, it will soon cease to have any power

over you. And here, as in many other cases, you will have occasion for all that decision of character which is so important in a public man. I could almost venture to prognosticate whether you would do much to purpose in future life, if I only knew with what degree of rigour you adhere to your plan of study. If you are unsteady and undecided in regard to this, you will probably be so in every important occupation as long as you live.

11. Let your most important studies be assigned to those hours in which you perceive your mind to be in a state most favourable to exertion. No one rule can be laid down which will suit all. The tastes of different individuals with respect to seasons of study, are as different as their tastes with regard to articles of food; and the former must, to a certain degree, like the latter, be indulged. With some, the best hours for study are very early in the morning; with others in the forenoon; and with a third class, during the retirement and stillness of the evening. If there be a material difference with you, ascertain it, by a fair and thorough experiment, and distribute your time accordingly. Carefully consult the powers and bias of your own mind, and you cannot be much at a loss about the proper distribution.

12. Let the proportion of time assigned to each study, be determined by its relative importance. This counsel is so obvious, and so weighty, that neither illustration nor enforcement can be necessary. To a divine, every one sees that the study of the Bible, and of Didactic and Polemic Theology, is most essential. But how often are these postponed to studies of far less moment!

13. Do not embrace too much in your plan of study. Some diversity of objects in a course of study is desirable. Variety relieves and refreshes the mind. But where the number of departments is so great as to distract, and to keep up a constant fever of pursuit, the effect cannot fail of being unfavourable. To how many studies you may with advantage attend, in a single day, or week, depends so much on the circumstances in which the student is placed, and the peculiarity of his mind, that no other general rule can be laid down than this, viz: That no one ought to undertake more than he can accomplish without hurry, perturbation, or fatigue.

14. Let even your light reading be such as shall exert a favourable influence on your professional studies. A candidate for the sacred office, and even he who already fills that office, must have, and ought to have, his light reading; that is, a kind of reading, which, while it is really calculated to enlarge, enlighten and polish the mind, does not require the same severe application with many of the more important subjects and books of study. Works of imagination, taste and entertainment, belong, of course, to this class. If you had time enough, without neglecting better things, I should say, read all the first-rate works of this class that you can obtain. But you have not time. Life is short; and duties far more momentous, both of study and of action, demand the much larger portion of your attention. You must, therefore, be content with a selection, and even a small selection, from the first-rate list. Now, my advice is, that this selection be made with a sacred reference to its bearing on your professional studies. Let your choice fall on

such works as those of Shakspeare, Milton, Addison, Pope, Young, Thomson, Cowper, Johnson, &c.; and also on the best productions of the class of biography and travels. These, while they relax and refresh the mind, wearied by severe application, tend to fill it with noble sentiments; to make it familiar with the most masterly diction; and to furnish that kind of information which may be every day brought to bear upon the duties of the sacred office. Whereas some other works, nearly as powerful in conception, and fascinating in style, abound in images and a spirit, which the less they are known, or the sooner they are forgotten, by a minister of the gospel, the better it will be for his heart, if not also for his head.

15. I would advise you to exclude novels from your light reading altogether. I throw this counsel into a separate section, for the purpose of making it more emphatical. There have been ministers who were, habitually, among the most devoted readers of novels to be found. But I hardly need say, that they were not, in general, the most diligent and exemplary in the discharge of their parochial duties. I am not insensible of the powerful talents and fascination displayed in many of the first class of novels. But on this very account, as well as others, I would banish them from the study of a gospel minister. I consider them as an article, which, like tobacco, and ardent spirits, if a man use at all, he will probably be tempted to use excessively. And, therefore, I would say, "Touch not, taste not, handle not." No one, however grave his character or pursuits, if he once give way to this sort of reading, can ever be sure he will not go to excess: and every man who abounds in

novel reading, even though he be a clergyman, will suffer both intellectual and moral injury of no trivial import.

16. Never pass a day, if you can avoid it, to the end of life, without reading more or less of Latin, Greek and Hebrew. You will scarcely believe, without having made the experiment, how little time bestowed on this object, every day, will keep up, and insensibly extend a very comfortable degree of acquaintance with the languages which I have mentioned. After you quit the seminary, and indeed after the second year of your residence in it, you will probably cease to bestow any formal or long-continued attention, at any one time, on this object. The consequence will be, unless you adopt the plan which I now recommend, that, in a short time, you will become rusty in these languages. But if, from the time that you cease to attend to them every day as a task, you make a point of reading, if it be only two or three sentences of each language, with strict accuracy, daily, the result cannot fail of being greatly to your advantage. For this purpose, assign some time when you can with most certainty calculate on freedom from interruption. A few minutes at a time well husbanded will suffice. You will not ask me, I am sure, of what solid use a familiarity with these languages will be to you. If I thought a theological student capable of entertaining a doubt as to this point, I should really consider his understanding as manifesting too much weakness or obliquity to be a proper object of reasoning.

17. Be a close student through life. It is as wonderful as it is humiliating, how entirely habits of study are abandoned by many clerical men, almost as

soon as what may be called their initiatory course is closed. From that time, they seem to think it sufficient, if they read and think enough, each week, to address their people twice from the pulpit, on the sabbath, in a common-place way. Thenceforward they make no solid addition to their stock of knowledge. Their minds become lean and inactive. Instead of causing "their profiting to appear unto all," every time they enter the sacred desk, they become more and more jejune and uninteresting. With the habit, they lose all taste for study. Their leisure hours are spent in worldly cares, or in gossipping, rather than among their books. They invite premature intellectual torpor and debility. They cease to instruct their hearers, and soon become a dead weight, instead of a comfort and blessing to their congregations. Such is the history of many a minister who had good natural talents; and concerning whom the expectations of his friends were raised; but who could never be persuaded to love study. Rely upon it, no minister will ever be, for any length of time together, really acceptable and popular as a preacher, who is not a constant and diligent student; and who does not "feed his hearers with knowledge and with understanding." Keep up this habit with unabated vigour even to extreme old age, if you shall ever reach it. Strength of mind is promoted and retained by nothing so much as persevering exercise. Many judges, and other secular men, retain their intellectual powers unimpaired to the age of seventy, or even later. But the mass of ministers, after fifty-five, make no more mental efforts; preach over their old sermons, and study little. The consequence is, that, at sixty, they are commonly beginning very perceptibly to decline in intellectual vigour, and sometimes greatly to the injury of the cause of religion.

Make a point then of being a "hard student" as long as you live. Keep up the habit of reading much, reflecting much, and writing much, as long as you have strength enough to open a book, or wield a pen. Content not yourself with merely that kind of study which will qualify you to prepare your sermons with success; but let your constant aim be to make rich and solid additions to your stores of professional knowledge. For this purpose constantly keep under perusal some great standard work. And never consider yourself as having gotten through a year well, unless you have carefully read seven or eight such works, in addition to all your other studies. This will render your sermonizing more easy and delightful to yourself, and more profitable to others. It will keep up the activity and tone of your mind. It will avert premature dotage; and better qualify you, in every respect, to do your Master's work.

18. Do not, however, confine yourself to the perusal of books strictly professional. Endeavour, as far as practicable, to keep pace with the current literature of the day, by reading the most important new books which appear. Be careful, also, to maintain a constant familiarity with your college studies. There is a shameful negligence on the part of many young clergymen as to this matter. If you live, you will probably be, one day, a trustee, or a visitor of some college or academy; and you may often be called upon to examine students on all the branches of knowledge taught in those institutions. And will you not

disgrace yourself, if you shall have become so rusty in those studies as to be wholly unable to do it, or to do it in a very bungling and inadequate manner? Besides, you know not to what station God in his providence may call you. It is the part of a wise man to be prepared for any one. During a considerable part of the eighteenth century, in the days of Dickinson, Burr, Edwards, Davies, Finley, Ewing, Allison, Wilson, Witherspoon, Nisbet, Smith, Macwhorter, and a number of others who might be mentioned, we had a very honourable proportion of ministers in our church, whose classical and scientific attainments and general literature, were so rich and mature that they were well qualified for the highest literary as well as ecclesiastical stations; and acted as conservators of literature in their respective neighbourhoods. Whether we have as many now, in proportion to our numbers, who are thus qualified, I will not at present decide. But do what in you lies, that the Church may have one such individual in yourself.

19. Always have some reading, or some other intellectual employment, to fill up the small spaces of time which would otherwise be lost. To the man of real wisdom, every moment is precious. To waste even single minutes, therefore, appears to him unspeakably more foolish than throwing away gold. Yet, in the lives of the most industrious, many minutes will occur, in the course of every day, which must inevitably be wasted, unless some expedient be adopted to furnish means for filling up every vacant moment, however unexpectedly it may occur. For this purpose, I would advise you always to carry a Bible in your pocket, and some other port-

able book of value, which may be taken up for a few moments, wherever you may happen to be, and laid down again without material disadvantage. And when you go from home, always take with you books enough, and of the proper character, for the profitable employment of your time, while waiting at taverns, or travelling in public conveyances, in which many an hour is lost by the improvident man. If you are only awake to the importance of this subject, and have your attention vigilantly directed to the economical use of time, it is wonderful how much of it may be easily saved from utter waste.

20. Study much with your pen in hand. Keep several blank books on your shelves. One of these should be a common-place book, in which you should enter references to the volume, chapter, and page, in which any remarkably just sentiments, or able discussions, are to be found. This is, undoubtedly, a method greatly preferable to that which is adopted by many; I mean the method of laboriously transcribing long passages from books; which ought never to be done unless with respect to such books as you may not be able to see again. If you possess, or can easily procure a book, a reference to the passage which strikes you, under its appropriate title, in a volume kept for that purpose, is quite sufficient, and much less laborious and exhausting. It is a good thing, too, while the contents of a book of sterling value are fresh in your memory, to throw on paper a compend or synopsis of the scope, plan, and reasoning. This will not only tend to fix them in your memory; but may also serve, if filed and preserved, some important purpose afterwards. And, finally, in an in-

terleaved Bible be careful to enter, in a small, neat hand, all the striking criticisms, and expositions of scripture, which you may meet with in the course of your reading, or your attendance on the preaching of others.

21. It will be, in many cases, a great saving of time, if you learn the character of books, from good judges, before you read them. As no one has time or strength to read every book that can be found, on a given subject, and as it would not be worth his while if he had, it is desirable for a student, at the outset of a particular investigation, to find out, from those on whom he can rely, what writers have treated on the subject which he wishes to explore, with most ability. I have often been distressed to see inexperienced but zealous readers, wasting weeks and perhaps months, in reading inferior, and even paltry books, when those which were far more worthy of their attention, might have been had with equal ease. And an additional reason for regret occurs, when a student whose funds are extremely scanty, expends a portion of them in the purchase of works scarcely deserving a perusal. A conversation with some learned friend in reference to a contemplated book, may not only enable you to judge of its relative value, but may really prepare you to read it with far more advantage than you would otherwise have done.

22. Never pursue study to the point of exhaustion, or even of very sensible fatigue. There is so far from being any economy in this, that it is the most injudicious waste of time and strength that can well be imagined. The probability is that you will lose ten times more than you will gain by it. Every mo-

ment that you spend in study after the mind becomes jaded, is worse than thrown away. But I have seen so many instances in which youthful students were deaf to all warning on this subject; so many instances in which, under the impression that they could bear any degree of application to study with impunity, they madly went on, until the firmest constitutions were broken down, — in some instances irreparably; that I despair of doing much good by the most solemn repetition of this counsel. No one, in an ordinary state of health, ought to spend more than six or seven hours a day in close study. If to these be added two or three more of light reading, there will be as much time devoted to intellectual exertion, as any one ought ever to think of. For one that can bear more, as a habit, without injury, five or six cannot endure so much. Will students never learn but by the destruction of their health, that it is much better to leave off study, while their minds continue elastic, and their animal spirits unwearied; than, for the sake of gaining a few hours, to run the risk of a prostration of strength, which may exclude them from their books for years, and deprive them of all comfortable health for the remainder of life?

23. Never study much by night. Begin with the dawn of day, and improve every moment of daylight that you can secure. But be extremely cautious of night-studies. I have known them to injure incurably the eyes and the general health of many unwary students, before they apprehended the least danger. Study to a late hour at night ought never to be indulged at all, by any one who values his health. Two hours' sleep before midnight are worth three, if not

four, after it. And he who frequently allows himself to remain at his studies after eleven o'clock in the evening, is probably laying up in store for himself bitter repentance.

24. Let me advise you to do all your writing in a standing posture. If you write at a common table, the probability is, that you will contract a crooked, half-bent mode of sitting, which will materially injure your health. Writing-chairs are very much in vogue with many students. But if I am not greatly deceived, they are pestiferous things, which do ten times as much injury as they do good. It is almost impossible to write on them without incurring an unequal and mischievous pressure on one side. Indeed, a gentleman of much experience and observation, lately assured me that he had procured the banishment of such chairs from an important literary institution with which he was connected, on account of the serious mischief which he had found them produce to the persons and general health of many students. If you write standing and guard against pressing your breast bone on the edge of the desk, but rest altogether on your arms, I am persuaded you will find it a method attended with fewer inconveniences and dangers than any other. On this plan, no part of the body is in a constrained posture, and the circulation is unobstructed. Besides, if you read sitting, as most people do, it will create an agreeable variety, if you rise when you begin to write.

25. Whenever you are called upon to make particular exertion in study, let it always be accompanied with special abstemiousness with regard to food. Every one who is addicted to a sedentary employ-

ment, and especially a student, ought habitually to live on a much more slender diet than those whose occupations are more active. And this point demands the greater attention on the part of students, because, with many, intense application to study, instead of diminishing the appetite for food, rather gives it an additional or morbid keenness; so that, at such a season, they are tempted to more than common indulgence in eating. But whenever you find it necessary to make a mental effort, in reading or writing, more than usually severe and long continued, let it ever be accompanied with more than usual abstemiousness. This will render the effort more easy, at the time, and less exhausting in its effects. It will impart to your mind a serenity, a vigour, and an aptitude for exertion, always perceptible, and often delightful; and it will commonly enable you to perform the same amount of work, not only better, but also in less time. It is true, managing the business of abstinence requires the exercise of much caution and judgment. If carried too far, it may destroy the health; but this, I believe, is seldom done. Every one who is wise enough to make the experiment, must observe and judge for himself how far it will be for the advantage both of his bodily and mental health to carry it. But I am very confident that, among all the physical auxiliaries of which a student may avail himself, there is none more rational, or more potent, than this.

26. You must not think me whimsical, if I tell you, that some have found their minds more active and vigorous in consequence of putting on clean clothes, and attending to circumstances of personal cleanliness. I could name more than one minister, who, whenever

they wish to make special efforts, wash their hands and face, put on clean linen, and dress themselves as if for company—declaring that they scarcely ever fail to find sensible aid from this preparation for study. I feel no difficulty in believing that this aid is more than imaginary. That there is a close connection between the body and the mind, we all know. And that he who wishes to study to advantage, will find his object promoted by every thing which removes defilement, obstruction, oppression, or any kind of discomfort from his body, would seem to be one of the most rational conclusions.

27. While I think it proper to throw out these hints, which may possibly promote your comfort, when you are called to make special efforts in study; I consider it as my duty, at the same time, to put you on your guard against one mistake, which to a minister of the gospel, may be a serious one. I refer to the popular notion among many students, that men of genius can work, and ought to attempt to work, only at those seasons which they call seasons of inspiration. That is, seasons in which their minds are in a state of peculiar alertness, and aptitude for intellectual labour. I am far from denying that there are such seasons, with most men, perhaps with all men; and have no doubt that with some, they are much more strongly marked than with others. When they do occur, there is no question that every one is bound to make the most of them. But what I deny is, that theological students, or ministers of the gospel, ought, in ordinary cases, to wait for such seasons. Time is too short, and souls too precious, for this. With them, the necessity for intellectual labour occurs, not only statedly,

but almost constantly. If their work be done at all, it must be generally done within a given number of hours; and this must be the habit of their lives. It is of the utmost importance to them, therefore, that they be, as much as possible, at all times ready for their appropriate labour. And although it is certain that they will not be, at all times, in a state of feeling equally favourable to either intellectual or bodily effort; yet the effort ought not, in common, to be forborne on that account. And, after all, if you conduct your studies in a judicious manner, as to plans and hours; and, especially, if you practise with wisdom, that occasional, and even habitual abstemiousness, which I recommended in a preceding section, rely upon it, your seasons of inspiration will occur much more frequently than you suppose, or than liberal feeders commonly experience.

28. Make a point of keeping every thing in your study in a state of perfect neatness and regularity. Whether your books be few or many, keep them in their places, and in perfect order. Let all your manuscripts be so arranged as that you shall be able to lay your hand upon any one of them in a moment. Tie your pamphlets in bundles, in a certain order understood by yourself, and as soon as possible, get them bound in convenient volumes. Fold, label, and deposit in proper drawers, all loose papers, so as to be at no loss to find any one of them whenever called for. And, in general, let every thing in your study bear the marks of order, system, and perfect neatness. You can have no conception, without having made the experiment, how much time and trouble will be saved by this plan. When you are tempted to think, that

you have not time to put a book or paper which you have been using, into its proper place, ask yourself whether you will probably find it convenient a week or a month afterwards, to spend an hour in searching for that, which half a minute would have sufficed for depositing in its appropriate situation? Let me advise you also to preserve and file copies of all your important letters; and where you cannot find time for this, to keep, at least, a distinct memorandum of the dates, principal contents, conveyance, &c., of all such letters. You will, in the end, save more time by this regularity than you can now easily imagine.

29. With one more counsel I shall close this letter; and that I am more at a loss to frame in a satisfactory manner than any of the preceding. It is that you endeavour to guard against those incessant interruptions of study by company, which, unless you take measures to prevent, will not fail to consume a large part of your time, and often to distress you exceedingly. I have more than hinted at this subject in a former letter. But it is one of those, the evil of which, I fear, even "line upon line" will not be sufficient to obviate. Whether you consider your comfort or your improvement, you ought, undoubtedly, to take hold of this matter with a firm hand. Some of the students of the seminary are so extremely modest, that when a number of their fellow-students drop into their rooms, one after another, and divert them from study for four or five hours together, they cannot summon resolution enough to give the least hint of the distress which it occasions them; but perhaps sit several hours, in a state little short of agony, submitting to the encroachments of those reckless in-

truders, who, instead of interrupting others, ought themselves to be busy. There are various ways of shaking off these marauders on the time of honest people. One is, as I stated in a former letter, to lock your door, and be deaf to all their knocking. Another is, from the moment they seat themselves, to maintain a rigid silence; or, at least, to answer them only in monosyllables. A third plan is, as soon as any unseasonable visitor sits down, to begin to converse with him on the study in which you happen to be engaged; to ply him vigorously with questions in relation to it, which shall put to a severe test his own acquaintance with it. I once knew a young man who adopted this method, and who resisted every attempt to change the subject; and he very seldom failed to clear his apartment of loungers. But some are thoughtless or iron-hearted enough not to regard any of these plans. With such, the only effectual resort seems to be to state, in so many words, the urgency of your engagements, and your wish to be left alone. One advantage of taking strong measures in the outset on this subject, will be, that by such measures your fellow-students will most speedily learn your cue in reference to the matter in question, and soon cease to give you trouble. The remedy may be painful; but it will be likely to effect the most expeditious and complete cure.

LETTER IX.

Take fast hold of instruction; let her not go: for she is thy life.
PROV. iv. 13.

HABITS IN THE LECTURE-ROOM.

MY DEAR YOUNG FRIEND:—It may be supposed, at first view, that the deportment of a student in the lecture-room might well be left to instructions and correctives applied on the spot. When the student is immediately under the eye of the professor, and in a situation in which a gentle hint or admonition may be instantly directed to the occurrence which is supposed to demand it; where, it may be asked, is the necessity of laying down a set of formal counsels on paper? I have two reasons for not passing over this part of my subject without particular notice.

One reason is, that to a professor who has the least delicacy of feeling, it is always painful to admonish an ingenuous and pious youth of any aberration from strict propriety, in the presence of his companions. Such an admonition, however well intended, and well administered, may inflict a deep wound on the feelings of him who receives it. And if, to avoid this evil, it be administered in private, one of its most valuable benefits is lost, viz: that of putting others on their guard against a similar fault.

But a second and still stronger reason is, that it is much better, if possible, to prevent such faults from occurring, than to correct them when committed. My object is, not to wait until I see improprieties, inadvertently or otherwise indulged, and then to apply the corrective; but to put conscientious young men on their guard, beforehand, against indulging them, and thus obviate the necessity of inflicting pain on either side.

You must not suppose, from the aggregate of these counsels, that I have been accustomed to see the frequent occurrence of ill-breeding or disorder in our lecture-rooms. Far from it. On the contrary, the remarkable infrequency of any call for animadversion, or the slightest form of discipline in our Institution, after the experience of many years, has been a source of peculiar satisfaction, and, I hope, an occasion of cordial thankfulness. Yet there are theological students of cultivated minds, and of unfeigned piety, who bring with them from college, or from the academy, certain habits in the lecture-room, which, though not criminal, are some of them unseemly, and all disadvantageous; and of which, from mere inconsideration, or inexperience, they see not the evil. A few of those habits I wish to point out, and to place in the light in which much observation convinces me they ought to be contemplated.

I am the more disposed to consider some of these habits in detail, because the correction of them now will be of use to you throughout life. Similar improprieties may be indulged in other places besides the lecture-room; and the spirit of my remarks will apply to all situations and practices analogous to those which are noticed in detail.

1. Never allow yourself to be absent from a lecture, when you can possibly avoid it. Some students, who mean to be attentive and regular, are occasionally induced, by insufficient causes, to absent themselves entirely from the lecture-room, when they ought to be there. An interruption of company; the slightest indisposition; a party of pleasure; the writing of a letter, which might be postponed; a fit of drowsiness; and even the fascination of a new book, are allowed, each in its turn, to detain them from being present when some important exercise in their course is passed. From causes of this kind, I have known students to miss seven or eight lectures during a single session. And more than once it unfortunately happened, that a portion of the lectures thus lost was precisely the most radical and indispensable of the whole number, the loss of which imposed upon them the most serious disadvantage through all that came afterwards. In fact, the loss of one lecture may be productive of evil not easily calculated. Now, no student can possibly know beforehand, when this may be the case; and very unjust is he both to himself and his teacher, who ever allows himself to miss a lecture at which it is possible for him to be present.

2. Make a point of appearing in the lecture-room, at the prescribed time, with perfect punctuality. Let no company, engagement, or obstacle of any kind, short of absolute necessity, prevent this. The evils of coming late to a lecture are numerous. He who does so, of course loses the prayer, which precedes

every exercise in the seminary; a loss, which, by the pious mind, will not be deemed small. He also loses, I need not add, all that part of the lecture which is delivered before he enters the room. Now, this part may be essential to the right understanding of all that follows; so that to lose it is, in effect, to lose the whole. But this is not all. The student, by entering the apartment after a lecture is begun, disturbs his fellow-students, by diverting their attention; by the noise which unavoidably attends his coming in, and seating himself; and perhaps, by whispering to his nearest neighbour, to ascertain what the subject is, under discussion, and what has been said. He also disturbs the professor, by the noise which attends his entrance, and by forcing on his mind the painful impression, that there is at least one of his hearers, who, from ignorance of what has gone before, cannot possibly go with him, satisfactorily and fully, in what is to follow. This is so important a matter, that I must beg your attention to it with peculiar emphasis. Invariably make such calculations as will enable you to be present several minutes before, rather than a single minute after, the proper time. In truth, I have been so painfully impressed with the mischiefs resulting from a late attendance on any exercises of the seminary, that I have often sincerely wished, if a student did not enter before the first sentence of the lecture were delivered, he might not come at all. In some cases, indeed, it may be otherwise; but in many others, such would be my deliberate opinion.

I should do injustice to you, and to the subject, if I did not add, that all my experience in this institution enables me to say, that, almost without exception, those students who have been most honourably distinguished for talents, mature knowledge, decision of character, and subsequent usefulness in the ministry, have manifested a degree of punctuality in relation to this matter truly remarkable.

3. If you would acquire the virtue of entire punctuality in your attendance on the exercises of the seminary, you must learn the important art of dismissing intrusive company without ceremony. This is a hard lesson to learn for a young and modest man; but he must learn it if he would discharge his duty as a public man; and the sooner he begins to reduce it to practice, the better. You will often be visited by those who have nothing to do themselves, and who, of course, will not be apt to recollect that you ought to be busy. Endeavour to acquire that decision of character which will enable you, gently, but firmly, to dismiss such persons, when the hour for lecture arrives. What can be more reasonable than to say to such a visitor, when the bell rings—"That is my signal, sir; you will have the goodness to excuse me?" Whether you wish to discharge present duty, or to form a habit, the value of which will be developed in after life, the gain will far more than counterbalance all the irksome feeling, or social loss, which may attend the dismission.

4. There is one practice in the seminary, which very often interferes with punctual attendance on the exercises of the institution. I refer to the practice of the more advanced students, who may be licensed to preach several months before they leave us, and who, in many cases, make engagements to preach which very materially interfere, from time to time,

with their appropriate duties as students. This is a mischievous practice. There is, indeed, a real advantage in the pupils of the seminary being licensed a short time before the completion of their course, that they may have an opportunity of actually appearing in the pulpit, in the presence of their professors, and fellow-students, and receiving their friendly remarks. But when such licentiates have so little firmness of mind as to yield to every solicitation to preach, and thereby to break in frequently on their proper engagements in the seminary, their license is worse than useless ; and the privilege which it gives ought rather to be deprecated than coveted by a diligent student.

5. Never allow yourself to enter the lecture-room in a slovenly dress — in any dress in which you might not appear decently in the street. If I mistake not, you have sometimes seen very worthy students appear among their companions in that kind of striking dishabille which might have been expected if they had five minutes before quitted their beds. There is something in this kind of appearance by no means respectful, either to their fellow-students, or their professors. I am far from being pleased to see theological students fond of elegance, or even of formality, in their dress. Decent neatness is all I ask. But surely this may be demanded whenever they come together to attend on any public duty. Besides the considerations already suggested, they know not but that, on such an occasion, several strangers may be present, who may receive an impression concerning the seminary in general, from the appearance of two or three individuals among the pupils.

6. While you are in the lecture-room, let your atten-

tion be closely and immovably fixed upon all that is said and done. Some theological students are so inconsiderate as to allow themselves to bring to the seminary the habit, in reference to this point, which they unwisely formed at college, or at the academy, of considering themselves as not particularly interested in any thing that passes, excepting that which is immediately addressed to themselves. Nothing but the strangest want of reflection can tolerate such a thought, or the habit which flows from it. Surely every member of a class is just as much interested in every thing which drops from the lips of the professor, as he who is immediately interrogated, or addressed. Every question that is asked; every answer that is given; every difficulty that is solved; and every mistake that is committed or corrected, may be considered as the property of all alike; as equally calling for the attention of all; and as worthy, if possessed of any value, of being equally treasured up by all. In short, a mind awake, active, and eager, in the language of Solomon, to "take fast hold of instruction," and let none of it go, will derive advantage from every word that is uttered in the lecture-room, whether directed immediately to himself or to his companions. He will turn it all to gold; and make it redound, in some way, to the great cause of his improvement.

If every student were aware of the importance of this counsel, we should not be pained by those cases of evident absence of mind, which often occur; and those instances of languor, drowsiness, and even occasional slumber, which have been sometimes witnessed. We should see every one appearing to forget every thing else, in his all-absorbing attention to the subject immediately before him. And even when the remarks of the lecturer were not either as weighty or as interesting as might be wished, such a band of listening auditors as I have sometimes seen, by their eager looks, their pertinent questions, and their intelligent inferences, might animate dulness itself, and educe rich instruction from a lecture which scarcely rose even to mediocrity of character.

7. It is a bad practice to indulge in any kind of reading during a lecture. One of the rules of our seminary, indeed, absolutely prohibits all reading, during any recitation or lecture, excepting that which relates immediately to the subject under consideration. But I am more and more persuaded that no one ought ever to avail himself even of this exception: for it is manifest that no one can read a book on the same subject on which a lecture is proceeding, and at the same time attend to the lecturer. And if the pupil deliberately prefer the former to the latter, he had better be in his own apartment, employed in reading alone, than place himself in circumstances in which neither reading nor hearing can be enjoyed to the best advantage. As to the cases which now and then occur, in which something entirely foreign from the subject of the lecture is read, it is such a direct violation of the law of the seminary, and such a piece of disrespect to the professor who may happen to fill the chair, that no conscientious or well-bred student, who reflected a moment what he was about, could possibly allow himself to be guilty of a single act of the kind, much less to indulge in the practice.

8. All private conversation or whispering, during a

lecture, is a violation of good manners, as well as an infraction of an express law of the institution with which you are connected. I have known some students, who had an infirmity of this kind, which appeared altogether invincible. They seemed not to be capable of sitting five minutes in the lecture-room without whispering to all to whom they were near enough to annoy them in this manner. Whether they approved or disapproved comprehended or were unable to comprehend, what was said, it was equally the subject of this private communication. Sometimes, however, it had a respect to matters altogether foreign from those of the lecture. The mischiefs of such a practice are serious. It is manifest that while the individual is whispering to his neighbour, he cannot possibly attend to what is uttered, at the moment, from the professor's chair. It is also manifest, that the neighbour whom he addresses is equally taken off, during the same time, from that attention which is due to his instructor. Now the sentence or sentences thus lost, may be essential to a connected view of the subject. Of course, both parties, on such occasions, will be likely to understand it very imperfectly, to say the least. Accordingly, I have always remarked as a general fact, that your habitual whisperers were the poorest students in the classes to which they belonged; and that, when the day of examination came, they were seldom found to understand with accuracy any subject which was brought before them.

As to the pain which this practice cannot fail to give to the lecturer himself, I forbear to urge it; as a student whose feelings allow him to commit such an indelicacy, will not be likely to pay much respect to those of a professor. Yet such pain will inevitably be inflicted on the mind of a conscientious man, who is really interested in the improvement of his pupils.

Some who do not whisper, do worse. They scribble on pieces of paper what they have to say; hand them to the individuals whom they wish to address; and solicit from them answers in the same manner. This is worse, because it takes up more time, on both sides, to write a sentence, than it would to utter it orally; and of course, to accomplish every such communication, a larger amount of attention must be withdrawn from the appropriate duty of the hour.

Never allow yourself, therefore, on any occasion whatever, either to whisper, or to circulate billets, in the lecture-room, unless in a case of absolute necessity. In forty-nine cases out of fifty, what is communicated in this way, might be just as well left until the lecture is ended; and the inability to wait, almost always arises either from weakness of judgment, or puerile impatience. Not only avoid doing any thing of this kind yourself; but do not allow others to whisper, or to hand billets to you. If any make the attempt, repel it, by saying—"I wish to attend to the lecture."

9. Some, who do not allow themselves to whisper, are in the habit of frequently winking, nodding, or smiling, to one or more of those around them, to express either their approbation, or their doubt, of something which has been said. I have known this to be so much the habit of a few students, who have, at different periods, passed through our seminary, that they rendered themselves really conspicuous by it.

They no doubt meant that it should be considered as a mark of attention and talent; but I believe it seldom failed to receive a very different construction on the part of all sober-minded observers. As the practice in question is chargeable with most of the evils mentioned in the preceding section, I shall not repeat the detail: but would observe, that he who wishes to avail himself most completely of all the advantages of the lecture-room, ought to learn the art of sitting, with fixed attention, and unmoved countenance, throughout the whole of its exercises, and of giving no encouragement, even by look, or by the least response of the favourable kind, to those who act a different part.

10. Never place yourself in the lecture-room in a lounging or reclining posture. There are those who, though enjoying all the vigour of youth and health, appear never to be easy a moment but when in a posture partly recumbent. If they be seated on a bench, or any seat which admits of it, they raise their feet, and place them horizontally, and even stretch themselves at full length, as if preparing for a nap. Can any one who reflects a moment fail of perceiving that this manifests ill-breeding of a pretty gross kind? There are few cases in which any one ought to allow himself to sit, or rather lie, in such a posture, in the midst of his equals only; but to do it in the presence of any one whom he regards as his superior, is really an outrage on decorum. If you suppose that I go too far in this statement, rely on it, you altogether mistake. It is universally so viewed by well-bred people. And you may rest assured that gentlemen whose good opinion you would think worth possessing, have severely remarked on some few instances which

they have personally witnessed of the unseemly postures to which I refer. Learn, then, at all times, and quite as rigidly in the lecture-room as in the parlour, to sit upright, and in the posture of respectful attention. Decorum to your companions, and especially to the professor who may be addressing you, requires it; a regard to your health requires it; a proper care to avoid drowsiness requires it. Whenever a young man finds that to be comfortable he must lean, and lounge, and find some support for his back, and his feet, it is high time to feel that his habits call for immediate, and resolute correction.

11. Closely allied to the foregoing faults is another, which I have often observed with pain: I mean the habit of leaning forward, while seated in the lecture-room, and resting the head on the back of a chair, or bench, in front, as if for the purpose of sleep. When you place yourself in this posture, you will be apt, contrary to your own intention, to be betrayed into drowsiness. Even if this consequence do not follow, your fellow-students know not but that you are sleeping. And your professor must, of course, be subjected to the pain of doubting whether at least one of his auditory be not insensible to all he is saying. Can this be right in itself, to say nothing of the point of *etiquette*, as established among well-bred people? If I even had a severe headache, I would refrain from this practice. It looks so much like the vulgar lolling of a school-boy, or a college-lad, who has neither sufficient intellect, nor sufficient respect for himself or for any other person, to make him a listener, *arrectis auribus*, to that which is delivered.

12. When any thing is dropped by a professor, in

the course of a lecture, which is supposed to militate with the opinions of some pupil present, receive it with gravity and with a fixed countenance. If, instead of this, there be smiling, tittering, a dozen turning round at the same instant, to see how the pupil in question looks, and appears to feel — as is sometimes the case among ardent and inexperienced young men—there is a manifest and gross indelicacy, which, on a variety of accounts, ought to be avoided. It is ill treatment to the professor himself, who may not have intended the application thus unceremoniously made. It may be deeply embarrassing and painful to an ingenuous pupil. And it exhibits those who indulge in it, as borne away by an undignified puerility, altogether unworthy of their character. Allow me again to say, that learning the habit of maintaining, on all such occasions, a composed and grave countenance, is of no small importance in the formation of clerical manners.

13. When called upon to make remarks on the production of a fellow-student in the lecture-room, do it with perfect freedom, but with respectfulness and gravity. If you have occasion to make a remark of the unfavourable kind, let it be couched, as far as is consistent with candour, in kind and brotherly language. Pause a moment, before you offer it, and ask this question —" Is the criticism which I am about to offer, intended to display myself, or to benefit my brother?" " How should I feel, if it were made in reference to myself?" If you are conscious that it would wound your own feelings, do not, in ordinary cases, allow yourself to utter it. Not that we are to resolve never to give pain. It is sometimes unavoidable, if we would be faithful. But it should never be

inflicted unnecessarily; never more severely than is indispensable to the performance of duty; and always with as many characteristics of studied gentleness and benevolence as perfect honesty will permit.

14. Never allow yourself, on account of any ordinary avocation, to withdraw from the lecture-room, until the whole exercises shall have been completed. There is a disposition in many conscientious young men so to magnify the importance of trifles, which attract their attention, from day to day, and so to indulge the impatience which is apt to characterize that season of life, that they are constantly hurrying from one engagement to another, and often do not allow themselves to complete one, before they begin to run after another; so that they never gain the full benefit of any. This is a wretched habit, calculated to shed a baleful influence over the whole course of study, and, indeed, over the whole professional life. The admirable maxim of the old pensioner, De Witt, to "do one thing at a time," is of inestimable value. Act on the spirit of it continually; that is, be totally absorbed in your employment, for the time being, whatever it may be, and never leave it till it is completely and well done. Your studies will then be mature and profitable, and the results bear that solid, practical character, which incessant haste, and habits of immethodical and desultory attention, never can produce. Let it be your fixed habit, then, never to quit the lecture-room until its exercises are fully closed. If the instructions there delivered be of no value, you ought not to enter it at all. But if they be worth your attention, let no petty consideration ever tempt you to lose a hint or a word.

15. There is a practice indulged, not very frequently indeed, but more frequently, if I mistake not, than it ought to be. I mean that of calling out a student from the lecture-room, in the middle of a lecture or recitation, and sometimes on very slight occasions. That occasions may arise, which will fully justify such a step, no one can doubt. But that it should be ventured upon frequently, and for trivial purposes, merely to gratify a social visitor, or to indulge a fit of juvenile impatience, every one will perceive to be both injudicious, and a mischievous violation of order. It disturbs the officiating professor. It incommodes the whole class. It may suddenly take out of the room the very individual for whose benefit a particular explanation then in hand, had been intended, as I have known, more than once, to be the case; and thus do an injustice of which no one can fully estimate the amount. And all this, perhaps, to accomplish something either of no real importance, or which might just as well have been postponed until after the close of the exercise. I would advise you, then, to set your face against this practice, by testifying your disapprobation when it is done with respect to yourself, and by endeavouring to disseminate a sentiment adverse to it among your fellow-students.

16. I would advise you to take copious notes, on the spot, of all the lectures which you hear. This habit, when once established, will furnish an additional motive to perfect punctuality in being present at every lecture; for you will be unwilling to see a blank occurring in every half dozen pages in your note-book. It will constrain you to pay close attention to every word that is uttered when you are present. It

will aid you in acquiring the art of expressing yourself with brevity and precision. And it will enable you with ease to refresh your memory afterwards. I once knew a student who had a series of note-books, which contained the substance of all that he had studied at college, as well as afterwards in the seminary. And he assured me, that not only had the labour of forming them been of great advantage to him; but that he also considered them, at the time when he was speaking on the subject, as, on various accounts, among the most precious books in his library.

17. In fine, let every hour which you spend in the lecture-room, be considered as an hour of peculiar value. Remember that the business of a professor is not to think for you, but to excite you to think; to put you in possession of general principles; to start trains of thought; to state leading facts, rather than the minuter items of history; in short, to open a precious mine, to give you a specimen of its contents, and to unfold some of the best methods of exploring its boundless riches. This being done for you, all the rest must be accomplished by yourself. But in vain will any student hope to achieve much in the attainment of that which lectures cannot give him in detail, unless he bring to every lecture a mind awake, active, inquisitive, and greedy of knowledge; unless he carefully watch every sentence that is dropped, every opening for an important question and explanation; and every opportunity, however small, of extending his views of truth or duty. If students listened with such a spirit, the shortest and most meagre lecture would be thought a feast. O how remote from this is the dull, drowsy, uninterested mind which some bring

to the exercises of the class; a mind which, instead of eagerly seizing, examining and extending all that is presented to it, can hardly be stimulated to such a degree of attention as will enable it even to comprehend what is said at the time, much less to give any intelligent account of it afterwards. You may rest assured, that if you do not gain the art of bringing intense mental application to that which is presented to you from time to time, you will never accomplish much in any species of mental improvement.

LETTER X.

That thou mayest know how thou oughtest to behave thyself in the house of God. — 1 TIM. iii. 15.

HABITS IN THE PULPIT, AND IN THE HOUSE OF GOD.

MY DEAR YOUNG FRIEND: — The pulpit has been sometimes called the minister's throne. There he appears to perform the most important part of his public work. And there, if any where, he ought to be seen to advantage. His aspect, his attitudes, and his whole deportment, ought to correspond with the gravity and solemnity of his message. And while, on the one hand, every thing like pomp, ostentation, or mock dignity, should be avoided as hateful; on the other, all coarseness, levity, or vulgarity — every thing that borders on the ludicrous, or the want of real dignity, ought to be shunned with no less care. As you are soon, with the permission of Providence, to ascend the pulpit, I am anxious that you should have some just ideas how you ought to appear there. It is my purpose, therefore, in the present letter, to put you on your guard against a few of those faults which I have often observed ministers to commit in the sacred desk; and to offer a few plain counsels which may aid you in avoiding those faults.

1. Avoid all unnecessary expense of spirits, voice, and strength, immediately before going into the pulpit. Those who are not aware of the difficulties under which ministers labour, especially such of them as have weak lungs, or general delicacy of health, are apt to call upon them for services which require much effort, just before the commencement of the public service in the church. The consequence is, that they sometimes ascend the pulpit nearly as much exhausted, as, at other times, when they quit it. This cannot always be avoided; but it certainly ought in all cases to be avoided, when it can be consistently with duty. Guard against all unnecessary reading loud, and every thing which tends to produce exhaustion or weariness, especially of the lungs. Make a point of entering on the service of the sanctuary in all the freshness and fulness of your strength and spirits. In this case, you may hope to perform them with more vigour and animation; with more comfort to yourself; and with more profit to others. Whereas if you either inadvertently, or unavoidably, fatigue yourself before you go to the pulpit, your whole public work, on that occasion, will probably be dull and nerveless. Hence that preacher is extremely unwise, who sits up late on Saturday night, and exhausts himself in making preparations for the next day. Of all nights in the week, it is important that that, which immediately precedes the Sabbath, should be passed in unbroken sleep.

2. When you expect to preach, instead of eating more, rather eat less than on other days. I do not forget that no rules on this subject can be laid down, which will equally suit all persons. But, unless I am

greatly deceived, there are some general principles here, which admit of very few exceptions. And one of these I believe to be, that, when we are about to make a great exertion, especially in speaking, a state of repletion is so far from being advantageous, that it is directly the reverse. Try it when you will, you will find that, when your aliment on the Sabbath is more light in its quality, and smaller in quantity, than on other days, you will go through the labours of the day with more ease and vivacity, with far less subsequent fatigue, and feel much better the next day, than when you take an opposite course. Of all mistakes on this subject, that is the greatest, which dreams of deriving unusual strength and animation for the labours of the pulpit, from an usual indulgence in the use of solid food.

3. Never habituate yourself to the use of any of those tonics, nourishing draughts, and clearers of the voice, of which many make such abundant use. I have known some preachers, who abounded so much in the use of eggs, and honey, and mint-drops, and spirits of lavender, and wine, and sugar-candy, &c. &c., immediately before going to the pulpit, that, when abroad, and among those who were not accustomed to their habits, they were really troublesome guests. And I not long since read a work, entitled *Medicina Clerica*, from the pen of an English clergyman, in which the writer makes preparation for entering the pulpit so complicated a system; in which he recommends such a long list of drops, and lozenges, and stimulants, and remedies for hoarseness, and such an endless round of indulgences and plans for "ease and comfort," that the perusal of his book appears to me

much better adapted to teach a man how to make himself a hypochondriac, than a powerful, active preacher. The truth is, young preachers do not stand in need of any of these things, and ought not to use them. They are seldom necessary for any one who does not make them so, by improper management. If you ask me, what plan I would recommend for keeping the lips and mouth sufficiently moist, and for clearing the voice, in the pulpit, my answer is, I would recommend—just nothing at all. Avoid the use of any thing for this purpose. Guard against the miserable servitude of having a dozen little wants, all of which must be supplied before you can ascend the sacred desk. Endeavour, by temperance and exercise, to preserve in vigour your general health, and then, unless some organic disease should render some application to the mouth or throat necessary, you will do much better without any thing of the kind. The truth is, this is one of the numerous cases in which the more you make use of the auxiliaries of which I speak, the more indispensably necessary to your comfort they will be likely to become, until you may convert your study into an apothecary's shop, and render yourself a poor feeble valetudinarian, by the very efforts which you make to avoid the evil. On this subject I speak from experience. In the early part of my ministry, I abounded in the use of prescriptions for strengthening and clearing the voice. I soon discovered, however, that the only effect of them was to increase the difficulty which they were intended to remedy; and to render an increase both in the frequency and quantity of the applications indispensable. Alarmed at this discovery, I determined to lay them all aside. I did so; and found, when the first little inconvenience of the privation had passed away, that I was able to do better without than with them. And now, with a delightful independence of all my former little wants, for which I cannot be sufficiently thankful, I usually go to the pulpit more comfortably, without a single medical or dietetical application, than before with a host of them.

4. Go from your knees to the pulpit. The more thoroughly your mind is steeped, if I may be allowed the expression, in the spirit of prayer, and of communion with God, when you ascend the sacred desk, the more easy and delightful will it be to preach; the more rich and spiritual will your preaching be: the more fervent and natural your eloquence; and the greater the probability that what you say will be made a blessing. Be assured, my dear young friend, after all the rules and instructions which have been given on the subject of pulpit eloquence—and which in their place have great value—that which unspeakably outweighs all the rest in importance, is, that you go to the sanctuary with a heart full of your subject; warmed with love to your Master, and to immortal souls; remembering too, that the eye of the Master is upon you; and that of the sermon which you are about to deliver, you must soon give an account before his judgment-seat. With these sentiments in full force, it is always desirable, both for your own sake and that of others, that you should enter the pulpit. And I know of no means more likely to produce them, than humble importunity before the throne of grace.

5. Make a point of being as perfectly punctual as possible in attending at the appointed hour for public

service. A punctual minister makes a punctual congregation. Whereas if the minister be tardy, or variable, as to the time of his attendance, he scarcely ever fails to induce a similar habit on the part of his parishioners. The consequence of this is, that a considerable portion of them seldom arrive till the service is nearly half over; thereby diminishing their own profit, and disturbing the devotions of those who are more punctual than themselves. With regard to country congregations, other evils, quite as serious, flow from this unhappy practice. The people are frequently permitted by the minister to wait for his arrival half an hour, and sometimes longer, after the major part of them are assembled. This interval, instead of being spent profitably, by the mass of the attendants, is commonly passed in vain and unprofitable conversation, if not in that which is of a worse character; communications take place which render the minds of many wholly unfit for the solemn services which follow, and perhaps lead to injurious engagements, after those services are ended. Thus, in many cases, incalculable mischief is done. I would advise you to accustom the people, by your own example, to absolute punctuality. Endeavour to be always seated in the pulpit a few minutes before the arrival of the time appointed for commencing the service. Begin precisely at the time, or, at any rate, within five minutes after it, even if you have but a dozen hearers. Wait for no one. If this plan be adopted and persisted in, and notice given accordingly, you will soon be rid of all trouble from this source: and many precious hours will be saved to yourself, as well as to the people of your charge.

6. Let your mode of entering the house of God, and of walking along the aisle, toward the pulpit, be grave, dignified, and yet perfectly simple and unaffected. Few things are more unbecoming, than to see an ambassador of Christ, who enters the sanctuary for the purpose of conducting the devotions of a religious assembly, and of addressing them on the most momentous of all subjects, walking with hurried steps, or in a light, airy manner; looking over the house, as he enters it, as if in search of an acquaintance; and perhaps, even bowing to those who are seated near him as he passes. All this I have frequently seen, and never without disapprobation and disgust. How much more suitable, to manifest the spirit and feelings of the pulpit before you enter it; to approach it with a deliberate and grave step, with a serious and fixed countenance, and taking but little notice of any external objects around you! Do not, in these circumstances, even accost an individual, if you can easily avoid it. And instead of mounting the pulpit steps with a rapidity, or an affectation of gracefulness, approaching the artificial skip of a dancing-master, let it always be done with that mixture of gravity and gentleness, which I have elsewhere recommended as so important in every part of clerical manners.

7. Let every look, motion, and attitude in the pulpit correspond with the gravity of your character, and the solemn purpose for which you ascended it. Let there be no roving of the eyes over the assembly, as if to gratify curiosity, to search for acquaintances, or to indulge vanity at the sight of a crowd. Let there be no adjustment of the dress, as if you were anxious

about your personal appearance. Every thing of this kind should be done before you go thither, and afterwards entirely dismissed from the mind. Let there be no abrupt, rapid motions, as if you were hurried or agitated; no tossing about of books, or turning over their leaves in a hurried manner, as if vexed or impatient. But let every movement, and your whole demeanour, be of the calm, sedate, gentle character, becoming a mind withdrawn from the world and its scenes; a mind even withdrawn from its own secular feelings, and occupied with divine contemplations; a mind softened, tranquillized, and adapted to its holy employment. There is something as beautiful as it is impressive, in seeing the whole air, countenance and manner of a man of God, who is just about to deliver the message of his Master, corresponding with his office and his work: and without either affected solemnity, or any other species of affectation, evincing a heart absorbed with the great objects which he wishes to recommend to others.

8. I have noticed in some ministers a striking want of dignity in almost every thing that they did in the pulpit. If they had occasion to give any orders to the sexton; or to announce any public notification; or to address any one in the church, at some distance from the pulpit, it was done in a manner much more adapted to promote ridicule, than impressions corresponding with the sabbath and the house of God. If they had occasion to discharge saliva from their mouths, in the midst of the public service, it was accomplished very unceremoniously, throwing it about offensively, and perhaps with noise, without the use of a handkerchief. In short, their whole manner of

performing every thing they were called to do or say, was without taste, without that quiet and gentle dignity, which ought ever to mark what is done in the sacred desk. Carefully guard against such coarse, repulsive habits. Let nothing escape you, which may tend, either in matter or manner, to jar the feelings of the most fastidious member of the assembly who is reasonable, or to produce an emotion unfriendly to that solemn Christian composure which becomes the place.

9. Let not your commencement of the public service, either as to voice or manner, be abrupt, harsh, or loud; but studiously gentle and reverential. Offences against this obvious rule of propriety are exceedingly common. Every thing that looks like haste, or the want of due solemnity, never fails to repel correct minds. And every thing in the tones of the voice, which indicates the absence of that sacred awe which ought to fill the mind in entering on the duty of dispensing sacred things, is no less obvious and repulsive. Let your whole manner, in first rising in the pulpit, be in harmony with the occasion and the place.

10. Be not in haste to pass from one part of the service to another, before the preceding is finished. It is by no means uncommon to see the occupant of a pulpit rise for prayer, before the psalm is completed; and still more frequently, rise to commence his sermon, while the praises of God are going on. Nay, while the last verse of the psalm or hymn was singing, I have known several who always stood up; turned over the leaves of the Bible; adjusted marks for passages to which they wished to refer; and seemed to be entirely absorbed in something entirely different

from that part of the service which was then going on. I must confess that this strikes me as a great impropriety. Is the conductor of the public service to consider himself as taking a part in it or not? If he do, then surely he ought not to pass from one to another, until the former be finished. While he is eagerly engaged in searching for passages of scripture, he cannot be really uniting with his fellow-worshippers in singing the praises of God from the heart, however his lips and voice may be employed. Besides, where is the need of so much expedition? Why should you be in haste to pass on to another exercise, until the preceding is completed? If the worship of God were irksome, and you wished to bring it to a close as soon as possible; or if you believed your sermon to be much better than prayer or praise, you might be in a hurry to pass from the latter to the former. But as you would not be willing to avow either of these, let nothing that would imply either mark the progress of the public service.

11. But sometimes a still more striking indecorum occurs. It is that of a minister who, when standing in the pulpit, while a brother is officiating in prayer, has been occupied, a number of minutes before the prayer was ended, in looking for the psalm which was to succeed, or for the chapter which was to be read; and actually rustling the leaves for that purpose, in a manner audible, as well as visible, to the greater part of the congregation. It is difficult to speak of such a practice in terms of sufficiently strong reprobation. It is indeed, an offence against decorum so flagrant that it is wonderful how any one who had the least desire

either to be, or to be thought devout, could possibly fall into it.

12. Let me advise you, in public prayer always to close your eyes. I should not mention this, were it not that some ministers of our church, and some of no inconsiderable eminence, have been in the habit of conducting public prayer with their eyes open, to the great annoyance of many who witnessed the practice; and were it not also, that the celebrated and truly excellent Dr. Doddridge, in his "Lectures on Preaching, &c.," seems to give it the sanction of his advice. I am persuaded that if you can, without great inconvenience to yourself, keep your eyes constantly shut in this exercise, it will be found much preferable to the opposite method. To many persons, the appearance of the eyes open in prayer is really painful. And when they are kept open, it is extremely difficult, especially to some individuals, to keep them from wandering to different objects, and parts of the church, and thus, in some degree, interfering with that entire abstraction of the thoughts from sensible objects, which is certainly desirable.

13. Study to administer the sacraments of the church in a manner adapted to make a distinct and solemn impression. Let there be no appearance of coarseness, haste, or carelessness in your mode of administering those peculiarly interesting ordinances. As they mean much in reality; so let them be seen to mean much in your hands. When you are about to administer the ordinance of baptism, either to adults, or infants, be careful to inform the persons concerned, unless you are perfectly sure that they are informed beforehand, of all the questions which you

intend to address to them; where and how they are to stand, &c.; as these are points with respect to which the usages of churches are not entirely uniform. In short, try to guard against their being taken by surprise, or embarrassed by any part of the service. In like manner, in the administration of the Lord's Supper, whether the communicants sit at tables or in pews, take care to have every thing so far prepared and adjusted beforehand, as that there may be nothing likely to occur to jar the feelings, to incommode, or to impair the solemnity of the scene. Let there be no undue haste; no omission of what is necessary for the comfort of the communicants and others; but every thing studiously ordered in such a manner as to render the whole occasion, as far as possible, solemn, impressive, and edifying to all classes who may witness it.

14. Guard against making your public services too long. The opposite to this advice is a fault which often occurs, and which is always unfriendly to edification. Whenever weariness begins, edification terminates. It was well said by Whitefield, that a sermon of more than an hour long, though preached by an angel, would appear tedious, unless the hearers were angels too. Where there is more than one service statedly performed, no sermon ought ever, on an ordinary occasion, to be more than forty-five minutes in length; nor ought the whole service, at any one time, to be longer than an hour and a half. And if, at any time, you are compelled, by special circumstances, to preach longer, let all the other parts of the service be, in a corresponding degree, abridged. Some ministers manifest a degree of thoughtlessness, or

want of judgment, on this subject, truly wonderful. If at any time they are betrayed into an inordinate tediousness in their sermons, they seldom fail, at the same time, to make the portion of scripture read, the prayers, and the psalms, all in like proportion tedious. This is extremely ill-judged, and often interferes most essentially with the edification of many hearers. It appears to me proper to urge this advice with especial earnestness, in reference to those occasions on which the Lord's Supper is dispensed. At such peculiarly solemn and interesting seasons, when the services are unavoidably much longer than those of an ordinary sabbath, I have often been surprised to see clergymen take so little care to abridge those parts of the service which easily admit of being shortened. On such occasions, by making the sermon shorter than usual, and by lopping off a small portion from each of the other exercises, a very convenient length of the whole may be readily attained.

15. Never render yourself remarkable by continually making a display of a white handkerchief in the pulpit. I say, by making a display of it. To have such a handkerchief, if convenient, in the pulpit, and to use it on proper occasions, and in a proper way, are by no means objectionable. But to hold it up frequently and in a flourishing manner, as if to invite the notice of the congregation, is a practice unworthy of a man of sense. Indeed, with regard to every part of your dress, or other appendage of your person, never allow it, on any occasion, to have the appearance of engaging a single thought.

16. When you have occasion to reprove any disorderly person in the house of God, guard against in-

dulging or betraying irascible feeling. It is peculiarly unseemly, and out of season, for a minister of the gospel, in the pulpit, and in the very act of exhorting men to obey the commands of God, to lose his temper, and give way to that which may even possibly be regarded as an effusion of anger. Do not make your reproofs from the pulpit very frequent, or else they will become cheap. When you think yourself called in duty to administer a reproof, do it seriously and solemnly, but mildly. Sometimes it is best to come to a full stop, and look at the individual offending, in perfect silence, until every eye shall be directed toward him. At other times, it may be proper to request the sexton to attend to those persons who are disturbing the congregation, and to direct them, if they cannot be persuaded to behave decently, to leave the assembly. Sometimes a pause, without naming or indicating any individual, and uttering a sentence or two on the importance of reverencing the name and worship of Jehovah, may answer every purpose. The cases, I presume, will ever be found few in which it can be necessary to administer a direct and personal rebuke. But, whatever may be the form of admonition which the case requires, deliver it in a grave, mild, and gentle manner. Never attempt to taunt the offenders by sarcasm, or to turn the laugh on them by wit. This might do very well in a secular assembly; but is not proper for a minister of religion, and in the house of God.

17. Let your deportment in quitting the pulpit, and withdrawing from the church, be of the same general character with that which was recommended in approaching and entering it. Retire as soon as you

can, gravely, silently, and alone. Discountenance the practice which I have known some ministers to indulge to a considerable extent; I mean that of stopping to converse with a number of individuals, at the close of the public service; with some, as a mere matter of social respect and ceremony; with others, perhaps, on the subject of the discourse just delivered; and with a third class on the subject of religion generally. In general, give no encouragement to any of these classes of persons to stop for the purpose of conversing with you at this unseasonable time. Not the first class; because mere social conversation is extremely apt, even on the Sabbath, and in the house of God, to degenerate into worldly chat, before we are aware, and to banish from the mind the most solemn subjects of contemplation in which we may have been engaged. Not even, in ordinary cases, the second and third classes; because, although it may, on some special occasions, be your duty to gratify those who may wish to remain a few minutes, for the purpose of conversing with you, and it might appear morose to decline it; yet yielding to a practice of that kind, may be very injurious. At the close of the public service, you will generally find yourself fatigued, and often exhausted. This is a very unfit condition in which to enter on conversation in reference to the most important of all subjects. And frequently has a minister, before he was aware, materially injured himself, by pausing to engage in conversation, while fatigued with a preceding service.

Besides, on the score of example, ministers ought, by all means, to be in the habit of retiring from the house of God to their place of abode, in serious and solemn silence. What would be the consequence, if every hearer, at the close of the public service, were to linger about the church, receiving and paying civilities; making social inquiries; hearing or telling news; or even conversing on the subject of the minister's discourse? Is it not evident that a scene of noise and disorder must ensue, and that the practical influence of the exercises of the sanctuary would probably be very transient? And shall a minister, by his own example, sanction any thing which, if it were to become general, would produce incalculable mischief? I have known many a congregation, especially in the country, the members of which were in the habit of spending a considerable time, both before the commencement and after the close of the public service, in social chat, and sometimes in that of a very light and unsuitable kind. And I must say, that, in general, when I have observed this, I have been strongly inclined to lay a large share of the blame at the door of their pastor. If a proper example had been, in all cases, set by him, such a practice could not have been long kept in countenance.

18. When you are seated in the pulpit with another minister, let your conversation with him be in a low and inaudible voice. I have known a minister, sitting in the pulpit with a clerical brother, to talk so loudly, that the sound of his voice might be heard almost over the whole church. I have known others, so far to forget themselves as not only to smile, but to laugh outright, at something which had been said in the course of this pulpit dialogue. Every thing of this kind makes an unpleasant impression, and ought to be avoided. Let all conversation in the pulpit be

conducted in a whisper, audible to none but those who are engaged in it; and let the most perfect gravity of countenance be constantly maintained. There is no doubt that cases may occur in which a smile in the pulpit may be very innocent. But how shall the members of a congregation know when, or how far, it is so in any particular instance? The motto of every Christian, and especially of every Christian minister, on all such occasions is, "Shun the very appearance of evil."

19. I know not a more suitable place than this for taking notice of another habit frequently indulged by clergymen. I mean the habit of conversing aloud, and sometimes even jocularly, at funerals. If ministers of religion find no convenient opening, at funerals, for making appropriate remarks "on the frailty of life, and the importance of being prepared for death and eternity," they at least owe it to decorum not to join in conversation calculated to banish such thoughts from their own minds, and those of others. I have often been surprised and pained to hear such conversations carried on in funeral assemblies, when several ministers of the gospel were present. If you cannot regulate the course of conversation more agreeably to your mind, it is far better to sit gravely silent. Let it be seen that there is at least one person present, who is engaged in serious meditation. Let me also advise you to observe the same rule when you are walking in procession at funerals, to the place of interment. I have seen ministers, in these circumstances, talking, and even laughing audibly, on indifferent subjects. Is not this a manifest indecorum? Surely it is not requiring too much to say, that when

you are conveying the dead to the "house appointed for all living," your subjects of discourse, your countenance, and your tones of voice, ought to be of that grave, thoughtful, and subdued character, which is in harmony with the scene.

20. Sometimes when a brother occupies your place in the pulpit, you may be called upon to make a prayer, either before or after sermon. Whenever this is the case, carefully avoid making the prayer a vehicle of flattery to him who has just preached, or who is about to perform that service. This is frequently done; and yet it is obviously, in a high degree, both criminal and contemptible. We may, indeed, sometimes, almost apply to it the language of an inspired apostle, on another occasion, and call it "lying to the Holy Ghost." Let no such impious sycophancy ever pollute those prayers in which a whole assembly are expected to join. Let me also put you on your guard against flattering a brother, who has just laboured for you, in a manner less impious, but still worthy of being totally condemned. I refer to the manner in which many ministers are in the habit of making their grateful acknowledgments to their brethren, for the official help afforded them; too frequently in the style of flattery, sometimes in that of a very gross kind; lauding their sermons in strong terms; and addressing them in a way which, if it do not minister to their vanity, it is because it is too fulsome to be mischievous. Shun every approach to this sin. To thank a brother for his services, if they be really valuable, is, in common, quite enough. If there be, in any case, a call to go further, and to express a favourable opinion of a sermon, let it be done

with studied moderation, and always rather fall below the truth than transcend it.

21. When you appear in the sanctuary as an ordinary hearer, let your deportment ever exemplify those rules of serious, meek, and respectful attention which you inculcate on others. It has been remarked, that some clergymen are among the most inattentive and irreverent hearers that enter the house of God. Perhaps one of the infelicities of their profession is, that they are too apt to hear as critics; to be constantly measuring the discourses of others, by those canons of composition which they have been in the habit of regarding as obligatory; and when these are palpably violated, to manifest by their looks and manners the disrespectful feelings which occupy their minds. Hence, they turn away from the preacher, as if desirous of escaping from the sound of his voice, gaze about the house, or lean down their heads, as if endeavouring to compose themselves to sleep. I have also known ministers who were in the constant habit of placing themselves, during public prayer conducted by others, in such postures, and to indulge in such employments, as have, to say the least, very little of the appearance of devotion. Some clergymen, during public prayer, are frequently, if not generally, employed in looking round the church, in adjusting their dress, in fixing their hair, and in constantly changing their posture, as if impatient of the continuance of the exercise. All this is indecorous in any one; but especially in a minister of the gospel. If he allow himself thus to act, what can be expected from the mass of hearers, who always look to those who sustain the sacred office to go before them in devotion,

purity, and every thing that is ornamental in Christian deportment?

To this point allow me to direct your particular attention. Let none have occasion to say, that your devotion is official, not personal; and that, when you are out of the pulpit, you can be as remote from the solemnity which becomes the house of God, as any of your neighbours. On the contrary, let your serious countenance, your wakeful, erect, fixed attention, your meek, respectful air, your universally devout manner, even when you are seated among others, as a common worshipper, manifest that you are yourself really engaged in those things which, from the pulpit, you recommend to others. Remember that, if your performances in the pulpit, from Sabbath to Sabbath, put to the test your ministerial gifts; your manner of attending on the service of the sanctuary, as a common worshipper, puts to an equally decisive test your Christian graces. When you join, then, in the devotions led by another, and listen to instruction from a brother's lips, endeavour to lay aside the feelings of the minister, and to sit, an humble, candid learner at the feet of the Saviour's servant; recollecting that, if you are saved, it must be by the same rich grace; and if edified and comforted, it must be by the same simple, precious, humbling truths and promises which you recommend to the most illiterate of your hearers. In a word, I am persuaded that ministers, by their exemplary manner of attending on the ministrations of others, may, and often do, preach as solemnly, and impress those around them as powerfully, as by the best services which they ever perform in the sacred desk.

22. Avoid much exposure to cold air immediately after leaving the pulpit. You ought to be aware that cold air received into your lungs, or striking on your body, while you are warm with speaking, is peculiarly dangerous, and may be productive of fatal mischief. Carefully avoid such exposure, especially in very damp or piercing weather. When you leave the church, in such weather, throw around your person a warm cloak. Hold it up in such a manner as completely to cover your mouth and nostrils; and take care to inhale none but the air which is enclosed, and the temperature of which is moderated, by your cloak. And, let me add, take all these precautions at night with very particular care. Some preachers, after having addressed crowded assemblies, in very cold weather, in the evening, do not scruple to ride home several miles, at a late hour. This is always dangerous, and ought never to be done without wrapping up with peculiar care, and using every precaution to guard your body and lungs against the night air.

23. When you have been a hearer, do not quit the church criticising the sermon, and especially in an audible voice. This is not unfrequently done; not always in the happiest manner; and sometimes, unfortunately, within the hearing of the preacher. The character of a criticising hearer of sermons, is not a very good one at best. He is not likely to obtain much practical benefit from hearing. And when he proclaims his criticisms, at the very door of the sanctuary, or on his way from it, he perhaps extends an injury to others. Always be a candid hearer of other men's sermons. When you can speak favourably of them, do it; but not noisily or publicly. When you

are constrained, if you say any thing, to censure, give utterance to your sentiments as gently and as privately as possible, consistently with Christian integrity.

24. Finally, as I advised you to go from your knees to the pulpit, so I would, with equal earnestness, advise that you go from the pulpit to your knees. If you are faithful, you will often exhort your hearers to retire from the church to their closets, to meditate, and implore the divine blessing on what they have heard. And why is it not equally the privilege and duty of ministers to meditate and implore a blessing on what they have said? Nay, has not the spiritual guide more numerous and more solemn reasons for following all his efforts with his prayers, than any other person? It was well remarked by an old divine, that "the minister who is more before his people in public, than he is before God for them in private, has little reason to expect a blessing on his labours."

LETTER XI.

And the apostles and elders came together for to consider of this matter. —ACTS xv. 6.

CONDUCT IN CHURCH JUDICATORIES.

MY DEAR YOUNG FRIEND:—I have repeatedly had occasion to observe, that every part of the deportment of a minister is important, both to himself and the church. He cannot be said, in the discharge of any official duty, to act for himself alone. In all that he does, the whole body of Christ has an interest. But this remark applies to no part of his duty more strongly, than that which he performs as a member of the judicatories of the church. When a minister takes his seat in any one of these judicatories, he places himself in a situation in which every thing that he says and does, may, for what he can tell, exert an influence to the remotest bounds of the church to which he belongs, and may have a bearing on the comfort, respectability and usefulness of his brethren, as well as himself, to an extent which no one, at present, can measure. In this situation, he is called continually to act with others, as well as for others; and almost every hour to give a touch more or less important, to the ark of God.

To suppose "a steward of the mysteries of God," capable of addressing himself to duties so peculiarly interesting and momentous as these, with levity or indifference, would be to suppose either a want of consideration, or a want of principle, truly deplorable. Here, if ever, he ought to be awake to all the solemnity of his situation; and to be anxious to summon to his aid all those dictates of wisdom and holy fidelity which he continually needs. He who does not feel deeply serious, when he is about to deliberate, with his brethren, on the great concerns of the Redeemer's kingdom, and to take steps which may vitally affect that kingdom, not only in a single congregation, but in many congregations, has little indeed of the spirit of a "watchman on the walls of Zion." And he who is not aware of the danger, that his own prejudices, passions, and folly may interpose an unhallowed influence in all his deliberations and discussions on these great concerns, will not be likely to be much employed in watching and praying against that influence.

I must say, that there appears to me much need of attention to this subject. It has seldom been my lot to witness the proceedings of any of the higher judicatories of the church, either as a member or spectator, without having occasion, as I thought, to lament that correct views and habits, in relation to this matter, were not more prevalent. I have seen excellent men expose themselves, give pain to others, and even embarrass ecclesiastical business, by mere inadvertence. And I should certainly have esteemed it a happy circumstance for myself, if I had been put on my guard, in early life, against many of those mistakes and faults into which I fell, from want of suitable instruction and training, on a point so deeply interesting to all who wish to see dignity, order, wisdom, brotherly love, and piety, marking the proceedings of every ecclesiastical body.

It will readily occur to you that there is an importance attached to this subject which is altogether peculiar. In state legislatures, in congress, and in most of the secular deliberative assemblies which convene, the time which may be spent in their sessions is not rigidly limited. If the debates be protracted, and they cannot complete their business in three or four weeks, they may take, if they see proper, double or treble that period. And if a high degree of heat, disorder, or even violence, should unfortunately mark their proceedings, decent people may deplore it, but the great interests of religion may not be materially compromitted, inasmuch as they are not religious bodies. But it is otherwise with our ecclesiastical judicatories. For various reasons, they cannot possibly continue to sit beyond a very few days. Every moment, therefore, is to them doubly precious. Of course, every moment's interruption, and every unnecessary, worthless speech, become serious evils; evils to the cause of Christ: and whenever heat, disorder or violence occurs among the ministers and elders of the church, religion bleeds at every pore. As ecclesiastical judicatories are purely religious bodies, so they ought to bear a religious character, in all their deliberations, and in every movement. Surely, then, this is a concern in which all our wisdom as men, and all our piety and prudence as Christians, are most solemnly put in requisition.

This subject is so extensive that I cannot undertake to consider it in its minute details. Permit me, however, to suggest a few general counsels; and to accompany each, as I proceed, with some brief explanatory or corroborative remarks. And

1. My first counsel is that you make a point of being perfectly punctual in attending on every judicatory of the church in which it is your duty to be present.

This is a duty of far more deep and vital importance than most ministers appear to imagine. The faithful discharge of it bears relations, and exerts an influence, which, unless I am deceived, are seldom duly considered. Among the many reasons which might be urged in favour of this opinion, the following are certainly entitled to your serious regard.

(1). Your ordination vows will demand constant attention to this duty. In that solemn hour, in which you kneel before God, and, surrounded by the church and her ministry, receive the imposition of "the hands of the presbytery," you will promise to be "subject to your brethren in the Lord," and to be "faithful and diligent in the discharge of all the public, as well as the private duties of your office." Now, there is scarcely any public duty more important than that for which I am pleading. Of course, he who neglects it violates his solemn engagements. Nor is this all. These judicatories form an essential feature of Presbyterian church government. To abolish them, would be to abolish Presbyterianism. Consequently, he who allows himself habitually and unnecessarily to neglect attendance on them—is unfaithful to his solemn profession—is no Presbyterian in fact, whatever he may be in name.

(2). If these ecclesiastical assemblies ought to be maintained, then it is plain that all who are properly members, ought to be punctual in their attendance, on the principles both of equity and benevolence. He who neglects them, thereby refuses to render his share of service to the church, and throws an additional and unequal burden on those of his brethren who make conscience of attending. Is this consistent with good morals, to say nothing of higher considerations? It is, certainly, not doing to others, as we would that they, in like circumstances, should do to us.

(3). A punctual attendance on the ecclesiastical judicatories to which a minister belongs, is indispensable to his attaining a high and desirable standing among his brethren, and enjoying their affectionate confidence. It is the remark of one of the wisest and most venerated ministers of the Presbyterian church now living, that "he has never known a minister, in our connection, who was either very useful, or very respectable, that did not give his presence at presbytery, synod, and assembly, whenever that duty became incumbent." *

The reasons are many and obvious. The minister who seldom appears among his brethren, in their ecclesiastical meetings, has, commonly, but little intercourse with them, as ministers, at all. He is, consequently, but little known to them. Of course, he cannot possibly enjoy much of their confidence, or have much influence among them. They see little of him in person; but they habitually witness his negli-

* Rev. Dr. Green. "Charge at the Ordination of Messrs. J B. Linn," &c. [Dr. Green died May 19th, 1848, in the 86th year of his age. *Ed. of the Board of Pub.*]

gence and deficiencies. Will these be likely to command either their respect or their love? The minister, then, who unnecessarily absents himself from the judicatories of the church, does a complicated injury to the cause of Christ; but he injures his own character, standing, and influence in the sacred office, quite as much, if not more than any other interest.

(4). A punctual attendance on the ecclesiastical assemblies under consideration, is the best school in the world in which to study church government. I know that you have read books, and heard lectures on this department of theological study. But the knowledge derived from books and lectures is apt to be theoretical, and to make but a slight impression on the mind. When you come to occupy your seat, and act your part in ecclesiastical judicatories, you see the great principles of church government, as it were, embodied and exhibited in actual cases. And being called upon closely to contemplate these cases, to study them, to view them under various aspects, and to listen to ample discussions on their real merits; we may be said, in these circumstances, to enjoy advantages for investigating principles, and having the results of investigation deeply and strongly impressed upon our minds, which no retired study can so well furnish. Whatever may have been your previous reading, never expect to find yourself expert in comprehending and applying the great doctrines of church government, unless you have studied them much on the floor of judicatories. If you carefully observe what passes, you will observe men of excellent minds, who are not in the habit of attending those judicatories, often betraying a degree of ignorance, on some of the very first principles of church discipline, as ludicrous as it is disreputable.

(5). Finally, a due attendance on the assemblies under consideration, is one of the best means of obtaining and constantly extending and improving a connected knowledge of the history of our church. Whatever other part of ecclesiastical history a minister is ignorant of, he ought certainly to be well acquainted with the history of his own church; and especially of that portion of it which is embraced within his own time. But even this portion will not be thoroughly gained and kept up by any member who is not in the constant habit of attending on the judicatories of his church. Before these assemblies all the principal facts are made to pass. And they appear there with a life and force much more impressive, much more likely to be remembered, and in connections and circumstances better adapted to leave their appropriate lessons, than if contemplated only by means of an oral statement, or a printed page. Show me a Presbyterian minister who is familiarly acquainted with the history of his own church, and especially since he entered her ministry, and I will, without hesitation, show you a man who has been constant and punctual in attending on her judicatories.

It is evident then, whether we consider the honour of our religion, the edification of the church, the fulfilment of our official vows, the duty which we owe to our fellow-servants, the promotion of our own respectability and influence among our clerical brethren, or the extension and improvement of our own ecclesiastical knowledge, we ought to make a point of appearing, as punctually as possible, in every judicatory of the church in which we have a right to occupy a seat.

2. Make a point, not only of attending every meeting, but also of being punctually present at the opening of the judicatory. It is possible that the first acts of business may be decidedly the most important. In this case, tardiness may be quite as injurious as total non-attendance. And even if this be not the case, as most commonly it is not; a variety of things may pass before your arrival, absolutely essential to an intelligent and connected view of the proceedings. Let no ordinary engagement interfere with perfect punctuality in this matter. Be on the ground among the earliest; and you will find more advantages connected with such a system than I can well enumerate. To say nothing of many other considerations, what right have you to occupy the time and swell the minutes of the judicatory by compelling them to receive and record your apologies for delinquency?

3. I would advise you to prepare for attendance on every judicatory, by serious retirement, meditation and prayer.

If every "creature" that we enjoy ought to be "sanctified by the word of God and prayer," surely this ought to be more especially the case with one of the most important official duties in which we can possibly engage. When we are about to meet with our fellow-servants, as a judicatory of Jesus Christ, to deliberate and consult respecting the interests of the Redeemer's kingdom; to act together in our public and ministerial character, not merely for the welfare of a single soul, but for that of many congregations, and perhaps, of the whole church with which we are connected; and when we know not how far the influence of what we say and do may extend; surely we ought to address ourselves to all such duties, with the most serious consideration, and with humble, importunate prayer for all that wisdom, and guidance, and strength which we need. I had almost said, if there be any occasion on which a man of enlightened piety should feel serious and devout, it ought to be on the approach of such an assembly.

Let me urge you, then, whenever you are about to attend any church judicatory, and especially those of the higher kind, in all the movements of which large and momentous interests are involved; to set apart a portion of time for special prayer, with a particular view to this object. If you be about to take your seat in a Synod or in the General Assembly, let the whole day before you set out, if practicable, be observed as a day of solemn prayer, accompanied with fasting. If the discharge of necessary duties preclude the possibility of this, as may sometimes be the case, make a point of redeeming at least one hour for special retirement and devotion, in reference to your anticipated engagement. And in this solemn hour, endeavour to ponder deeply in your heart, and to spread before the Lord, all the magnitude and difficulty of the work which you have in prospect; and all the temptations and dangers to which you may be exposed, from your own infirmities, and those of others. Pray that you may be inspired with heavenly wisdom in all the business that may come before you: that you may be enabled, in every case, to take just views of truth and duty; that you may be guarded from prejudice, from passion, and from every unhallowed temper: that you may be enabled always to act from the purest motives, and with a single eye to the Redeemer's honour: that you may be preserved from giving a wrong touch to the ark, either ignorantly or presumptuously; that you may not be permitted, unnecessarily or improperly, to wound the feelings of those with whom you may be called to act; and that, in all the proceedings of the judicatory, you may be enabled to judge and act in such a manner as that the peace, purity, and edification of the body of Christ may be happily promoted.

Nor ought you to forget, in these moments of humble and tender approach to the King of Zion, to pray for the brethren with whom you are about to act, as well as for yourself. Pray that they may be so enlightened, aided, sanctified, counselled and controlled in every thing; may be so guarded from the influence of erroneous views, and from the ebullitions of unhallowed feeling, that "all things may be done decently and in order," and may issue in the advancement of the great cause of truth and righteousness. If every member of ecclesiastical judicatories attended their meetings, respectively, under that kind of influence which such exercises, faithfully conducted, would be likely to inspire, how different would be their aspect and their results, from those which we frequently witness!

4. Not only engage in these exercises before the judicatory assembles; but endeavour every day, through the whole of its sessions, to repeat similar exercises in reference to this matter. Ponder much and frequently, more especially on the introduction of each new article of business, on the nature and

importance of the duties devolving on the body. Labour and pray without ceasing, that a deep sense of the majesty and glory of Sion's King; of the unspeakably interesting character of his kingdom; and of the solemnity of every step which has a bearing on that kingdom, may dwell upon your own mind, and the minds of others, in every part of the business in which you engage. If you desire to be constantly watchful, constantly wise, constantly aided and directed in the best manner, you must daily and hourly ask for it. I know of no situation in which you will more urgently need the constant supplies of heavenly grace, than when standing among the representatives of the church, to consult respecting her delicate and dearest interests.

5. When you take your seat in an ecclesiastical assembly, do not expect too much of the pleasing and edifying kind. I have known some young ministers, who the first time they attended such an assembly, were greatly disappointed, and even disgusted. They had formed to their own minds a picture of ideal excellence, which can never be realized in this imperfect world. It seemed not to have occurred to them, that diversity of opinion, and an ardent manner of expressing opinions, on both sides, would be likely, in any case, to mark the proceedings of ecclesiastical men. They forgot that even in the synod of Jerusalem, made up as it was of venerable apostles and elders, there was "much disputing." They forgot that Paul "withstood Peter to the face," because he thought that "he was to be blamed," on a certain matter of ecclesiastical business, to which probably the inspiration of neither extended. If things of this

24

kind occurred then, how much more may we expect them to occur now! Besides, it ought to be recollected, that, even when an assembly of pious men are entirely agreed respecting the general propriety of a certain measure, they may differ greatly, and not without reason, as to the best means of accomplishing it; and it were hard, indeed, to deprive them of the privilege of discussing, and even at considerable length, the probable tendency of the alternate means proposed. Every one acquainted with ecclesiastical bodies, knows that, not unfrequently, those who were most warmly in favour of a projected plan, and, in the outset, most impatient of opposition to it, have, after half a day's or a day's discussion of the subject, seen difficulties in the plan which they had not discerned before, and become quite as willing to abandon it as any persons present. Who can tell but that such a discussion, irksome as it sometimes is, may be the instrument of more good to the church of God than half a dozen common sermons? That this may be, and, indeed, often has been the case, I think there can be no reasonable doubt.

I know that some excellent men, of a querulous or fastidious turn of mind, frequently have in their mouths the complaint of the famous Gregory Nazianzen, who said that "he never saw any good resulting from synods or councils." This is the sentiment of a narrow or a cynical mind. Did no good result from the synod whose meeting and decrees are recorded in Acts xv.? Did no good result from the Council of Carthage, in 253; from that of Nice, in 325; from the synod of Dort, in 1618, or from the Assembly of Divines at Westminster, in 1643? My dear young friend, do not indulge in this querulous temper. Make allowance for the imperfections of men. If you see any thing wrong in a church court, you are not bound to approve it. Nay, in most cases, you are bound freely and openly to bear testimony against it. But to indulge a disposition to condemn all church courts in the gross, because we occasionally see what is undesirable in their proceedings, is just as unreasonable as to condemn all civil courts of justice, as useless or pernicious, because we now and then witness a revolting scene, arising from the want of skill or fidelity in those who conduct them. Let the government of the church be administered under what form it may, human frailty will attend the administration. While you mourn over this, let it not tempt you to become disaffected to the regular support of ecclesiastical government and discipline. See that as little as may be of this frailty be found with yourself; and, for the rest, pray without ceasing that it may be restrained, removed, or overruled for good.

6. When you have taken your seat in any judicatory, be conscientiously punctual in attending on all its sessions. Give yourself wholly to the business of the body.

There is a fault in this respect which is indulged so frequently, and to such an extent, as to produce an amount of evil truly formidable. It is well known, that a number of those who attend on the higher judicatories of the church, when they convene in large cities; and especially of those who are commissioned to sit in the General Assembly, employ only a part, and sometimes a very small part of their time, after taking their seats, in attending to the duties which devolve upon them as members They make no scruple of engaging in parties of pleasure, and in plans of secular business, which take them away, time after time, for a number of hours, or perhaps for a day together, from the body which they professedly came to attend; and for which, perhaps, they receive a compensation. And, even when they in a sort attend, they are scarcely ever punctually present at the hour of meeting; but generally from half an hour to an hour behind the time. The consequence is, that, when inquired for, they are frequently not to be found; and when they come in, it is often in the midst of a discussion, or in the midst of the reading of an important paper, without a knowledge of which the cause under consideration cannot possibly be understood. In these circumstances, with what face can a conscientious man stand up, and request such a paper to be read over again, and a statement of facts, it may be a long one, made before his arrival, to be repeated, to accommodate him, who has been criminally neglecting his duty? Yet he must either make this modest request, to the great annoyance of all the more punctual members; or forbear to vote when the cause is ultimately decided; or, what is still worse, for the sake of avoiding trouble, vote in the dark, and run the risk of giving his influence to the cause of falsehood or injustice.

From the moment, then, that you take your seat in any judicatory, I counsel you to make a point of being punctual and constant in your attendance on all its sessions. Never allow yourself to be absent a single moment, if you can possibly avoid it. Ever be among the number of those who make conscience of being present as early and as uniformly as the moderator; who never leave the body till he has descended from his chair; and who never fail to unite in those prayers for the divine presence and blessing which open and close every session. In short, be exclusively devoted to the business of the judicatory. As far as may be necessary for unfailing attendance until it is finished, lay aside every interfering engagement and care. The advantages of this habit are so numerous, so important, and so obvious, that I am persuaded it is not necessary to dwell upon them in detail.

7. When you are sitting in a judicatory, be uniformly attentive and devoted to the business, as it is going on.

It is very possible for a member of a judicatory to be punctually and constantly present at every season; and yet to pay very little of such real attention to the business as deserves the name. Some sit reading a newspaper, or a new pamphlet; others are, a great part of the time, conversing with those who are so unfortunate as to sit near them; sometimes on the subject under discussion, but more frequently on one altogether foreign. And this, often, at the expense of disturbing the whole assembly; and, at any rate, at the expense of turning off the attention of all with whom they converse, for the time being, from the subject before the body. I have seen respectable and excellent men, who appeared to be incapable of sitting silent in a deliberative assembly for five minutes together; who rendered themselves conspicuous by whispering and laughing in the midst of the most solemn discussion; and who came, at length, to be shunned as a nuisance, by all who wished to pay a fixed and undivided attention to the business before the judicatory.

This is a fault which every one who regards either his reputation or his usefulness, ought to avoid. Let secular men, in their assemblies, walk about, and converse, and make a noise, while others are speaking. Let them be regardless of the feelings of their fellow-members; let them violate equally the laws of urbanity and benevolence, and run the risk of disturbing the whole body by their unceremonious expressions of indifference or contempt. It certainly ought not to be so in ecclesiastical bodies. There every member ought, even at the expense of no little pain to himself, to learn the important art of giving silent and close attention to every speaker, and to all that passes. Whenever he attempts to hold a private conversation, in the midst of business, with a fellow-member, his own attention is, of course, for the moment, withdrawn from what is going on; and he treats his fellow-member badly, by constraining him, perhaps against his inclination, to be guilty of the same ill manners with himself. I have often known a member, after having his own attention, and that of one or two others, thus withdrawn, for a few minutes, by a private conversation, to rise and ask questions, or make a speech, which he would never have thought of uttering, if he had heard what passed while his attention was diverted. Respect for your brethren, then; respect for yourself; and regard to the proper order and despatch of business, should all prompt you early to fix the habit of paying uninterrupted attention to the business of every judicatory in which you are sitting.

Resist every solicitation to the contrary, from whatever quarter it may come. Never allow yourself on any occasion, except one of the extremest urgency, to go into a deliberative assembly, and call out a member, in the midst of a debate, for the purpose of conversing with him; nor allow yourself, in similar circumstances, to be called out. During the ten minutes which may pass in such an absence, the most important statements and reasonings relating to the cause in hand, may be presented. They, of course, will be lost to you. And by giving your vote, without a knowledge of them, you may be quite as likely to trample on truth and justice as to support them. I have often wondered how conscientious men, when they reflected that, by occupying a seat in the judicatory, they had a solemn trust committed to them, could so frequently abuse it in the manner that has been suggested. Especially have I wondered to see this so frequently done in the General Assembly, by men formally delegated, as the representatives of presbyteries, to perform a certain duty; and above all, perhaps, by a man who was the only commissioner present to represent the presbytery from which he came! Surely such an one is peculiarly bound to be always present, to neglect nothing, and to let nothing that passes escape him.

8. When you take your seat in any judicatory, especially in one of the higher classes, I would earnestly recommend that you carry in your pocket a copy of the rules of the body, and that you carefully and repeatedly read them over before business commences.

Few young ministers, and indeed few of any age,

are so perfectly familiar with the rules of judicatories, as not to be the better for having their memories refreshed by repeated reperusals. This is evident from the frequency with which the plainest rules are violated, not by the inexperienced merely; but by those, who ought, long since, to have known better. Do not think it superfluous, then, to aid your memory by a new perusal every time you are called upon anew to take your seat in a church court. Endeavour to render the rules in question as familiar to your mind as the alphabet; so that at length, even an inadvertent infraction of them may be impracticable. The advantages which this will confer upon you in the transaction of business, will be numberless, and of inestimable value. It will not only prevent you from falling into many a blunder yourself; but will also give you an influence among your brethren, and impart a weight to your opinion on points of order, which no man ought to deem of small value. Besides; in the course of the business an appeal to the "Form of Government" of the church often becomes necessary. If you have no copy of your own in your pocket, you must walk from one part of the house to another to obtain a sight of it. This unavoidably gives rise to noise and disorder. Only suppose a number of members in this destitute situation, and under the necessity of doing the same thing, and how much confusion becomes inevitable!

9. I would earnestly advise every young minister to speak very little the first two or three times that he occupies a seat in the higher judicatories of the church.

The late venerable Dr. Rodgers of New York, often

mentioned to me, that during the first two or three sessions of the old Synod (then the highest judicatory of our church) which he attended when a young man, he never opened his lips, unless it were to ask a question, or, by a word or two, modestly to solicit information. And he often expressed the deepest disgust, when he saw young men, the very first time they appeared in a Synod or a General Assembly, making more frequent and longer speeches than, perhaps, any other individuals in the body. Many a young minister, in the outset of his official career, has lowered his own character for wisdom and discretion, a number of degrees, in the estimation of his brethren, by allowing himself to take such a course. So flagrant a violation of every principle of dignity and prudence is apt to be long remembered.

The art of transacting business wisely, expeditiously, and with suitable temper, in a deliberative assembly, is not to be learned in an hour, or a day. To do it well, requires close observation; considerable experience; watching the manner, course, and success of the best models; much attention to the discipline of our own feelings; and a frequent conning over the lesson, which we are always slow to learn, that other people have knowledge and wisdom, as well as we; and that opposing us, is not always infallible testimony that our opponent is wrong. All this requires time. The first two sessions of ecclesiastical bodies that you attend, then, are by no means too much for you to pass as a close, vigilant, silent learner. Rely on it, for any young minister to wish that distinguished precocity should mark his efforts as a speaker in church courts, is seldom, nay, never wise.

Your own good sense, my dear sir, will readily suggest to you, that the general rule which I have here laid down, is, in some cases, at least, to be followed with much allowance. Sometimes a very young minister may be the only member present from a quarter of the church from which important information is desired. In this case, he must give it, or it cannot be received. It may happen, too, that when a deeply interesting cause is about to be decided, a member who attends for the first time may be in possession of facts and views in relation to it which appear to him exceedingly important in leading to a just decision. In such a case he certainly ought not to shrink from the task of imparting them. But, in all cases whatsoever, in which a very young member rises in a Synod, or in a General Assembly, let it be manifest that he does it reluctantly. Let it be seen that he is actuated by an unavoidable call of duty. Let modesty and humility mark every word he utters. Let there be no impassioned oratory, no positiveness, and no reference to what has been said by others, but the most filial respectfulness.

10. During the first ten years of your ministry, do not, in ordinary cases, rise to express your opinion in church judicatories, until you have heard some of the more aged and experienced express theirs. If there be any situation in which we should suffer age to speak, and grey hairs to teach wisdom, it is in church courts, where experience and piety are the best counsellors. In the earlier periods of the General Assembly of the church of Scotland, young men seldom rose to speak until they were invited by the moderator, and never until a number of their superiors in age

had previously delivered their judgments. In later times the practice has been in a considerable degree different in that respectable body. In the Associations of New England, a very dignified example in this respect has been long set, and is still, it is believed, retained. My advice is that you imitate this example. The more carefully and uniformly you do so, the more likely will you be to judge wisely, to speak to the purpose, and to prove a blessing instead of a nuisance in every church court in which you appear.

11. Guard against very frequent, or very long speaking, in ecclesiastical judicatories, at any age.

No member of any deliberative assembly, either ecclesiastical or civil, ever allowed himself to be a very frequent or a very long speaker, without depressing his influence, and of course diminishing the respect with which he was heard. Whatever a man's talents may be, he must not be upon his feet on every question, or he will soon be made to feel that he cannot command the undivided and respectful attention of his audience on any question.

The celebrated Dr. Witherspoon spoke very seldom in church courts; and his speeches were very rarely longer than from ten to twenty-five or thirty minutes. He generally waited until he heard a number of other speakers, and until, from the debates on both sides, he was confident that he was in possession of all the principal facts, and of the principal arguments on which each party relied. Hence his speeches were always directly to the purpose; never tedious, and commonly in a high degree lucid and convincing. He was able, in this way, to disentangle the most complicated subjects, and to take the most impartial views;

and seldom failed of carrying with him a large majority of the body. Few men, indeed, can be compared with Dr. Witherspoon, who was entitled and expected to take the lead in every assembly of which he was a member, and who was, in every view, warranted in reserving himself for important occasions. Every one, of course, is not qualified to aim at that which he, often, most happily accomplished—to close a debate; to sum up both testimony and argument; and to wield the judgments of a hundred individuals. But still the leading principles upon which he acted, are those upon which every man ought to act. They were these—Never to rise until he had good reason to think that he understood the subject; never but when he had something really important to say; to say it in the shortest, clearest, and most unostentatious manner possible; and when he had done, to—sit down.

It is not uncommon for youthful and ardent speakers to "take the floor," as the parliamentary language is, at the very commencement of a debate. In this headlong course, they seldom fail to discover in a few minutes, that they are altogether unfurnished with the information requisite to an intelligent and just discussion of the subject. But this is not the worst. Having fully committed themselves by this precipitate expression of opinion, they feel it difficult, if not impossible, to retract; and are tempted to employ all their ingenuity, and to make many speeches, to patch and support their ill-commenced work. Many a florid and ingenious declamation, and many a final vote, have been thus thrown away upon a miserable effort to appear consistent, when a little later speaking, and a little less speaking, would have answered the purpose far better. Believe me, there are few situations in which it is more important to the speaker himself, as well as to the comfort and real benefit of the judicatory, to have his words few and well ordered.

12. Never rise to speak on any occasion, without solemnly examining your motives for speaking, reflecting distinctly on the presence of God, and silently but fervently imploring his blessing and aid. Be faithful with yourself. Set a guard, afresh, on your feelings and words. And beseech Him who has the hearts and the tongues of all in His hands, to preside over all that you say. If this were constantly done, how many hasty speeches; how many petulant speeches; how many ostentatious speeches; how many retaliating, passionate speeches, would be banished from the assemblies of the church!

13. Never insist on speaking when the call for the question becomes importunate.

He is very unwise who does this. When an assembly has become wearied, impatient, and unwilling to hear, the best speech, in most cases, is thrown away. It is not merely not heard respectfully, it is often not heard at all. Never attempt to speak in such a state of an ecclesiastical body, unless you are very sure that you have something new and weighty to offer. Frequent trespasses of this kind on the patience of a deliberative body, not only tend to diminish the influence of him who is guilty of them; but they also tend to irritate and exhaust the assembly, and to prevent the succeeding articles of business from being well done. He who wastes the time of such a body, is one of the worst foes to its comfort, its honour, and its usefulness.

14. On whatever occasion you may think it your duty to speak in an ecclesiastical judicatory, carefully avoid all harsh, satirical, sarcastical, acrimonious language. Let nothing escape you that is adapted to wound feelings, or to produce undue warmth.

It is not an uncommon thing for very worthy men, when they come to act in deliberative assemblies, to be extremely impatient of contradiction; to be always in a degree, and sometimes deeply, excited whenever they are opposed in their favourite plans. This arises, in some, from extreme nervous irritability, which, in spite of their better judgment, always throws them off their guard when the least opposition occurs. In others, unbridled peevishness, or arrogance, prompts them to consider every kind of resistance to the measures which they propose, as a personal affront, and treat it accordingly. Let me earnestly exhort you to set a strong guard against every thing of this kind. Whatever opposition may arise, study always to be composed and self-possessed, and endeavour to fix in your mind, once for all, that others have just as much right to differ from you, as you have to differ from them.

Again, some speakers, in ecclesiastical, as well as other assemblies, seem to consider it as lawful to use almost any kind of weapon that will enable them to carry their point. Hence they endeavour to be witty at the expense of their opposing brethren; they speak with extreme severity of their arguments, of their motives, and even of their persons; and express their astonishment that men of "common sense, and common honesty" should attempt to advocate sentiments so "palpably absurd," and so evidently "subversive of all sound principle." And it is well if they do not sometimes indulge in language still more coarse and opprobrious. Never give countenance, by your example, to this mode of conducting debate among brethren in Christ. Remember that ministers and elders, assembled in solemn council to deliberate on the interests of the Redeemer's kingdom, are neither bloody gladiators, nor artful pugilists, nor snarling politicians. Of course, none of the language or habits pardonable in such characters, ought ever to be witnessed among them. Never employ language toward any fellow-member which you would not be willing to have directed toward yourself. Treat every brother, and his arguments, in a respectful and fraternal manner. There is a respect due to their office and situation, which may not be always due to their persons. While you maintain your opinions with firmness, and express them with candour, load no man with reproaches for differing from you; impeach no motives; insinuate no unkind suspicions; make no one's person or reasoning an object of ridicule; carefully guard against every turn of thought or expression adapted to irritate. In a word, let the old maxim—"soft words and hard arguments;" or rather the scriptural injunction of constantly endeavouring to imitate "the meekness and gentleness of Christ," give character to every sentence you utter in an ecclesiastical assembly. That this manner of conducting debates in ecclesiastical courts is best adapted to promote peace, love, and edification, every one is ready to acknowledge. And further, that he who resolutely refuses to employ any other weapons than those of the purely Christian character which have been mentioned, is most likely to make friends, and to be respected even by his opponents, is quite as generally confessed. But this is not all. Such a man is more likely to gain the victory in argument, and thus to carry his point, than the sarcastic and acrimonious debater. Surely, then, the disposition to employ, in the conflicts of ecclesiastical assemblies, those poisoned weapons, to which the children of this world so often resort in their assemblies, is, of all propensities, one of the most inexcusable; since they are as injurious to the cause of him who employs them, as they are offensive to all pious and delicate minds.

It is impossible for me to avoid recollecting here some venerable ministers of our church, with whom it was my happiness to be acquainted in early life, and who, in reference to the point under consideration, left a noble example. They spoke, in judicatories, as men who remembered that they were servants of Christ, and were assembled to advance the interests of "pure and undefiled religion." No coarseness, abuse, sarcasm, or unseasonable levity ever escaped their lips. I have heard them reply to weak, petulant, and even highly offensive speeches, with a meekness, benevolence and dignity, which excited the admiration of all, and which more effectually mortified and humbled their indelicate opponents, than a thousand vollies in their own style could have done. Such men are too rare in any church. Would that their mantles might be found resting on the shoulders of many who came after them!

15. While you treat the opinions of every fellow-member with respect, you ought to treat those of the more aged and experienced with peculiar deference.

Remember that such men have not only seen more years than yourself, but that they have been long accustomed to the consideration of such questions, and the routine and difficulties of such business as may come before you. It is, therefore, not merely desirable that you should hear their opinions, if possible, on any subject under discussion, before you make up your mind upon it; but when they have uttered those opinions, it behoves you, however they may differ from your own, to treat them with the profoundest respect. And if you are constrained to express a different opinion, let it be done with modesty, and even with caution. Oppose them rather by stating the objections to their views which occur to your mind, and inquiring what can be offered for their removal, than by direct or confident attack. Let it be seen that you differ from them with reluctance, and with much diffidence. And when you refer to any thing which has been uttered by them, in which you cannot concur, let it be with something of that filial reverence with which you ought ever to regard their persons. While you do this, however, do not fall into the extreme of those, who, when they differ, in ecclesiastical assemblies, from an individual venerable for age or standing, do it with so many circuitous apologies, and so much fulsome flattery; protesting how much it pains them to oppose a father so "learned," so "pious," so "illustrious," &c., that every person of just taste is disgusted. Let your respect for their persons and opinions be manifested by your general air, tones, and manner, rather than by any direct eulogies on their character, which it is difficult to express in a happy manner, and which had better always be omitted.

16. Be careful to maintain habitual gravity in all ecclesiastical courts, and especially in those of the higher class. Can it require a moment's reasoning to show, that when the ministers and elders of the church of Christ are assembled to deliberate on the most deeply momentous and solemn interests which can possibly occupy the attention of mortals, they ought to be serious, sober, and to avoid every thing that approaches to levity? One would think that the very lowest standard of propriety that could be adopted by any thinking man, would require this. And yet, such is the frailty of our nature, and such the temptation frequently arising from the gregarious principle, if I may so express it, that in our larger ecclesiastical bodies, and especially in the General Assembly, it often happens that gravity is interrupted to a painful extent, and that some of the most devout men are frequently borne away by the power of sympathy. Indeed some ecclesiastical debaters avowedly act on the plan of carrying their point by almost any of those weapons which are admissible in secular assemblies, and, among the rest, by the broadest and most undisguised ridicule. Hence, if they can so manage as to excite a burst of laughter at the expense of an opponent, they are peculiarly gratified. I cannot believe that this is a proper mode of conducting ecclesiastical business. It is an offence, in my opinion, both against Christian dignity, and Christian benevolence.

17. Do not think me too minute, if I guard you against a frequent change of your seat, and much moving about, during the proceedings of an ecclesiastical assembly. There are those who appear, probably from a bad habit, rather than any thing else,

incapable of sitting still many minutes at a time, even in a church judicatory. You may see them, perhaps, in a dozen or twenty different parts of the house, in the course of one forenoon. This is a practice as undignified as it is mischievous. It is almost incompatible with fixed attention to the business of the body. It necesssarily leads to more or less noise and confusion, and thus interrupts the attention of others, as well as our own. What would be the consequence if every member of such an assembly were to be thus continually changing his place? It is evident that all composed attention to business would be impracticable. Rely upon it, that learning the art of sitting still in a deliberative assembly, is, in itself, a matter of no small value. Choose a seat, then, in the beginning, as much adapted to your convenience as you can select. Retain it, without some good reason for a change, as long as the body continues to sit. Be always found there. However irksome this may be at first, habit will soon reconcile, and afterwards attach you to the practice; and if generally practised, its advantages would be great indeed.

18. Remember that every thing which is intended to be well done in a church court, ought to be well prepared out of doors before it is introduced.

There are men, even good men, who take a sort of pride in being considered as the unprompted and unaided authors of certain favourite measures, which they wish to distinguish themselves by bringing forward. Hence they take counsel with none, suggest even their purpose to none, until it is made the subject of a public motion. There is a littleness in this, unworthy of a truly elevated mind; and it is as indiscreet as it is little. He who is about to introduce an important proposal into an ecclesiastical assembly, ought to remember that he can have no private or selfish interest in the proposed measure; and, therefore, that he ought not to desire to carry it, unless it be really adapted to promote the cause of truth and righteousness. And in order to ascertain this, he ought, in all cases, to be desirous of knowing how the aged, the wise, the experienced, and the pious, regard his projected measure. If they unanimously or generally disapprove it, he ought to be very certain of its wisdom, and of their being under a mistake, before he brings it forward.

Let me advise you, then, when you are about to bring any important plan or measure before a church judicatory, always to consult at least some of the most judicious, prudent, pious and influential members of the body, beforehand, out of doors; taking their opinions of the feasibility and usefulness of the plan; and, if they approve it, soliciting their countenance and aid in carrying it into effect. The advantages of this course are numerous. The measure will be more likely to succeed. It will probably be carried with more unanimity and comfort. Every wise adjustment in private, will both shorten and mollify debate in public. And if, in the course of this out-of-door consultation, there be so much opposition manifested, as to convince you that the proposed measure cannot succeed, the probability is, notwithstanding all your overweening fondness and zeal in its behalf, that it is less wise than you imagine, or, at least, ought to be postponed.

19. Perhaps you will smile when I gravely offer

another counsel on this subject, which is, that when engaged from day to day in the important business of an ecclesiastical judicatory, you should practise much self-denial, and even abstemiousness, with respect to the indulgences of the table. Perfect temperance in a minister of religion is, of course, at all times, a duty, and at all times important. But now I speak of a self-denial special and peculiar; of a restraint upon appetite more vigilant than usual, and for a great moral purpose. This is no easy matter. When large numbers of ministers and other ecclesiastical men are convened in a populous town, their meeting seldom fails to be attended with much hospitality, and not unfrequently with strong temptations to luxurious indulgence of the convivial kind. The consequence is, that after a hearty dinner, in which no common rule of temperance has been transgressed, the mind is less active, less prepared for intellectual or moral labour, and, of course, less fitted to discharge the duties of the judicatory. It will tend to obviate this evil, if you take considerably less than your usual quantity of aliment, during the whole continuance of the sessions of the judicatory. You will certainly, in this case, if your mind be properly intent on the business, enjoy yourself far more; and perform every duty more to your own satisfaction. Depend upon it, lightly as some may consider this thing, much feasting is very unfriendly to the discharge of duties in which a large portion of wisdom and piety is needed.

20. Let all your conduct in judicatories be marked with the most perfect candour and uprightness.

That a minister of the gospel, in an assembly of his brethren, should be guilty of gross dishonesty or falsehood, is a supposition so abhorrent to every right feeling, that I will not suppose it possible. Yet it is certain, that men, in the main upright and pious, do sometimes, in the transaction of ecclesiastical business, and especially in attempting to carry favourite measures, indulge in a species of indirect management, which minds delicately honourable, and strictly desirous of "shunning the very appearance of evil," would by no means have adopted. Such are all the little arts of concealment and deception which are sometimes practised even in ecclesiastical business;—revealing only part of a plan, and carefully drawing a veil over those features of it, which it is well known a large majority of the body would object to, if aware of the whole plan; making insidious proposals, under the name of concessions; in short, engaging in a constant system of covert generalship, for overreaching and entrapping those, who it is known would never co-operate, if they were made acquainted with the whole scheme.

It is surely unnecessary to employ argument to show that this is a hateful character, and that every Christian minister ought to abhor and avoid it. You are not bound, indeed, to tell every body your whole mind, on all subjects; not, perhaps, to disclose all the facts you know on a given subject under discussion. But you are bound to deceive no one; to overreach no one; to spread a trap for no man's feet or conscience; to avoid all crooked and disingenuous policy; to give no man occasion to say that you hoodwinked or cajoled him, by representations which, if not false, were insidious. On the contrary, let all your plans be such as you would be willing to avow to the whole world;

and let all the means which you employ for carrying them into effect, be such as perfect integrity, honour, and candour will justify. Never allow yourself either to propose a scheme, or to suggest means for its accomplishment, which you would not be willing ultimately to see emblazoned in every gazette in the country. Depend upon it, artifice, concealment, and evasion, are, nowhere, ultimately profitable to any man: but in an ecclesiastical assembly, there is a hatefulness about them which cannot be too strongly portrayed, and a mischief which never fails, sooner or later, to fall on the head of him who employs them.

21. When you succeed in carrying your point in a judicatory, never exult; never allow yourself to use a language or a tone expressive of triumph over an adversary. It is not the part of magnanimity to do this. It stirs up unhallowed feeling in those who are disappointed. It greatly adds to the pain of defeat; and sometimes inflicts wounds as lasting as life. Besides, if you proudly triumph, on carrying a favourite measure, it is a sad symptom against yourself. The measure itself may be right; but the state of your heart is plainly shown to be very much otherwise: and your success may not, after all, be crowned with the divine blessing. Enjoy success, then, with moderation, and with marked respect towards those who have been defeated. Treat them in such a manner as to alleviate, as much as possible, the pain of failure; and your success will be much more likely to be a real blessing to the church.

22. On the other hand, when you have failed, or find that you are likely to fail, to gain the cause which you advocate, be mild and submissive. To bear to be

outvoted with a good grace, is a hard lesson to learn; but every good politician ought to learn it as early as possible. Much more ought every Christian minister. When a point is carried against you, indulge no complaints; utter no reproaches; let not a word or look escape you that has a tendency to interrupt fraternal feeling. You are bound to admit at least the possibility that the majority are wiser than the minority. At any rate, knowing it to have been determined as Infinite Wisdom judged best, for the present, every murmur ought to be silenced. And, after all, before twelve months have passed over your head, you may be as ready to rejoice as any one else that it was decided as it was. I am free to confess that such has been, more than once, my own experience.

23. If you should ever be chosen moderator of the General Assembly, or of any of the higher judicatories of the church, consider yourself as called to a very responsible station, and address yourself to its duties with much humility, seriousness and prayer. Remember how much both the comfort, and the expedition of business, in such a body, depend on the moderator. If he be inexperienced, timid, irresolute, deficient in address or presence of mind, or unwilling to employ the authority vested in him, the proceedings will probably be without dignity, without order, and, perhaps, even without judgment or justice. For the most wise and honest body in the world, when they once fairly get into confusion, may do some of the most foolish things imaginable, and do them in the most disorderly manner. No man, therefore, ought to consent to be moderator of the General Assembly, who has not served a kind of apprenticeship to the office in pres-

byteries and synods, and who does not feel himself, in some tolerable degree, at home in the rules of the church.

But if you should be elected to the office, and should think proper to accept of it, enter on the duties of it with humble trust in God, and with the firmness of one who is inspired with a determination to perform that which is required of him without fear or favour. Make yourself perfectly familiar, by repeated perusals, with the rules by which you are to be governed. Enforce them on every member with rigour and impartiality. Be always punctual, to a moment, in your seat, at the hour to which the body stands adjourned. Let the prayers with which you open and close each sitting be such as shall tend to fill every mind with solemnity, with brotherly love, and with a deep sense of obligation to the Redeemer's kingdom, without indulging yourself in what is called praying at people, which is generally useless, and often very unhallowed work. Constantly keep on the desk before you a copy of the rules of the body, a copy of the form of Government of the Church, and a complete roll of the members. Keep accurate notes, not only of all the assignments of business for particular days, but also of every occurrence which it may be important for you to remember and call up afterwards. Never allow yourself, on any occasion, while occupying the chair, to take part in the debate. Treat every speaker with perfect respect, however weak you may consider his argument. Give fixed and undivided attention to every speaker, keeping your eye steadily directed to his, to the last word; not only for the purpose of paying respect to him, but also that you may be able to observe and interpose, in a moment, when he becomes disorderly or irrelevant. Allow no personalities, or wandering from the point on any account; but be very sure before you call a speaker to order for wandering, that he is not pursuing a very compact and connected argument, some of the parts of which are a little out of sight. Be firm and inexorable in applying the rules to the oldest and most venerable, as well as the youngest member; yet never indulge in harshness, or the least disrespect to any one. Never permit the least altercation to take place between the moderator and any member: when any thing of this kind appears to be commencing or threatened, remind the individual that it cannot be allowed; that his remedy is to appeal to the body, without debate. In stating questions, and in deciding points of order, be as perfectly impartial as possible; never permitting a word to escape you that shall indicate your opinion as to the merits of the question before the judicatory; but keeping the scales perfectly even, as to both sides of the house. Remember that the business of the moderator is to maintain order, and to secure to every member the perfect enjoyment of his privileges in debate. In appointing committees also be impartial. Where there are parties, let strict justice be done to both sides. Never allow any one to whisper to the moderator while a member is speaking, or a vote taking; as it may have the appearance of listening to improper influence. In a word, exercise all the authority vested in you with perfect politeness, but at the same time with perfect firmness. I have only to add, that it is very seldom proper, if at all, for the moderator to place another person in his chair, and descend to the floor, for the purpose of taking part in a debate. It has sometimes been done; and there is certainly no absolute rule of the church against it. But it is by no means expedient. The best judges have decided against its propriety. And it may not be easy for the moderator, when he resumes the chair, to convince the members that he is perfectly impartial in stating the question and taking a vote on a point which he has taken part in discussing. Besides, why should he do it? If he has any thing important to say, he can surely put it into the mouth of a friend to be uttered, as well as by himself.

24. To sum up all in a word: endeavour so to treat every brother, and so to conduct yourself on every occasion, as shall be adapted to make the judicatory, so far as you are concerned, a scene of Christian affection and pleasure, and a nursery of every hallowed feeling. It is impossible, in such an assembly as that of a court of Christ, to have a set of rules, framed beforehand, sufficiently numerous and minute to meet every specific case. But if there be a heart full of love to Christ, and of love to his servants and his kingdom; if there be a deep impression of the all-seeing eye of God, and a solemn anticipation of his judgment-seat; if there be a mild, amiable, benevolent spirit in full exercise; if there be a sincere, disinterested desire to "follow the things which make for peace, and the things wherewith one may edify another;" if there be a sincere desire to give the business throughout a religious, and not a secular aspect: in a word, if there be no other banner set up in the camp than that of Jesus Christ, and no other end pursued than his glory; then the meetings of the judicatories

will be delightful scenes. The members will know no other strife, than who shall love the Redeemer most, and who shall serve him with the warmest zeal. Their differences of opinion will produce no alienation of feeling. Their debates will ever be carried on with mutual respect and love. They will separate with warmer affection than they met; will return to their respective charges with increased attachment to their Master and his work; and will look forward to another meeting with a glow of delight. My dear friend, let it always be your study and prayer, whenever you attend such an assembly, to contribute your full share to the production of these happy results.

25. After having read over the foregoing counsels, do not imagine that it will be an easy thing to follow them. I have no doubt that the substance of them will readily commend itself to your judgment, as obviously worthy of regard; and that you will resolve to bear the whole code in mind, whenever, in future, you enter an ecclesiastical judicatory. But be not too sanguine of success in this matter. It is one of the most difficult things in the world to follow the best and plainest rules; especially when you are called to deliberate and act with a number of others. In a large assembly many feelings are excited, which in solitude lie dormant. Pride, vanity, ambition, envy, jealousy, the irascible principle, and a thousand unfortunate sensibilities, which your fellow-members will either designedly or inadvertently attack, may, when you are off your guard, as it were, spring a mine under your feet, and contrary to your fixed purpose, betray you into language or conduct, which you will long recollect with mortification. Remember your own weak-

ness. Be jealous of your own heart, and watch it with intense vigilance. Have no confidence in your own ability to avert or overcome temptation. Constantly look for strength and wisdom to a higher source. I again repeat, not only pray for light and guidance from above, before you take your seat in such assemblies, as before advised; but through all their various and complicated business, "pray without ceasing," that you may be directed and guarded, and sanctified in every thing; that you may be preserved from the sudden onsets of unhallowed passion; and that you may have grace given you to act in conformity with those rules which you heartily approve, and desire to follow.

26. I think it must be impossible to read with any attention the foregoing counsels, without perceiving how erroneous is the principle on which many of our presbyteries proceed in choosing their commissioners to the General Assembly. The principle referred to is that of simple unqualified rotation, without reference to age, experience, or any personal qualification. Hence it often happens, and, acting on this plan, often must happen, that all the delegates, from some presbyteries, are young men who never saw the body before. Of course, they are not at home with regard to the rules and habits of the Assembly, and, therefore, cannot represent to the best advantage the presbyteries by which they are commissioned. More than once have I seen the interests of a particular section of the church really suffer, in consequence of the delegates from that section being all young men, who knew so little of the Assembly, and of its mode of transacting business, that they were not qualified to

conduct the matters intrusted to their care. If you should live to take a seat in any presbytery, I would advise that you endeavour to promote the adoption of something like the following plan. Let half your commissioners, every year, be men of some experience, who have been repeatedly members of the Assembly before; and the other half such young men, as have been at least five or six years in the ministry, and, of course, somewhat familiar, during that time, with the proceedings of presbyteries and synods. Acting upon this plan, the younger members, when they reach a certain age, will go in their turn, and be gradually trained to the work; and will be, at the same time, always accompanied by fathers, familiar with the habits of the body, and capable of giving to their juniors salutary counsel. When I was a young man, this plan was much more acted upon than it is at present. I had been nearly eight years an ordained minister before I ever received a commission to the General Assembly.

LETTER XII.

Entreat — the elder women as mothers; the younger as sisters, with all purity. — 1 Tim. v. 2.

FEMALE SOCIETY, MARRIAGE, ETC.

My dear young friend: — A clergyman will, of course, have much and constant occasion to be in the company of females. They form a most interesting and active part of every church. Many things may be accomplished by their pious agency, which could scarcely be attained in any other way. And happy, indeed, is that minister of the gospel, who, by wisdom, fidelity, prudence, and Christian delicacy, is enabled to conciliate the esteem, and to acquire and maintain the unlimited confidence of his female parishioners, and of other persons of worth of that sex, with whom he may be called in Providence to associate. He who fails of doing this, cannot either be very acceptable or very useful; while he who succeeds in attaining it, not only possesses one of the most valuable pledges of permanent popularity, but also enjoys advantages for doing good of the richest kind. The female part of every congregation have, in general, an influence, which, while it cannot be defined, cannot, at the same time, be resisted. And, for the most part, this influence, I believe, is as just in its ultimate award, as it is sovereign in its sway.

That department of clerical manners and habits, then, which has a respect to females, is at once, one of the most delicate and important that can pass under review. I am aware, too, of the great difficulty of treating this subject, especially in reference to unmarried clergymen, in a profitable manner. While it is a subject concerning which counsel is more frequently needed than almost any other; it is one, at the same time, in which feeling and caprice are so apt to triumph over reason, that, when counsel is most urgently needed, it is seldom heard, or, at least, seldom properly weighed. What else, indeed, can be expected, when so large a portion of mankind, and especially of the young, and even of the conscientious and pious, seem to think that here, if ever, inclination ought to bear a sovereign sway; and that listening to the dictates of prudence, is a sort of high treason against that refined system of "sentimentalism" which they suppose ought absolutely to govern in such cases. This is being weak and foolish, if the expression may be allowed, upon principle. And hence, I have known, again and again, some of the most sober-minded and excellent people of my acquaintance giving themselves up to matrimonial partialities and connections manifestly unworthy of persons in their senses, and so perfectly deaf to all the suggestions of wisdom, that they deserved the discipline of the rod just as much as children at school.

I do not deny that ardent affection is necessary to matrimonial happiness; and am as ready to grant, as the most sentimental of my youthful acquaintance, that marriages contracted on the ground of mercenary calculation, or even from the mere dictates of cold prudence, promise little conjugal enjoyment. But does it follow from this concession, that a reflecting man, and especially a man of religious principle, ought to allow himself to fall in love with the first pretty face he sees, without the least reference to his highest obligations, and without the least knowledge of the temper, intellect, principles, habits and manners of the individual? Surely a man ought as sacredly to take care, before marriage, on whom he bestows his affections, as afterwards that he confine them to the object whom he has chosen. There are limits, then, beyond which inclination ought not to be allowed to govern in this matter. So I should decide in the case of any one who meant to act the part of a rational being.

But a minister of the gospel is peculiarly bound to summon to his consideration, on this whole subject, a solemn reference to his official character, duties, and usefulness, as well as to his personal taste. And he who allows himself to make a sacrifice of the former to the latter, is unfaithful to himself, and to his God. Whatever others may do, when he thinks of selecting a partner for life, he should have before him his high office, and all the interests of the Redeemer's kingdom to which he has devoted himself, as well as his own personal gratification. Happy is the man who, in this interesting concern, is favoured with "that wisdom which cometh down from above," and is enabled perfectly to unite the tenderest impulses of affection with the sternest dictates of duty!

1. In reference to this subject, my first leading

suggestion is, that there are some clergymen who ought never to marry. While I firmly believe, that the doctrine which enjoins celibacy on the clergy generally, is, as the apostle styles it, "a doctrine of devils," and that it has led, and must always lead, to the most enormous evils; I have, at the same time, no doubt, that the minister who deliberately resolves to spend his days as an evangelist, or an evangelical itinerant, ought, if he can be happy in a single state, to continue in that state. I am of the opinion that neither Wesley nor Whitefield, for example, ought ever to have married. They were both, indeed, strangely injudicious in the selection of a partner; but I doubt whether any woman could have been happy with either of them herself, or have made either of them happy, as long as they pursued the course of life to which they were devoted. I think, too, I could name some individuals now living, in our own country, whose usefulness is greatly extended by their declining to entangle themselves with those worldly cares which the conjugal relation seldom fails to induce. I know not that you have in view any such plan of ministerial labour. If you have, and if you can be comfortable in a life of celibacy, I would advise you never to marry. In this case, you may give yourself more entirely to your work; your movements, however incessant, may be untrammelled; much less will suffice for your decent support, than if you had a family; and thus you may afford essential aid to many congregations, from which you would be in a great measure shut out, if you were bound by domestic ties. There ought to be a few such ministers in every church of large extent. Yet no one ought to be constrained, or even persuaded, to choose such a plan of life. Nor should any one adopt it, unless it be the object of his deliberate and devout preference. And even after having adopted it, for a time, he ought to feel himself at full liberty to retract, and assume the conjugal bond, whenever he is fully persuaded that he can serve the church better by taking this course.

2. My next counsel, however, is, that, in general, every settled minister should consider it as his duty, as well as his privilege, to be a married man. I give this advice, because I am deliberately of the opinion, that the matrimonial connection, when formed in wisdom, and in the fear of God, is by far the happiest union which the society of this world furnishes; and which, when really happy, approaches nearer than any other to the bliss of better society on high. I am so far from thinking that a state of celibacy is a state of greater "perfection" than any other, as some religionists have taught, that I am wholly unable to read the second chapter of Genesis, to say nothing of any other Scripture, without coming to a directly opposite conclusion. But, while all the considerations verifying the early declaration of our Maker, that it is not good for a man to be alone, which apply to other men, apply equally to him; there are additional considerations, which show that a happy matrimonial union is of peculiar importance to a minister. If he be married, his female parishioners will have more confidence in him, and feel more freedom in approaching him. He will himself, also, in this case, be delivered from a great many embarrassments and temptations which would otherwise beset his ministerial intercourse with

the younger females of his congregation. A man who knows, from experience, what domestic affections, duties, and trials import, will know better how to enter into the feelings and wants of his people on similar subjects, than would be possible for one in a different situation. A pastor, though unmarried, might, and undoubtedly ought, on suitable occasions, to preach on the duties of husbands and wives, parents and children, &c.; yet it is manifest that, on this class of subjects, a bachelor will commonly be a less skilful, as well as a less impressive preacher, than he who is not only a pious, exemplary divine, but also an exemplary husband and father.

If, therefore, you have nothing else in view than your ministerial usefulness, I should say, if you become a settled pastor, by all means be married. The celebrated Richard Baxter, somewhere in his practical works, asks this question — "Ought a clergyman to marry?" His answer is —" Yes; but let him think, and think, and think again, before he does it." So say I. For if there be an important step in the course of a minister's life, this, certainly, is one. The following sentences from Dr. Clarke's valuable "Letter to a Methodist Preacher," before quoted, though couched in strong language, are yet, I think, not too strong. "Marriage to you can never be an indifferent thing: it will make or mar you; it will be a blessing or a curse to you. It will either help you to heaven, drive you to hell, or be a heart-rending cross to you while you live. Nor will a bad or improper marriage affect yourself alone: it may be the ruin of every child that issues from it. And, dreadful as this is, it may not rest there; they may propagate the plague to interminable generations, and millions be injured, if not lost, by your improper or vicious marriage. Take this step, then, with that godly fear, and scrupulous caution, which a man should do, who feels that he has his all at stake."

3. Be not in too much haste to form a matrimonial engagement, and especially to be married. I say a matrimonial engagement, because, though not all, yet a number of the evils which result from a premature marriage, frequently flow from a premature affiance. When a theological student marries before he has closed his preparatory studies, and, of course, before he has any certain prospect of a settlement, he runs the risk, not only of embarrassment and retarding his professional career, both as to comfort and usefulness; but is really in danger of drawing on himself something like professional ruin. He could hardly take a step more directly calculated to interrupt his studies, if not to cut them short; and even while they nominally continue, to render them less composed, deep and successful. But this is not the worst. When a candidate for the ministry prematurely marries, he exposes himself to the strongest temptation to seek license to preach before he ought, and before he otherwise would; to press forward to ordination, and a pastoral charge, before he has passed through that leisurely training, both as a student and a licentiate, which is of incalculable importance; and even to indulge a degree of impatient urgency in obtaining a settlement, which may lower his dignity in the view of those who observe it, and even interfere essentially with all his professional prospects. I have repeatedly known instances in which the premature marriages

of theological students have impeded them in their studies to a distressing degree ; have been the means of hurrying them into the ministry before they were at all prepared for it; have led them to take measures for obtaining settlements, which their own impartial judgments, in other circumstances, would have rejected with scorn; and in a word, for many years, proved such an incumbrance to them, such an obstacle both to their comfort and usefulness, as they could never be persuaded to believe possible, until taught by painful experience. It is true, this is not always the consequence of forming matrimonial contracts or connections with indiscreet haste. But, if I mistake not, it is in a majority of cases; and I am clearly of the opinion that there is no profession more likely to suffer by such imprudent haste than the clerical.

Besides, no candidate for the sacred office can tell, till he actually enters it, where the Head of the church may cast his lot. He ought to hold himself ready to follow implicitly the leadings of Providence. But if he be already married, or under a matrimonial engagement, before he comes to this point in his course, it may be utterly impracticable for him to go in the direction which he most fondly desires, and which all his pious friends consider as, in itself, most desirable. Or it may be, that, in spite of every difficulty which his marriage or engagement presents, he may be shut up to a particular course; and then he may find himself compelled to take a beloved companion into a situation which she never anticipated; for which she is by no means prepared, either in spirit or habits; and in which she can never be happy.

For these and for many other reasons, I should

strongly advise that you guard against all engagements of this kind, until your professional studies are completed, and you have a fair prospect of a speedy settlement, or, at least, of being able to decide where you are likely to be ultimately placed. You may think this advice of small importance now; but if you act in opposition to it, I venture to predict, that you will review your conduct with bitter repentance at a future day.

4. Carefully guard against exciting expectations of a matrimonial intention, when you have no such serious purpose. You are, probably, not ignorant, that young clergymen are considered as one of those classes of suitors who are apt to be peculiarly popular with the female sex. And, truly, it would be a great reflection on their judgment if it were not so. For, in the case of young men of your profession, there is all that pledge of piety, virtue, conjugal fidelity and kindness, and general respectability of character, that official duty and engagements can give. Is it strange, then, that many young ladies of enlightened minds, and virtuous sentiments, should manifest a preference, other things being equal, to promising candidates for this profession? I should, indeed, think it strange if it were otherwise. Alas! that their confidence should have been sometimes misplaced; and that even clergymen should have been found capable of making unkind and miserable husbands!

Let it also be remembered, that as young ladies of pious amiable character are predisposed, as a matter of course, to think favourably of the general moral qualities of young clergymen, and, in many cases, to regard what are supposed to be advances on their part with a propitious eye; so there is another consideration which is worthy of your notice. When a young minister pays attentions to a young female, which have the appearance of being particular, they are apt to go for much more than the same attentions would, if paid by a secular man. The latter, it is understood, may, perhaps, have in view, in such attentions, his own present amusement only. But the fair presumption is, that the former has too much honour, integrity, and purity of principle, to sport, for one hour, with the feelings of a female acquaintance. An equal degree of attention from him, therefore, will be apt to be considered as meaning more, than from a person of another profession.

Let your whole deportment, my young friend, fully justify this presumption in favour of the clerical character. While you treat every female, with whom you may become acquainted, and who may be entitled to such treatment, with respect and due attention, carefully guard against every thing like particular attention, unless you have serious thoughts of seeking a matrimonial union. To act a part intended to excite the expectations, and ensnare the affections, of an ingenuous female, when you had no real intention of offering her your own heart and hand, would be a compound of meanness and wickedness of which I am confident you will never be deliberately guilty. But I have known young ministers to pursue, inadvertently, a course of conduct which led to this unhappy result. They have greatly respected a particular female acquaintance, and taken more pleasure in her company, than in that of any other of her sex in the neighbourhood; and have been thus led to be frequent in their visits, without the remotest thought of a matrimonial connection; and taking for granted that it would be so understood on all hands. It is dangerous thus to act. The peace of an unsuspecting and estimable individual may thus be unintentionally, indeed, but totally destroyed. Remember that more scrupulous delicacy, caution, and self-denial are required, and are really due, from young men of your profession than of any other. Never visit frequently where you are not willing to realize the most serious expectations that can be formed: and when you discover, or think you discover, that such expectations exist, without any proper ground, immediately adopt such a course of conduct as will, respectfully and delicately, but effectually, terminate them. Only suppose the case of the female in question to be that of a sister of your own, and then every Christian and manly feeling will dictate the proper course.

There is a tendency on the part of amiable and intelligent young ministers, to form what they call special friendships, with young females of fine understandings and amiable manners. These friendships are formally understood, in the beginning, by both parties, not to have matrimony for their object. Still they are carried on with many effusions of refined sentiment; the epithets of brother and sister are agreed to be employed in their intercourse; an epistolary correspondence is kept up; and every thing wears the aspect of what is commonly styled "courtship." Let me warn you against every thing of this kind, unless you are perfectly willing and desirous to marry the individual in question. Such "friendships" have a tendency to ensnare, and finally to embarrass the parties themselves. They seldom fail of making an erroneous impression on others. And I am confident "the winding up" is rarely satisfactory to all concerned. I always regret to see an epistolary correspondence going on between a young minister and a young female, when he professes to have no intention or desire of marrying.

5. Be on your guard against the advice and interference of notorious match-makers. There are such persons in every community. They are your forward, sanguine, and often well-meaning busy-bodies, who have a wife or a husband ready for almost every unmarried individual of their acquaintance; and who appear always willing to incur the responsibility of being the known contrivers of a match. Never court the assistance, or put yourself in the power, of such a pestiferous race. They may, sometimes, indeed, amidst many failures, be instrumental in forming a happy connection. But trust them not. Never put yourself implicitly under their guidance. Nay more, if you are not extremely vigilant, they will be apt to entrap you, before you are aware of it, into a situation from which you will find it difficult to retreat. Of this I have known some of the most striking and melancholy examples. Let no single individual dictate to you on such a subject. Consult, not many, but several judicious friends, especially pious friends, with a sincere desire and willingness to take sound advice. It is, surely, a matter of sufficient importance to engage all the deliberation, the inquiry, and the prayer which you have an opportunity of bestowing upon it.

6. In seeking a matrimonial union, bear in mind

the inestimable importance of piety in a clergyman's wife. I say the inestimable importance; because I am verily persuaded, that no one who has not made the experiment can adequately estimate the importance of genuine and even eminent piety in one who is intended to be a "help meet" for a minister of the gospel. However great the other excellencies of his wife may be, yet if she have not real piety, she cannot be a "helper" in the most important of all interests. She cannot aid him in the conflicts of the spiritual life. She cannot stimulate him in devotion when he is languid; or sympathize with him when he is dejected and comfortless. She cannot counsel and excite him in the delicate and arduous duties of his office. She cannot strengthen his hands among the people of his charge, by appearing foremost among the sisters of the church, in every pious, benevolent, and laudable undertaking in which they engage. She cannot exert a proper influence in "training up her children in the nurture and admonition of the Lord." In a word, she must so utterly fail of affording him the least aid, in all that large portion of his duties and conflicts which pertain to the spiritual welfare of himself, his family, and the souls committed to his care; and, if not an aid, must be so frequently a snare and a drawback in reference to all these interests, that, methinks, a conscientious man, entering on the work of the holy ministry, will be extremely unwilling to form a connection, to say the least, promising so little of either comfort or advantage.

Let me earnestly exhort you, then, in seeking a wife, to look for one of unfeigned and ardent piety. Nothing that she can possess ought to be considered as a compensation for the want of this great characteristic. However beautiful, however amiable, however intelligent, however extensively read, and however polished in her manners, if she lack the "one thing needful," she will be essentially deficient as a companion for an ambassador of Christ. But if, with other qualities, which may fairly be presupposed, she whom you choose for a wife be a person possessed of enlightened, active piety, you will find her a treasure beyond all price; a comforter in trials; a counsellor in study, in labour, and in perplexity; a soother of your care-worn hours; a suitable guide of the best interests of your household in your absence; an efficient helper in a variety of respects, incapable of being specified; and, above all, a happy medium of intercourse, and pledge of confidence, between you, and the pious females of your congregation. I have often known the pious wives of clergymen exert an influence so manifest, so extensive, and so happy, within the pastoral charges of their husbands, that, in some cases there were those who felt constrained to doubt whether the pastors or their companions were, all things considered, the more useful. But you cannot be made, at present, to see the whole importance of this matter. If you wish to find your own personal piety nurtured, your comfort increased, your influence extended, and your usefulness doubled, never think seriously of any other than a pious wife. All experience, you may rely upon it, speaks this language. I have never yet known a minister who appeared to know much of the religion of the heart himself, who did not, as he advanced in his course, manifest a growing sense of the great importance of securing a spiritual helper in the companion of his life.

7. You will not fail, I trust, to consider good sense, and prudence also, as indispensable qualities in a clergyman's wife. Whatever piety the object of your choice may possess; yet if she be a person of weak mind, and strikingly deficient in practical discretion, she will perpetually mortify you, and probably do you more harm than good among the people of your charge. She will seldom fail, by her precipitancy, her rashness, her imprudent speeches, and her childish deportment, to weaken your hands, and counteract some of your best efforts. Or the most favourable supposition is, that, when her character is once fairly understood, she will be considered as harmless, and do you no positive injury. Surely something better than this ought to be sought and expected by him who is about to choose a companion for life; a mother for his offspring; a "guide of his house;" a lightener of his cares; and a counsellor of his most confidential hours. Who can tell the importance of having, in so near a friend, sound, practical wisdom, and habitual prudence? To a clergyman it is highly desirable that his wife should have good sense and piety enough to be a helper even in his professional duties; but that she should have the principal management of all his domestic concerns, will follow as a matter of course. For this purpose, every one sees that wisdom, prudence, and energy too, are indispensable.

8. I scarcely need to add, that you will, no doubt, consider good temper, and amiable manners, as holding a very important place in the qualifications of her who is to be a "help-meet" for a minister. It has

often been remarked, that no clergyman ever married a wife of a remarkably weak understanding, without severely repenting it. With this I agree. But I am inclined to think that a wayward temper, and repulsive manners, in a wife, are more destructive of domestic happiness, and especially that of a clergyman, than even folly itself.

It is of the utmost importance, that the wife of a public man have that amiable, bland, accommodating disposition ; that habitual equanimity and benevolence, which will dispose her at all times to consult her husband's comfort, and to receive with a kind welcome all his friends and visitants. If her temper be irascible, discontented, querulous or vindictive, she will not only create many a bitter hour under her own roof; but will also alienate the friends of him whom she has the deepest possible interest in sustaining, and present an additional obstacle to the favourable influence of his best exertions. Many a minister has had his usefulness in a great measure prostrated, and some have been driven from comfortable settlements, by the acerbity and perverseness of female tempers. And, on the other hand, it is but justice, and equally to my purpose, to add, that, in many cases, a clergyman of weak mind, or unhappy natural temper himself, has been most happily influenced from day to day, and in a great measure sustained in dignity and usefulness, by the affability, prudence, and address of an amiable wife.

9. Good health and a good flow of spirits in a wife are of incalculable importance to any man ; but to a minister of the gospel they are, obviously, of peculiar importance. I will not suppose you capable of being

so insane as to wed a known valetudinarian; in other words, voluntarily to connect yourself with an incumbrance, rather than a help, for life. Your companion may become sickly, after marriage. If this should be the case, submit to it without a murmur, and cherish her with growing affection, just as you would wish her to do, if your own health should fail. But pray do not begin with a nursling. An invalid of either sex ought, undoubtedly, to receive your compassion, and, as far as practicable, your benevolent attention; but in seeking a wife, I shall take for granted that you wish to obtain a companion by whom your own enjoyment and usefulness will be increased. But surely there is a miserable prospect of either of these objects being, to any extent, attained, when any one commences his conjugal career with a companion, whose frail, morbid frame, and continually recurring indisposition, are ominous of the sick room, rather than of the cheerful, active housewife, as long as she lives. Nay, more; not only seek a wife of good health, and some activity and energy; but one who has also a good flow of animal spirits. How inestimably important to an intellectual and moral labourer, that he have a companion who will be able habitually to cheer him in his gloom; to encourage him in sickness; to incite him in his languid hours; and to banish the clouds which occasionally obscure his prospect, by the fascination of a smiling countenance, which "doeth good like a medicine!"

10. You will, no doubt, have observed that, in the foregoing list of requisites, I have said nothing of personal beauty. For this, my reasons are various. There is no danger of this quality having less influ-

ence than it ought to have, in the choice of a wife. All the danger is on the other side. It is a fading flower; soon passing away, and leaving the intellectual and moral qualities, the grand requisites to conjugal felicity. Even while it lasts, it enters much less into the essence of connubial bliss, than the youthful imagination is apt to suppose. Some of the happiest marriages I have ever known were cases in which the wife was remarkably homely, rather than beautiful; but in which her moral beauty was very conspicuous. While, therefore, it is, doubtless, desirable that the woman with whom you hope to spend your life, should have a face and person entirely agreeable to you; I trust you will not be unwise enough to consider a "set of features and complexion," as all in all in your choice. In less than half a dozen years after you have become a husband, every thing of this nature will be lost in the more important considerations of the understanding, the temper, the heart, and the practical duties of domestic life.

11. I solemnly warn you against marrying for money. And by this I mean something more than is commonly intended by the expression. To be influenced, in forming a matrimonial connection, solely or chiefly, by the consideration of property, and not by genuine affection, I hold to be a complicated wickedness; a sin against God, against nature, and against domestic enjoyment; and it is no less a folly than a sin. Such marriages are scarcely every happy; and no wonder that the frown of heaven, as well as the disapprobation of all the wise and good, should rest upon them. But I would go further, and say, to a

young clergyman, by no means marry a lady of very large estate, even if you can love her sincerely. Her property will, without something like a miracle, be a snare to you. She will probably expect to live in splendour; to see much company; and to adopt a style of equipage and expense by no means friendly to Christian simplicity and spirituality. This will be fatal to your ministerial fidelity and comfort. Besides, the very care and anxiety unavoidable in managing a large estate, would make your heart and hands so full of the world, as wholly to interfere with exclusive consecration to the duties of your office. I say again, then, be not in haste to wed a large worldly property. In one case only would I allow such a step, viz., where the female who brought the property was decidedly pious; disposed to be plain and simple in her habits; and not likely to ensnare a servant of Christ, by worldly cares and parade. But who can be sure that this will be the case with her whom he marries? The best way is to avoid the danger altogether. In giving this advice, however, I acknowledge, I have little hope that it will be considered as wise, and far less that it will be followed. But if you go counter to it, you will bring on yourself many a heart-ache, which will convince you of its wisdom afterwards. I have known of one instance of a clergyman declining a matrimonial connection of the most attractive character from motives such as these; but he was a man of singular piety, disinterestedness, and magnanimity.

12. Recollect that there is no step in life, in which you stand more in need of constant divine direction, than in choosing a wife. Perhaps I ought rather to

say, that there is no temporal step in which you stand so much in need of the guidance of infinite Wisdom. To marry without cordial affection is madness. To marry without sacredly listening to the dictates of prudence, as to the piety, the good sense, the good temper, and the amiable manners of the individual selected, is equal madness. How shall the demands of both be satisfied? Especially since this, of all the subjects which come before the mind, is that concerning which caprice, fancy, and passion are, perhaps, most apt to blind the judgment, and bear a sovereign sway? For my part, when I recollect these things, I am constrained to ask, can there be a subject concerning which you more urgently need guidance from above? Can there be a subject in regard to which it behoves you more implicitly to cast yourself on the teaching and the control of God, and more importunately to beg him to choose for you? To this momentous matter, let me, with peculiar emphasis, apply that precious precept and promise of God's word;—"Acknowledge him in all thy ways, and he will direct thy steps." Beseech him with unwearied importunity to go before you; to guard you against the confidence of self-will, and the government of unhallowed passion; to point out the proper object; to direct your choice in mercy; and to preside over every step in your progress. He can, and if you importunately ask him, you have reason to hope, he will, guide your eye; control your feelings; lead you by his providence; remove difficulties; and conduct you to a union for which you will have reason to praise him for ever. If God were more acknowledged and honoured in forming matrimonial connections, we should see more happy marriages. But if, instead of this, in seeking a wife, you forget the best Counsellor; conduct your inquiries more by the eye than the ear; think only of those qualities which please the fancy; depend on effecting an entire revolution in a character confessed not to be, at present, at all suitable; and turn away from the warnings of piety and experience; —why, then, you will probably find your acquisition a scourge instead of a blessing, and all your anticipated joys turned into gall and wormwood.

13. Beware of violating a matrimonial engagement after having formed it. I have sometimes doubted whether there were on the minds of many conscientious young men, a sufficiently deep impression of the evil of this conduct. The same levity of feeling which is apt to prevail in forming such contracts, is too apt to be indulged in breaking them. And hence, some who claim strong sensibility to the point of honour, and even of piety, after entering into a solemn contract of this kind, have not scrupled unceremoniously to violate it, and perhaps in a manner and in circumstances extremely revolting to delicate minds. Such cases are always deeply to be deplored; and, where an individual of your profession is concerned, cannot fail to inflict a severe wound on religion. I do not say, that a solemnly betrothed party may in no case whatever break off an engagement before marriage. For I have no doubt that new facts may sometimes arise, and important discoveries be made, which will fully justify such a step. But, in my opinion, by far the greater part of the cases of such conduct which occur, are utterly unjustifiable and deserve lasting censure. It is no valid plea to

say that affection has cooled. That may be an evidence that there was juvenile folly and haste in the engagement; but by no means proves that it may be violated at pleasure. Suppose affection to cool after marriage; what then? Truly it is an unhappy dilemma; but still it only proves that the man was precipitate at first, and inconstant afterwards; but neither branch of character will add much to his reputation among the wise and the good. The remedy for all this is obvious. Be careful in inquiring. Be deliberate and prayerful in choosing. When you have made the choice, and stand in the situation of one betrothed, no more admit the thought of violating the engagement, than you would think of deserting a wife and half a dozen children. And even if the most serious considerations arise, to make a rupture of the contract, in your view, necessary, you ought to regard it as one of the greatest misfortunes of your life; and, like the English prelate, who had committed an accidental homicide, to keep an annual day of humiliation and fasting in memory of it to the latest year of your course.

14. From the hour that you become a husband, let it be your care to set an edifying example of conjugal excellence. As a clergyman ought to be the most pious man in his parish; to go before all his people in the exemplification of every Christian grace and virtue; so he ought to make a point of being the best husband in his parish, of endeavouring to excel all others in affection, kindness, attention, and every conjugal and domestic virtue. Unfortunately this is not always the case. Some clergymen, who preach well on the duties of husbands and wives, are, not-

withstanding, austere, harsh, tyrannical, and unkind in their own families. Whenever this is the case, it can seldom fail to be known; and, when known, can never fail to diminish, in some degree, their official influence. But, I need not say, that your daily and hourly happiness, still more than your reputation, will be involved in this matter. It would be unseasonable here to attempt even the most cursory detail of conjugal duties. Suffice it to say, that if you should not love your wife enough to make the most unceasing attentions and kindness to her delightful; if you should not have an affection for her so strong as to prompt you to be continually contriving something for her happiness, even at the expense of self-denial and sacrifice on your part; if the feelings of your heart should not spontaneously dispose you to bear with her infirmities, to cover her faults, to comply with all her reasonable wishes, and to respect and honour her in the presence of your family, as well as of strangers; I say, if you should not have a love for your wife which will prompt you, without constraint, to do all this, it will be vain to give you counsels on the subject. But with such a governing attachment as I have supposed, all this will be easy, natural, and pleasant. Do not, however, expect perfect bliss with any woman, however lovely or excellent. As you are yourself a fallen and depraved creature, you must expect to find her so too. And as she will certainly see much requiring to be overlooked and forgiven in you, so you must be willing to overlook and forgive, if you hope to receive the same favour. Even if you find yourself somewhat disappointed in the woman of your choice, do not imagine that this will release you from the obligation to treat her with unremitting kindness and attention. Suppose her to be somewhat disappointed in you; would that release her from the obligation to make you an affectionate and attentive wife? Surely if there be any one who is bound to contemplate this whole subject through the medium of Christian principle and Christian duty, it is a minister of the gospel.

But there are two faults to which attentive husbands are frequently liable. The one is, indulging in undue fondness, and even caresses, before company. This is disgusting in any one, but in a clergyman peculiarly so. The other is, paying to a wife in company that punctilious and extreme attention, which is really a kind of overacting, and which seldom fails to be unfavourably noticed. While you avoid both these faults, maintain that easy, unaffected attention, that cordial yet dignified kindness, which indicate a deep-seated and pure attachment.

15. The conduct proper to be observed by the wives and daughters of clergymen, is worthy of your most serious attention. That they ought to study to be exemplary beyond the degree which is required of those in the ordinary walks of life, I suppose all will concede. As to the precise details of this example, there will probably be some diversity of opinion. In the following hints, I give you the result of some experience, and of the strongest convictions. I represent the subject as worthy of your serious attention, because I take for granted that any woman whom you would consent to marry, may be expected to regard your wishes, properly expressed, with sacred attention. If there be any clergyman's wife who wraps herself

up in a cold indifference to the friends, the interests, and the congregation of her husband, and who feels herself at liberty to depart from that line of conduct which is obviously calculated to strengthen his hold on the affections of his people, and to promote his general comfort, usefulness and honour, I can only say, that, in my view, whatever her other accomplishments may be, she labours under either a weakness of judgment or a defect of principle, which cannot but render her a pitiable object among all sober-minded observers.

Whatever may be your temporal circumstances, let your wife, and your daughters, if God should give you any, be studiously plain in their dress. Let no marked expensiveness; no devotedness to fashion; no flaring colours; no symptoms of inordinate attention to ornament, ever appear among the members of your family. On the contrary, let simplicity, modesty, economy, and the absence of all ostentation, in this respect, be among their invariable characteristics. I give this advice under a deep persuasion, not only of its justice, but also of its importance. And I do not give it merely because, by following it, much unnecessary expense may annually be saved. This, indeed, in a Christian family, demands constant attention. But the counsel before us ought to be followed from other, and far higher motives:—for the purpose of setting an example of simplicity and economy; for the purpose of repressing those inordinate sacrifices to "bodily adorning" which are apt so criminally, and so mischievously, to prevail in all polished society: and for the purpose, too, of consulting the feelings of the less fashionable part of most congregations, who are always pained, and justly pained, at seeing the members of their minister's families dress in a splendid style. And if you imagine that the most gay and wealthy part of a pastor's congregation would esteem any member of his family the less for dressing in the manner advised, you were never more egregiously deceived in your life.

That a clergyman's wife ought also to feel that she bears an important relation to the families under his pastoral care, will, I suppose, be readily granted. How far, indeed, she ought to aim at going, in the important work of visiting those families, cannot be definitely prescribed. This will, of course, depend very much on the situation of her own family, her health, her degree of leisure, &c. But that a pious and prudent woman can accomplish a vast amount of good, by visiting among the people of her companion's charge; especially among the females; not forgetting the plainest and poorest any more than the most wealthy; and that it is her duty to do as much of this as her circumstances will admit, none I hope will be disposed to doubt.

I will only add, that it is of immense importance to a clergyman, that his wife not only have, in general, good sense, and prudence, as before inculcated, but that she, and all the members of his family, should be aware that it is peculiarly incumbent on them, as a matter of decorum, as well as duty, to be "grave, sober, no slanderers," habitually and delicately reserved with respect to every thing which concerns either his personal or official duties, and constantly on their guard against every thing, in speech or behaviour, which may, even by possibility, implicate his character or usefulness. I wish the wives and children of clergymen felt as they ought, the undoubted truth, that every instance of levity or indiscretion on their part, is not only wrong in itself, but tends also, in ways which they little think of, to depress the reputation of those whom it is, in every respect, their highest interest to honour.

16. Before marriage, as well as afterwards, exercise great delicacy in conversing with females. There are clergymen, both single and married, who are not sufficiently attentive to this point. Every thing that approaches to fondling with females; frequently taking hold of their hands; leaning on, or over their persons; saluting them; retiring much with them into private apartments; often taking solitary walks with them; corresponding with them by letter, &c.—are all practices of which clergymen, young or old, ought to be extremely cautious, and more especially in respect to married females. In a word, in all your associations with the other sex, let your delicacy be of the most scrupulous kind. Shun not only the reality, but even the appearance of evil. And remember that the very confidence, with respect to purity, which is commonly placed in a clergyman's character, while it is, in some respects, highly advantageous, may become a snare to him in a variety of ways easily conceivable.

The importance of perfect delicacy of language, on the part of a clergyman, in conversing with females, has been urged in a preceding letter. I shall not, therefore, now enlarge on the subject, further than to say, that, for any one to use an expression, in their presence, which borders on the indecent, or approaches even to double entendre, is to forfeit the character of a gentleman; but for a minister of religion to be guilty of any thing of this kind, is peculiarly base. There is no need, however, of my adding another syllable in support of so plain a dictate of common decorum.

The manner in which you converse with women, and especially with young women, on the subject of experimental religion, will be worthy of your particular attention. Here the text which stands at the head of this letter is strictly applicable. "Entreat—the elder women as mothers; the younger as sisters, with all purity." Do not affect privacy in your conversations with either, more than the nature of the case may render absolutely necessary. And, as often as you can, avail yourself of the aid of those "mothers in Israel," whose piety, experience, and influence render them capable of eminent usefulness among anxious inquirers of their own sex.

17. Let all the time that you spend in the society of females be employed as much as possible in useful conversation. When young men of the world converse with females, they commonly, of design, dwell on frivolous subjects, because they suppose no other to be adapted to the capacity of that sex. As this will not be your opinion, if you derive your sentiments from the Bible; so I trust your practice will be different. Never imagine that to talk on light and vain subjects, is to accommodate yourself to females. They will neither respect nor thank you for the accommodation. Women are just as capable as others of comprehending and discussing to advantage, most subjects which ought to be introduced into any company. And there are many subjects of great im-

portance, which they are able to treat in a more striking manner, and with a more delicate touch, than most men. Avail yourself of this fact. Try to turn every moment that you spend in their society to good account, both for yourself and for them. Especially let religion, and the great subjects connected with it, form as much as possible, when in their company, the leading topic of conversation. You cannot take a better method, at once, to promote their improvement and your own, and to gain their confidence.

18. Never allow yourself to adopt those contemptuous expressions concerning the female sex generally, which licentious men are so apt to indulge, and which some good men are prone, inconsiderately, to employ. That men who have little or no principle themselves, and who have no real acquaintance with any but the most worthless portion of the other sex, should be fond of throwing out reproaches against the character of women, as a body, is not wonderful. But when I hear a man of knowledge and piety, and, above all, a clergyman, doing this, I generally conclude, either that he is a weak man; that he has kept bad company; or that he is revenging some supposed ill-treatment from an individual female, or some unhappy connection or occurrence in earlier life. Be assured, my young friend, this is foolish conduct. No truly wise man was ever guilty of it. That there is more intellectual culture among men than women, is evident. But that there is more native intellectual soundness and justness of mind among the former than the latter, I do not believe. And that there is, decisively, more moral excellence among women, in general, in Christian countries, than among the other

sex, I am deliberately persuaded. If this, or any thing like this, be true, then the practice of speaking lightly of women, is not just in itself; is not agreeable to the word of God; and is not adapted to promote the great interests of virtue and piety in the world. It can answer no other purpose than to harden licentiousness in its folly; to mislead the young; to depreciate, in the view of many, a most precious part of the church of Christ; and to present an unnecessary obstacle in the way of their usefulness.

19. I have only to add, as a final counsel, growing out of all that has been said on the subject, that you endeavour to maintain a constant and firm influence on the minds of the pious females, wherever you reside. Depend upon it, this is worth all the care and pains you may take for its attainment. If you do not stand well with the female portion of your pastoral charge, as I remarked in the introduction to this letter, your prospect of usefulness in the ministry will be very small. If you ask me how the influence which I recommend shall be gained and preserved, I answer, not by flattery; not by any indirect or crooked arts; but by the faithful and able discharge of all your public duties; by a private conversation, pure, delicate, and dignified; and by treating your female parishioners with that respectful and appropriate attention which the word of God, and the interests of his kingdom, evidently command. We live in an age in which pious females take a far more active part in promoting the spread of the gospel, than was common half a century ago. Their associations, for a variety of humane and evangelical purposes, you will be prepared, I trust, in common with every enlightened

minister of Christ, to patronize and honour. If you do this; if you encourage your own wife—if you shall be so happy as to have a pious one—to take the lead in every laudable enterprise among her own sex; and if your own deportment be, in all respects, such as becomes the Christian minister and gentleman, I will answer for your acquiring and maintaining as much of the influence of which I speak, as you ought to have, and for your finding it one of the most valuable auxiliaries in the exercise of your ministry.

LETTER XIII.

Let your moderation be known unto all men. — PHILIP.

DRESS — STYLE OF LIVING — PECUNIARY CONCERNS.

MY DEAR YOUNG FRIEND: — It may seem, at first view, scarcely necessary, or even proper, in addressing a candidate for the ministry in the Presbyterian church, to dwell on the subjects which appear at the head of this letter. It is well known that the temporal circumstances of our ministers are very rarely affluent, and seldom even comfortably easy. Much labour, small salaries, and habitual self-denial, are, in general, the lot of those who, in our church, aspire to the precious privilege of serving Christ in the "ministry of reconciliation." Why then, it may be asked, should it be deemed proper to discuss a set of subjects which can be considered as claiming the particular attention of those only whose resources enable them to command some of the luxuries of life?

This objection is by no means solid. A few of our ministers, especially those who reside in great cities, and other populous places, have the means of living somewhat splendidly, and are often placed under very strong temptations to do so. Some, who are differently situated, have a natural and almost irresistible propensity to show and parade, which they strain every nerve to indulge; and there are even those in the sacred profession, who, though extremely poor, are so criminally unwise and prodigal, as to plunge themselves into debt for the gratification of this propensity. Surely a few words applicable to each of these classes may be neither unseasonable nor useless.

Perhaps the most serious difficulties in relation to this point are those which beset the city clergyman; especially if his pastoral charge include a number of fashionable and wealthy females, and if the provision which they make for his temporal support be, at the same time, pretty liberal. If to these circumstances be added that of his family being strongly predisposed to expensive dress and gay company, the consequences can scarcely fail of being very unhappy. Not a few ministers, by yielding to temptations of this kind, have grieved the hearts of the pious; weakened their own hands; and laid up in store for themselves the bitterest, but unavailing, repentance. As you know not the situation in which you may be placed; and as it is desirable that every young minister should be armed beforehand against the temptations which may assail him, I trust you will be willing to listen to a few suggestions, derived from some observation and experience, and offered under the most solemn impression that they are worthy of your serious regard. Rely upon it, that, however unfavourably some of them may now impress your mind, you will hereafter find in them more both of truth and importance, than it is possible for any one to perceive, who has seen so little, comparatively, as you have, of human life.

1. To begin with your own dress. Wherever your lot may be cast, whether in the country or in a city, let your dress be always plain, but at the same time, whole, neat, and clean. Never make it an object of primary or engrossing attention; but at the same time never neglect it. Even if your residence be ever so retired, never appear in public without setting a good example to your flock in this, as well as in every other respect. Recollect that one of the advantages of the Lord's day, and of public worship, is that they afford, at once, an opportunity and an inducement to lay aside the dust and dirt of the week, in a physical. as well as moral sense, and to appear clad in habiliments which indicate attention, industry, and neatness. And as the minister of the gospel is a public character, and must necessarily, in a great measure, live in public, it is desirable that he should appear every day, when he is in company at all, very much as he ought to appear on the Sabbath. Let your dress, then, be always simple, unostentatious and economical; but let it not be slovenly. Even if it be coarse, and you cannot afford to have it otherwise; still let it be free from all disgusting defilement. Imagine not that any degree of piety or talents will atone for total negligence of this matter. Be assured that any man, who is filthy, or even slovenly in his person, however striking may be his accomplishments in other respects, will find his character and influence depressed in proportion to the degree in which this evil prevails. Such a fault never did, and never will exist, in any case, with entire impunity.

It is the duty of a minister to spend a part of almost every day, if not in public, at least in social intercourse: and he knows not at what hour he may be called upon to converse with the most polished and ceremonious of his parishioners or neighbours. Now, in conversing with such individuals, it is surely desirable that there be nothing in his person calculated to repel them, or to diminish his influence over them; nothing adapted to give them an idea of filthiness or vulgarity; but, as far as possible, of the reverse. I am decidedly of the opinion, therefore, that some clergymen, who can very well afford to do otherwise, have been entirely too negligent of this matter, in appearing in public. I was once acquainted with a minister of our church, who was not only in very comfortable circumstances, but rather entitled to be called rich, who was so culpably negligent of his dress, and, on a particular occasion, appeared in habiliments so unworthy of his character, that a pious lady was on the point of procuring a suit of clothes for him, when she learned, to her surprise, that he was not poor, and that he would certainly be offended by an offer of such charity. He was an uncommonly pious, active minister; but he had, as to the point of slovenliness in dress, a constitutional infirmity; which, you can readily perceive, might have drawn both himself and others into a very embarrassing situation.

I trust you will endeavour to guard against any kind of excess on this subject. On the one hand, to see a minister of the gospel finical, or addicted to the love of splendour or finery in dress; to see, in a word, any thing about his person which discovers a special attention to fashion or ornament in clothing, or a peculiar desire to make a good appearance in this respect, is certainly unworthy of his character. But, on the other hand, to see such a degree of negligence in reference to this matter as is inconsistent with cleanliness, and with a decent respect for those with whom he associates, is equally disreputable, and quite as unfriendly to his usefulness. Why should an enlightened, prudent man, allow himself to run into either extreme?

2. If you should ever have a family, the dress of those who belong to it will be worthy of your particular attention. I have already adverted to this subject in the last letter. But a few additional suggestions in reference to it, in this connection, may not be entirely superfluous. Not only ought the female part of a clergyman's family to avoid every thing that looks like devotedness to fashionable dress; every thing dazzling, or "dashing," as the popular style is; but no such folly ought to appear, as far as it can be avoided, in the dress of any of his household. A disposition to load even his youngest children with tawdry or useless ornament, ought not to be indulged. To make them conspicuous by red shoes, waving plumes, and expensive, showy decorations of any kind, may gratify parental vanity; but cannot minister to the rational comfort of either parents or children; and may make an impression on the minds of some plain or poor parishioners which is very far from being desirable. Besides, the tendency to indulge in excessive gaiety and ornament of dress, is so general, and, in many cases, a source of so much evil, as remarked in a former letter, that a minister ought studiously to set an example of plainness and simplicity in this respect, in all to whom his influence extends, for the purpose of promoting a similar habit

in others. And the more able he is, on the score of expense, to indulge the inclinations of his family, the more useful will his example be likely to prove.

3. If you live to have a house of your own, let your furniture, and all your equipage be of the plain and simple kind. Most of the considerations urged in the preceding paragraph, apply here with equal force. There is so strong a tendency, in many persons who can ill afford it, to lavish expense on splendid furniture and fashionable equipage of every kind, that every well-wisher to the cause of good morals, to say nothing of religion, ought to throw the whole weight of his character into the scale of the strictest moderation. Even if you should be able, without inconvenience, to indulge the most refined taste in matters of this kind, by all means forbear to do it. Let it be seen that your heart is not set on such objects; that you deliberately prefer simplicity and plainness; and that you conscientiously choose to devote the money which might have been spent in splendid but useless decoration to the support of the infinitely more important interests of humanity and religion.

For example; if you should feel yourself able to keep any kind of carriage, always prefer a plain to an elegant or showy one. In purchasing horses, recollect that sound, substantial, decent-looking animals are more suitable for a minister of the gospel, than those which are remarkable for their beauty, which must, of course, be much more costly, without being really more useful; and in the use of which his parishioners would often be tempted to remark, that their minister was peculiarly fond of fine horses. The same principle will apply to every article of personal or domestic accommodation. Make a point of never expending a cent for show, or mere useless decoration; but all for solid utility and convenience. Nay, of two articles of exactly the same utility and price, always prefer that which is plain and unostentatious, to that which is highly ornamented, merely because it is plain. I have never known a clergyman to deviate materially from this plan of living, to affect splendour, to launch out into a system of dazzling expenditure, calculated to excite the envy or the admiration of a staring multitude, without seriously depressing both his reputation and his usefulness among all reflecting people. Indeed, to see a minister of the gospel ambitious of finery, and carried away with baubles and show, is revolting even to the devotees of the world themselves, who see at once how inconsistent it is with his sacred profession.

4. Never allow yourself to live beyond your income. He who does this must either contract debts without a rational prospect of paying them, or he must expect to have them discharged by the hand of charity; either of which is unworthy of the ministerial character. However scanty, therefore, your income may be, rigidly reduce your expenditure within its limits. It is not disreputable to be poor; but it is highly disreputable to be prodigal of other people's money. Indeed it appears to me that few things can more flagrantly evince the want of principle, than living luxuriously on property not our own. A writer in the "Christian Observer" expresses himself on this subject in the following language, which does not appear to me at all too strong: "A clergyman, overwhelmed with debts to his parishioners, whether his

debts arise from vanity, or from improvidence, loses his influence over their minds; and it is well if he be not also guilty, as too many persons who heedlessly plunge into debt are, of artifices, evasions, and perhaps worse offences, which must bring him into contempt, and utterly destroy the spiritual effect of his ministrations. However rigid the economy called for by a clergyman's circumstances, to that degree of economy he is conscientiously bound to submit; and every step beyond it, except under inevitable visitations of Providence, is an advance towards disgrace and ruin, both as a man and a minister."

5. Manage all your expenses with a wise economy. I wish to lay particular stress on the word wise. Every one must perceive that economy is a relative term. That which might be very properly so termed in one, would deserve the name of exceptionable parsimony in another, or of criminal prodigality in a third. Wise economy consists in maintaining a just balance between that which we have to spend, on the one hand, and that which we really need to spend on the other. Pecuniary embarrassments, in the case of clergymen, as well as others, frequently arise, not so much from general prodigality, as from expenditures which are not necessary. One of the best methods of keeping your expenses within the limits of your income is, never to purchase any thing, however cheap or tempting the article may be, unless you really need it. He who rigidly and prudently adheres to this rule, will seldom find the state of his finances very seriously deranged; and will generally have something to spare for the calls of charity.

6. Carefully guard against every thing approaching

to meanness in the management of your pecuniary affairs. Frugality is always, and in all persons, a virtue; but extreme and unseasonable parsimony is always censurable and degrading. Rely on it, a sordid, niggardly spirit was never useful to any one. Its savings are pitiful; its gains are mean; and, like most other vices, it generally defeats its own purpose; inducing, perhaps, the very evil which it aims to avoid. Many a man, by low and unmanly attempts to save, has been plunged into unexpected and heavy expenses. Never resort to any means of making money, inconsistent with the dignity of the clerical office, or which you would feel reluctant to have universally known. I have heard of clergymen, who, for the sake of some petty gains, carried on, privately, a disreputable little trade in articles of daily consumption, by pursuing which, with extreme exactness and parsimony, they were enabled to make a few cents each day. But it always depressed, and, in some instances, totally ruined, their characters as ministers of religion.

7. Conscientiously avoid every thing crooked, or even questionable, in your pecuniary transactions. It is not enough that a minister of the gospel sacredly guard against every thing in his dealings really fraudulent, and of which the laws of the land can take hold. He is here, as in all other concerns, to shun every approach to that which is incorrect, or even to that of the correctness of which there can be the least reasonable doubt. If there be any speculation or purchase, of the perfect fairness of which there is a popular question, however strong may be your own conviction of its fairness, have nothing to do with it. To go forward in such an enterprise may be injurious;

but to withdraw from it entirely is always safe. Whatever may be your opinion on the subject of what is called usury, either as to the Bible meaning of the term, or the wisdom of human laws in reference to it, never allow yourself to engage in any transaction, which immediately or remotely bears the least alliance to the usurious character. In short, never permit yourself to be concerned in any pecuniary affair, which, if, by any unforeseen occurrence, it should hereafter be dragged before the public, could possibly implicate either your probity or honour in the minds of the most scrupulous. Remember that, in all cases whatever, it is infinitely better to suffer wrong, than to do wrong; and that many things which would not be at all noticed in another man, may, in a minister of the gospel, be considered as far from reputable.

8. There are some advantages in keeping a regular account of your expenditures. You must by no means suppose that this practice is confined to men of a parsimonious spirit. Some of the most judicious, and even liberal managers of their pecuniary affairs that I have ever known, were in the constant habit of keeping such an account. The purposes which it may answer are various, and by no means unworthy of regard. It will be likely very materially to promote a general spirit of system and order in your finances. It may not only serve as a salutary check on unnecessary expenses; but it may enable you to solve many important questions respecting the cost of living; and it may form a record of no small value, both as a matter of curiosity and of instruction, in subsequent years of your life. Such a record has often furnished the means of ascertaining dates, and important facts,

to an extent not at all contemplated at the time of its formation. A man, therefore, of habitual order in his affairs, ought to be able to say, how much he receives, and how much he expends, in every year of his life; and what are the date and amount of every important purchase that he makes.

9. Persons of small pecuniary means, as clergymen generally are, should make a point of paying ready money for every thing they buy. Those who purchase on credit never fail to pay more for what they buy than others. If you wish to live economically, therefore, never go in debt for any thing. Never keep running accounts for your domestic supplies. You may thus save a large per centage on your annual expenditure. Nor is this all. When you pay the cash for every thing, you know how your money is going, and can take every step with intelligence and distinct calculation. But when you suffer accounts, in half a dozen places, to accumulate, for six or twelve months together, the probability is, that you will find an amount rising up against you at the end of this time, altogether unexpected, and which you are not prepared to meet. The history of the pecuniary embarrassments of many a clergyman may be traced to this source. One who has already plunged himself into difficulty by indiscretion, may not be able to act agreeably to this advice; but by wise management at the outset, it may be generally done.

10. Set a good example to your parishioners, and to all around you, in contributing to charitable and pious objects. You will often have occasion, both in public and private, to inculcate on others the exercise of Christian liberality. Indeed, I have frequently

thought that attention to this duty was not urged by ministers, either from the pulpit, or in private, as much, by any means, as its importance demands. But what will be the appearance, if while you strongly recommend this duty in words, you set no example of the discharge of it in your habits? It is true, ministers can seldom give much to charitable and pious objects. Of silver and gold they commonly have but little to bestow on any thing beyond the daily provision of food and raiment. But if they exercise a just economy, they may and will have a little. And if that little be suitably divided, and cheerfully bestowed; if you show a readiness to the utmost of your ability, and beyond your ability, to contribute to the promotion of the Redeemer's kingdom, you will give one of the best possible evidences of your sincerity and zeal.

11. Do not indulge a habit of undue solicitude, and especially of frequent complaint, respecting your temporal support. Where there is either an inordinate love of property, or a querulous temper, the subjects of salary, perquisites, &c., will be apt to engage more attention, and to be more frequently the topics of conversation, than a minister of the gospel ought ever to allow them to be. Never converse on subjects of this kind, unless it becomes absolutely necessary; and then let it be done sparingly, and with a few confidential friends only. You may rest assured, that dwelling much on his pecuniary affairs, in intercourse with his parishioners, never promoted the real benefit of a clergyman, either as to his purse or his reputation. All that can be done, to any advantage, in providing for the temporal com-

fort of a pastor, may, I am persuaded, be commonly done, quite as effectually, by dropping a hint, now and then, to a discreet friend, and much more to the honour of religion, than by the most unceasing complaints, and the most importunate solicitations.

12. Be not in the habit of proposing to your congregation to make subscriptions or donations for your support, besides your salary. Some distinguished ministers, both in Europe and America, who had liberal salaries, have been repeatedly guilty of this indiscretion. Either improvidently falling in debt, or being called to meet some extraordinary expenditure, they openly solicited, or indirectly encouraged, one private subscription after another for their own relief. This is seldom expedient, and often it is exceedingly injurious. Where any thing of this kind, on a special occasion, once in a minister's life, is spontaneously, and without his knowledge, set on foot by a few friends, and carried into execution with a delicate privacy, it may be accepted without any injurious consequences. But if he solicit it; or if it be repeated from time to time, it cannot fail, insensibly, to depress his standing with his people. It brings him before their view too much in the character of a pauper; and if he be presented to them in this character again and again, in spite of everything that can be said or done to the contrary, he will occupy a less respectable place in their feelings. No man who ministers at the altar, ought ever to consider a decent support, imparted by those whom he serves, as charity. It is nothing but his due. And yet, there is a certain spirit of independence which his own reputation, and the honour of religion,

equally call upon him to maintain. The character of an habitual beggar for himself, is a miserable one for a minister of the gospel.

13. Never leave a congregation on account of the smallness of your salary, if you can possibly avoid it. Every minister ought to expect from his people a comfortable support; not that which will enable him to live in luxury; but which will place him above want, and deliver him from those perplexing cares, which a very inconvenient scantiness of provision cannot fail to produce. If your congregation should be entirely able to give you such a support as I have described, and yet decline or neglect to do it, you ought to take the earliest favourable opportunity to leave them. The workman is worthy of his meat. And where, in such circumstances, it is withheld, those who are capable of deliberately withholding it ought to feel the consequences of their unchristian parsimony. There is neither justice nor charity in remaining with a people who will permit a faithful minister to starve, while they are abundantly able to "minister to his necessities."

But if you should ever be connected with a small and poor congregation; a society of an attentive and affectionate character; earnestly desirous of furnishing you with a comfortable support, but really unable to afford it; be not ready to leave such a people. Nay, if you are happy and useful among them, never think of deserting them on account of pecuniary considerations, as long as you can avoid it. Remain with them; cherish them; and rather beg for them than of them. This is almost the only case, in which I would advise a minister of the gospel to resort, for a part of his time, to some secular employment, which might supply the deficiency of an inadequate salary, and enable him to remain where he otherwise could not live, among a willing but poor people. Stay with such a people as long as God, in his Providence, renders it practicable; be willing to deny and exert yourself for their benefit; and let your removal from them to accept of a better support, be your last resort.

14. If you should ever be compelled to resort to any secular employment, for the purpose of supplying the deficiency of a small salary, let it be an employment as much as possible in harmony with the ministerial character. There have been clergymen, who, finding their salaries altogether inadequate to the decent support of their families, even in the most economical manner, and resolving to devote a part of their time to some employment, the product of which should supply the deficiency in their official income, have made a choice of employment truly unhappy. Some have been either acting or dormant partners in distilleries. Others have engaged in large mercantile business. A third class, in manufactories. And a fourth in speculating on notes, bonds, or some other species of property. And the history of these pursuits has generally been, that, while a few have succeeded, grown rich, and become completely secularized; the majority have been deceived, ensnared, and plunged into bankruptcy, and perhaps a total wreck of Christian and ministerial character. Of the whole number who take this course, I suspect, a very small portion, indeed, attained their professed object with comfort and reputation.

Against all such plans and employments, therefore, I would warn you. If your object should honestly be, what is commonly, in such cases, professed, viz., not by any means to grow rich; but merely to make such a moderate addition to your scanty income, as may enable you barely to support your family with comfort; then choose, as an auxiliary, some employment, which will interfere as little as possible with your ministry; which will tend as little as may be to impart a worldly influence to your mind; and which may coincide, in a considerable degree, with your ministerial duties. Such an employment is the education of youth. Such an employment, also, is the editing and sale of pious books. These objects of attention are so far from being hostile to moral and even evangelical duty, that they fall in with it entirely, and may be rendered essentially subservient to the great end of all ministerial labour. They have, also, this further advantage, that the gains which they yield are commonly small and regular, and are, of course, not so apt to betray the mind into a deeply secular spirit. Next to the employments which I have mentioned, perhaps that of conducting a small and compact farm may fall in more happily than most others with the duty of the sacred office.

15. If you should be enabled to lay up any portion of property, for the comfort of your family, never allow it to engross your thoughts, or to be the frequent subject of your conversation in company. He who has commenced, on ever so small a scale, the work of accumulating property, and who has occasion, from time to time, to invest his savings in some productive manner, is often tempted to converse on the subject

with undue frequency and solicitude, when he falls in company with those who are considered as well versed in financial concerns. And in a country of active commercial character, he will meet with such company so frequently, that he will be tempted almost every day to converse on the subject. Thus his own mind will be apt to become more and more occupied and ensnared with secular concerns, and he will betray the unhappy fact to those around him, to the dishonour of his holy vocation.

Do not allow yourself, then, in company, to talk frequently or freely on the price of stocks—the rise, fall, and prospects of moneyed institutions—the most popular and eligible investments, &c., &c. If any thing on these subjects worthy of notice be uttered in your presence, you may quietly listen to it, without entering deeply into the conversation as a matter of personal interest. If you need information to enable you to act, seek it privately from those who are most competent to inform you, and most worthy of your confidence. But do not exhibit yourself as the zealous devotee of such things. Few habits, not openly criminal, are more revolting, than to hear a minister of the gospel, in mixed companies, talking like a bank director or stockjobber. It ought to be one of the great objects of his life to turn off the minds of men from inordinate attention to these transient possessions, and to endeavour to fasten them on higher and better treasures.

16. If you should possess any property, guard against investing it in such a manner as will be likely to implicate you in frequent litigation, and compel you frequently to resort to legal coercion. This is

highly undesirable to any man; but to a minister of the gospel, it is absolutely ruinous on the score of reputation. It is the practice of many to invest their property in notes, in bonds, and mortgages, and in various forms of private security. This plan may answer very well for him whose disposition and character permit him frequently to contend, and to resort to legal measures; but it is by no means suitable to one who can hardly take the proper steps, in the plainest case, to obtain his just due, without subjecting himself to invidious remark, and from no quarter more commonly or severely than from those worldly men, who are themselves, every day, plunged and steeped in such proceedings. Men in other stations, of the best character, may sue their debtors, may foreclose mortgages, and get what is rightly their own, without injury to their reputation. But a clergyman cannot. He is expected to bear with endless delays; to forgive debts, where it is not entirely convenient to pay them; and to surrender claims where the richest man in the land would not be expected to do it. On all these accounts, and others which might be mentioned, be not fond of investing property in any kind of private securities, unless they are of a peculiarly firm and eligible kind. Public stocks, of the most secure character, are greatly preferable; because the interest on them is paid the moment it is due, without dunning or trouble; because they may be turned into cash at any hour; and because neither holding nor selling them is likely to drag their owner before the public view in a commercial attitude. For the same reason, be not fond of investing property in small tenements, the renting of which will be apt to bring you in constant collision with tenants, who more than half the time will be unable or unwilling to pay you your rent. Such property you will always find to give you much trouble, and yield you little profit. Whereas the true policy of every minister of the gospel is, to place all his property as far as practicable, in such a situation as will give him the least possible trouble, or even care, occupy as little as may be of his time, and render his moderate profits regular and certain.

17. Finally, guard with the utmost vigilance against the encroachments of a grasping, mercenary spirit. That a minister should desire to be furnished with a decent and comfortable support for his beloved family; that he should even be desirous, if it be the will of God, to leave something behind him to preserve a widow and children from utter beggary, every man who has a family, and domestic feelings, will think both natural and reasonable. But the moment one who occupies the sacred office goes beyond this moderate and reasonable wish; the moment a strong and governing desire of accumulating property takes possession of his mind, he may bid adieu to all steady ministerial zeal, to all exemplary devotedness to his Master's work. Preach with orthodoxy, and some degree of animation, he may; visit his parishioners, to a certain extent, he may; but a devoted labourer in the vineyard; a labourer who has one great object in view,—the extension and glory of his Master's kingdom, and who makes all his pursuits subservient to that object, he will not be. Few things, rely upon it, are more hostile to the spirit of piety, and of ministerial fidelity, than a spirit of worldly acquisition. It is just as

true of a minister as of any other professing Christian,—that "no man can serve two masters." If you should ever be so unhappy and criminal, as to give yourself up to the spirit of worldly gain, it will eat out the vitals of your comfort, your zeal and your usefulness. It will exhibit you, like Samson to the Philistines, a poor, enervated, despoiled object. It is just as impossible for a man to be a great accumulator of property, and at the same time a faithful, devoted minister of Christ, as it is to establish a fellowship between light and darkness, Christ and Belial.

LETTER XIV.

Let all things be done decently and in order. — 1 Cor. xiv. 40

MISCELLANEOUS COUNSELS.

My dear young friend: — I cannot consent to close this manual, although, perhaps, already too much protracted, without calling your attention to a few counsels not included in any of the foregoing letters. In stating these, I shall not be studious of any regular order.

1. Be careful to form the habit of scrupulous punctuality to all your engagements. The importance of this habit is very great, as already mentioned, even while you are a student in the seminary. But if you should live to be clothed with the sacred office, and to form the numerous and diversified engagements which will be likely to mark every week, if not every day, of your subsequent course, you will see, if I mistake not, a degree of importance attached to this matter, not easily calculated. When you have appointed a day and an hour for the performance of any duty, or to meet other persons on business, you have made a contract, which cannot be innocently broken, unless the providence of God render the fulfilment of it impossible. Every time you are

guilty of such violation, you may greatly incommode, and even seriously injure, one or more individuals, and sometimes many individuals, by compelling them to waste precious time in waiting for you. What right have you to do this? Is it not as real a robbery as taking a purse? How men, professing to be conscientious, and to have any just estimate of the value of time, can allow themselves to act thus, I have always been at a loss to understand. There is a degree of complicated mischief about it, which, whatever others may do, clergymen ought certainly to abhor. Let me entreat you, whether you regard your duty or your reputation; your own time, or the time of others;—to be rigorously punctual to every appointment. Establish a character for punctuality, and you will find the great advantage of it, not only in obtaining the confidence of those with whom you may be called to transact business; but also in promoting a similar habit among those with whom you associate. Like other virtues, the one of which I speak propagates itself, and is, eminently, its own reward.

2. You will never accomplish much, either in study or in action, without a large share of what may be called decision of character. By this quality, I mean that bold, steady, persevering firmness of purpose, and ardour of pursuit, which stand opposed to timidity, indolence and irresolution:—that unwavering confidence in the rectitude and importance of his pursuit, which prompts a man to press forward in it, with a constancy which nothing can shake; with a courage, which nothing can intimidate; and with a resolution which nothing can divert. This decision of character

appeared, pre-eminently, in Luther, in Calvin, in Wesley, in Whitefield, in Howard, and in many other men, whose history and services will readily occur to your recollection. It led them to surmount opposition, to brave dangers, to undergo the most indefatigable labour, to fulfil their engagements with punctuality, whatever it might cost them to do so, and to pursue the object which conscience told them was right, without hesitation, and without turning to the right hand or the left, until it was attained.

There is nothing which a public man needs more than a large portion of this spirit, impelled and regulated by Christian principle. If he be feeble and wavering in his purposes; inconstant in his pursuits; easily discouraged, and diverted from them; and frequently persuaded to abandon undertakings ardently begun, and to enter on others, only to abandon them in like manner;—he may make many promises and much noise; but he will do little. He will never be ready for his work; never punctual to his appointments; never either energetic or persevering in his exertions. If you are willing to be such a man, I altogether mistake your character. Yet thousands really bear this stamp, who are far from intending it. If you wish to do much for the church, and for your generation, be not obstinate, but be firm; be not blustering, but systematic, decisive and persevering. Be deliberate and wise in resolving; but determined, unyielding and indefatigable in execution. Do not let every idle individual, or every trivial difficulty, break in upon your plans, or fritter away your time. Remember that your time is short; your work great; the necessities of immortal souls unspeakably urgent;

and the judgment-seat of Christ immediately in prospect. If you really act in the spirit of these considerations, you will accomplish more in a month, than a timid, pliant, irresolute, procrastinating man, however pious, in six months, or a year.

3. Maintain the constant and persevering habit of early rising. This habit is conducive, to an extent which few appear to be aware of, to the health and activity, both of the body and of the mind. It has been often observed, that those who are remarkable for health and long life, have been almost always early risers. A disposition to lie long in bed in the morning, is, at once, a symptom and a cause of feeble digestion, of nervous debility, and of general languor. Whereas early rising is commonly connected with sound sleep; with elasticity of body and mind; and with habits of activity, which are greatly conducive both to health and comfort. Nor is this practice less conducive to success in mental improvement. It not only tends to give a daily spring to the mind, but also to make a very important addition to your studying hours. He who is called to engage in much mental exertion, and is, at the same time, liable to many interruptions, ought to make a point of securing several hours of unbroken study, before he will be liable to the calls of the earliest visitant. Often as the following remark of Dr. Doddridge has been repeated, I cannot forbear once more to transcribe it. "I will here record," says he, "the observation which I have found of great use to myself, to which, I may say, that the production of this work, and most of my other writings, is owing; viz., that the difference between rising at five and at seven of the clock in the morning,

for a space of forty years, supposing a man to go to bed at the same hour at night, is nearly equivalent to the addition of ten years to a man's life, of which (supposing the two hours in question to be spent) eight hours every day should be employed in study and devotion." Let me exhort you, therefore, at all seasons of the year, to rise early; in winter before it is light, and in summer with the sun. In cold weather, kindle your own fire; and in warm, walk out, work in your garden, or in some other situation, exercise your limbs, and inhale the fresh air. Before you take your breakfast, you ought always to have spent, according to the season of the year, from one to two hours in devotion, in study, and in some active recreation in the open air.

You may rely upon it, that a faithful adherence to this course, though at first irksome, will be in the end pleasant; will be conducive to good health, and good spirits; and will enable you to accomplish far more of your appropriate work than can ever be accomplished by the tardy riser, who finds himself, the whole day, running and struggling in vain, to regain the lost hours of the morning. But if you would be an early riser, you must retire early to bed. These are correlative duties which cannot be separated.

4. Few young men that I have ever seen, appeared to me to have any just impression either of the importance, or of the proper methods, of preserving their health. My original intention was to devote a whole letter to this subject; but finding the volume unexpectedly to swell under my hands, and becoming more conscious, the longer I reflected on the subject

of my inability to do justice to it in detail, I shall content myself with a few short paragraphs.

There are two extremes to which young men are prone in relation to this matter. The one is, to imagine that the citadel of their health is impregnable—that no care of it is necessary—that they may take any liberties with it, and lay any burdens upon it, that they please. The other is, to suppose that great scrupulousness of attention to this subject is desirable—that a multitude of rigid cautions; a frequent resort to medicine; guarding against all exposure to cold and damp weather; much wrapping up, &c. &c., are indispensable. He who acts upon either of these plans will probably soon render himself a miserable invalid for life, if he do not speedily cut short his days. Scarcely any young man, who has led an active life, in the pure air of the country, and who commences study with firm and florid health, is aware of the danger which he encounters in sitting down to close intellectual application. I have known a constitution the most robust, in six or twelve months after this change of habit was commenced, suddenly give way, and become utterly broken and prostrated. The truth is, the more active the previous habits, and the more vigorous the frame of a youthful individual, when he sits down to close study; the greater need is there, in many cases, for the exercise of caution, and for keeping up, at least for a time, a set of rules, as to exercise, nearly approximating to his former habits. The transition from an active to a sedentary life, must be made very gradually, if you would make it safely.

My counsel in reference to health shall all be

summed up in four advices, viz. Be strictly temperate with regard to aliment. Take every day a large portion of gentle exercise. Carefully guard against all intestinal constipation. And always avoid too much warmth, both in your clothing and your apartment, quite as vigilantly as you would too much cold.

With regard to the first; remember that temperance in you is a very different thing from temperance in a day-labourer. The latter may, in common, safely and even profitably take two or three times the amount of aliment that can be ventured upon by a sedentary man. If a given portion of solid food oppress you, gradually diminish the quantity, carefully watching the effect, until you ascertain the quantity which is best suited to your constitution, and after which you feel most strong, active, and comfortable, both in body and mind. It is plain that this matter can be regulated only by the individual himself; and that it requires daily watchfulness and resolution. Many students, I have no doubt, bring themselves to a premature grave, by over-eating, as effectually as others by intemperate drinking. The effects of the former species of excess are not quite so manifest, or quite so disreputable, as those of the latter; but, in a multitude of cases, they are no less fatal. He who is so infatuated as to persist in taking but little exercise, ought certainly to eat but little. And he who takes no exercise, ought often to ask himself, how far that inspired Scripture applies to his case—"If any man will not work, neither shall he eat." The answer of Charles Scarborough, physician to Charles II., to one of the courtiers of that monarch, is worthy of being remembered—"You must eat less, or take more exercise, or take physic, or be sick." Recollect, too, that our religion enjoins not only prayer, but fasting also. By this I understand to be meant, not metaphorical or moral abstinence, as some have strangely imagined, but literal abstinence from food. How often this abstinence should take place, I presume not to say. Let every one judge for himself. But that the frequent recurrence of it would be as favourable to the health and enjoyment of a student, as to his spiritual benefit, I have not the smallest doubt.

The importance of taking a large portion of gentle exercise every day can scarcely be overrated. Every student who wishes to preserve good health and spirits ought to be moving about in the open air from three to four hours daily. You may live with less, and, perhaps, enjoy tolerable health. But if you wish fully to possess the *mens sana in corpore sano*, of which the Latin poet speaks, rely upon it, with most students, less will not answer. Your exercise ought to be gentle. Some students, after exhausting themselves by a protracted season of severe study, start from their seats, issue forth, and engage in some violent exercise, which throws them into a profuse perspiration, from which they can scarcely emerge with impunity. In many cases, they had much better have continued to sit still. Your exercise ought to bear a strict proportion to your constitution and your habits. Gentle exercise diffused through four hours, is much better adapted to a sedentary man than a concentration of the same amount of motion within the space of one hour. It is also worthy of remark, that exercise taken either immediately before or immediately after eating, is both less comfortable, and less valuable, than if at least an hour of rest intervene. No prudent traveller will feed his horse immediately after his arrival at the place of baiting, or, if he can avoid it, put him on the road again as soon as he has swallowed his food. The same principle applies to all animal nature.

My third advice has a respect to intestinal constipation. There can be no health where this is suffered long to continue. And yet it is a point to which few inexperienced students are as attentive as they ought to be. They either neglect it, until a decisive indisposition convinces them of their folly; or they are very frequently endeavouring to remove it by the use of medicine. Both methods of treating the difficulty are miserably ill-judged. Medicine ought to be the last resort; and is seldom necessary unless where there has been great mismanagement. Exercise, abstemiousness, and the judicious use of mild, dietetical aperients, form the system which a little experience will show you to be the best.

The temperature of your room, and of your body, is the last point in reference to health to which I shall request your attention. A student, whose robustness is almost always in some degree impaired by sedentary habits, ought never to allow himself, if he can avoid it, to be in the least degree chilly, when he is sitting still. But it is quite as unfriendly to health to allow himself to be over-heated, either by the atmosphere of a room excessively warmed, or by too great a load of clothing. Every thing of this kind ought to be carefully avoided. So far as experience, in relation to my own case, goes, I am constrained to say, that excessive heat has been quite as often, to me, the source of disease as excessive cold. He who is about to take a long walk, in the course of which, he has an opportunity of keeping himself warm by constant, vigorous motion, ought just as carefully to avoid covering himself with an over-coat, while his walk continues, as he ought to be to avoid sitting in a cold place, or in a draft of air, at the end of his walk without it.

You will gather from the foregoing remarks, that my plan for preserving health, is by no means that of tampering with medicines, which is much more likely to make a valetudinarian, than a man of good health; but that of employing wisely and vigilantly the art of prevention. You have now, through divine favour, a good constitution. Try to keep it, by avoiding every species of excess, and by watching every approach of derangement; and, under the blessing of God, all will be well.

5. Never permit yourself to get into a whining, complaining habit, when speaking of your bodily health. You and I know some clergymen, both young and old, who have, by some means, gotten into the unhappy practice, whenever they are asked, by an acquaintance, how they do, of playing the invalid, in rather a ludicrous manner; continually complaining of more or less indisposition; giving a minute history of their little ailments and difficulties; and really appearing to take a kind of comfort from being listened to in a narrative of their own sufferings. Carefully guard against this habit. It is disgusting in itself; troublesome, and in no respect attractive, to your friends; calculated to gain strength by indulgence; and, in the end, to increase the real evils, and to turn into real, the imaginary evils of which it complains.

Unless there be something very peculiar in the state of your health, answer all inquiries respecting it in a single sentence. Trouble nobody but your physician with a minute detail of your pains, and aches, and infirmities; not merely because it is, to many, a revolting story; but because the influence of this habit on your own mind, when indulged to a considerable extent, cannot fail of being unhappy. Talking much about your complaints, will lead you to think much of them; and thinking much of them, will almost infallibly lead to an increase of their power, whether real or imaginary; and finally make you a miserable bundle of complaints and infirmities. Cultivate a cheerful temper, and it will diffuse a happy influence over your whole character.

6. Wherever vou reside, endeavour always to acquire and maintain an influence with young men. They are the hope of the church and of the state; and he who becomes instrumental in imbuing their minds with sentiments of wisdom, virtue and piety, is one of the greatest benefactors of his species. They are, therefore, worthy of your special and unwearied attention. Take every opportunity of becoming acquainted with them, and of conversing with them in a kind and friendly manner. Manifest an interest in their education, in their studies, and in all their temporal as well as spiritual concerns. Endeavour to have the serious and pious of their number united in associations of a moral and religious character; that they may know one another; that they may be prepared to act together; and that they may be as generally as possible brought under a good influence, and inured to good habits. Often meet and advise with

them, and endeavour to engage them in laudable and useful employments. Encourage them to visit you; and exert yourself to render their visits pleasant as well as profitable. Distinctly address them now and then, in a respectful and affectionate manner, in your public discourses. Make them the frequent objects of public prayer, especially in prayer-meetings. In short, employ every Christian method of attaching them to your person and ministry, and of inducing them to take an early interest in the affairs of the church. If you should live in a city, or populous town, keep a watchful eye on all young men who may remove to the place of your residence. Take the earliest opportunity of visiting them; of gaining their confidence, and bringing them within the sphere, and under the power, of hallowed principles. I know of no way in which an ambassador of Christ will be more likely to establish a beneficial influence, and to promote the extension of the Redeemer's kingdom, than by wisely and faithfully acting in conformity with this advice.

7. When you are introduced into the ministry, endeavour always, throughout life, to be on good terms with your clerical brethren. You have known lawyers and physicians who were always on hostile terms with their professional brethren. Like Ishmael of old, their hands were against every one, and every one's hands against them. But I presume you never knew such an individual who was truly respectable. The incessant disposition to vituperate and repel which this character supposes, must be considered as indicating either a want of principle, or an obliquity of temper, of the most unhappy kind. Show me a lawyer or physician who is for ever abusing his

brethren, and I will show you a man unworthy of their love or confidence. The same rule applies, perhaps with peculiar force, to ministers of the gospel. The religion which they teach is a system of love; and the great cause which they profess to seek is the cause of order, union, happiness, and salvation, temporal and eternal. Ministers, therefore, not only ought to be united in affection; but just so far as they are honest, and in earnest, in the great cause which they profess to love, they will be so united. As you value your own peace, comfort and usefulness; and as you wish well to the peace and edification of the church, cultivate a spirit of Christian love, and affectionate intercourse, with all who bear the sacred office. and especially with those of our own church. Visit them; honour them; co-operate with them; and put far from you every thing which tends to generate coldness or strife among them. Your own happiness, and the advancement of the Redeemer's kingdom, are more concerned in this thing than you are probably aware.

8. Never allow yourself to be a politician. Never attend political meetings; never harangue in political companies; never scribble political paragraphs; never connect yourself with political parties; nay, do not indulge in much conversation on politics, even with your friends. Ministers of the gospel, and those who are preparing for the ministry, have infinitely more important work to do. And rely upon it, that, in all cases, the more of a politician you are, the less will be your comfort and your usefulness as an ambassador of Jesus Christ.

9. Let your recreations be always such as become

your profession. That clerical men need recreation as much as others, and in some respects more, is too evident to be denied. Yet I need not say, that many of those amusements which are considered as innocent by worldly people, are out of the question for you. Happily our lot is cast in an age, and in a country, in which public sentiment as well as the word of God very unequivocally prohibits them. There is, however, an ample range of choice still left for any reasonable man. All that become a grave Christian, fall within this range. It will readily occur to you that the active discharge of many of his parochial duties, may be rendered by a pastor, and, if zealously engaged in, will become, some of his most precious recreations. But more than this will be necessary. Riding and walking, of course, in all their varieties, belong to the admissible class. To these I would especially add gardening, as one of the most rational, delightful, and profitable of the whole list. Man in his first and most perfect state was placed in a garden; and in proportion as men imbibe correct sentiments and cultivate a just taste, they will be glad to get back to the same employment. It is desirable to every student to have some recreation, which will not only be salutary, but also pleasant and attractive. If you engage with a moderate and well regulated zeal in the culture of vegetables and shrubbery, you will not probably find them to draw you away from your books a single hour more than will be useful to your health. And if you desire your gardening, as well as your walking and riding to be doubly agreeable, as well as doubly advantageous, try to gain at least such an elementary knowledge of botany and mineralogy as will give you an additional interest in every plant you cultivate, and in every fossil on which you tread.

10. Never allow yourself to be in a hurry. Clergymen who are active and faithful, have commonly so much to do, that, unless they are extremely diligent and orderly in their affairs, they will often be painfully hurried; and that which a public man does in a hurry, is commonly ill done. Few men were ever more busy than the late Mr. John Wesley; yet he significantly remarked, that "although often in haste, he was never in a hurry." The distinction was a just one. He had always a number of engagements on hand, and was obliged to pass rapidly from one to another. But, amidst them all, he maintained that composure of mind, which enabled him to do each thoroughly and well. This is an important art. Learn it as speedily as you can. To do so completely you must have Mr. Wesley's order, his industry, his habitual composure of mind, and his decision of character. He who allows himself in lounging and laziness at one time, must necessarily be in a hurry at another. And he who has not the strictest order in his affairs, must either be half his time distracted with hurry, or leave one half of his duty undone.

11. Never permit yourself to be concerned about popularity. Never inquire, nor be anxious to hear what is said of you. Popularity seldom fails to fly from him who inordinately seeks it; and is never so likely to be attained as by him who gives himself no concern about it. You have reason to be thankful that your lot is cast in a country in which we have no religious establishment, for the support of ministers independently, or in spite of public opinion. But

while this is a great blessing, it becomes, indirectly, a source of frequent and strong temptation. The temptation is that of deferring more to public sentiment, to popular praise and censure, than we ought. Be habitually on your guard against this temptation. Your business is to guide public opinion, not to let it guide you. Never let your course be prescribed by a previous calculation whom you shall please, and whom displease. Manifest no desire to hear either the praise or the blame which may be expressed concerning you. On the one hand, if the language of praise be addressed or reported to you, be not elated by it; for, in nine cases out of ten, there is much insincerity, or much injudiciousness and folly mingled with it. On the other hand, if you become the object of censure, let it neither depress nor irritate you. If it be just, thankfully profit by it; and if it be unmerited, still carry it to the throne of grace, and inquire whether some good use cannot be made of it. Remember that he who does his duty faithfully, affectionately, and perseveringly, will seldom fail of obtaining as much popularity as he ought to have; and that all that popularity which rests upon any other basis is unworthy of being either sought or prized.

12. When you become the object of ill-natured attacks, be not ready to take any public notice of them. That extreme sensibility to censure, which prompts public men, and especially ministers, to repel by a public reply the smallest assault which is made upon them, ought by no means to be cherished. Such replies, in a great majority of cases, rather give importance to the assailant than real protection or honour to the assaulted. Slander, in a multitude of cases,

cannot be killed; but, according to the old proverb, when let alone it will soon die of itself. Seldom undertake, therefore, to defend yourself against rude or malignant attacks. Never do it in haste or without consultation. In most cases such attacks will be harmless, unless you make them otherwise. Very rarely has any man been "written down" but by himself.

13. Be cautious and sparing in assigning public reasons for your conduct. Try to ascertain, in every case, what your duty is, and endeavour to perform it; but having done so, leave it, for the most part, to speak for itself. Undertaking to satisfy the public by assigning reasons for what we do, is often only presenting a broader front for ill-nature or malignity to strike at. As long as people only guess at your motives or reasons, their censure may be somewhat restrained. But that which you offer by way of explanation or of justification, may give them a handle against you, as little thought of by yourself, as it is gratifying to them. The action itself might have passed very well; some one or more out of half a dozen reasons for it, may possibly give mortal offence. This remark applies, perhaps, to no class of men more strongly than ministers of the gospel, who are usually connected with large bodies of people, all taking an interest, and feeling as if they had a right to express opinions, concerning every thing they say and do. In such circumstances, the shortest and safest course is to act rightly; offering but little by way of explanation; accustoming those around you to confide in your wisdom, and committing the whole to "Him who judgeth righteously."

14. It is a good rule of prudence for a public man

to be as much on his guard against his friends as against his enemies. If I were asked whether public men were more frequently injured by their enemies or their friends, I should certainly, and with confidence, reply, by the latter. Be thankful for friends; love them; be grateful to them; and be always ready with fidelity to serve them. But recollect that you ought to guard quite as vigilantly against their indiscretion, their folly, and their selfishness, as against the malice of your enemies. That general who wishes to succeed in his great military movements, must often conceal his purposes quite as carefully from his own army, as from that of the enemy. So it is, to a great extent, with every public man. Never commit delicate matters to many in number, even of your best friends; and never forget, that you are in quite as much danger from the tongues of those who love you most, as from the hostility of your bitterest opposers.

15. In travelling among strangers, guard against every thing that may savour of a forward or obtrusive spirit. There are two extremes in relation to this point, into one or the other of which public men are prone to fall. Some retreat to the most private recess of the vehicle in which they travel, or the hotel in which they lodge, and wrap themselves up in the silence and impenetrable reserve of one who wishes to escape from all intercourse with his species. Others are forward, talkative, and apparently desirous of making themselves known to every individual with whom they travel, and engaging with prominence in every conversation that occurs. The former is a monkish plan of proceeding, by which an intelligent man loses many pleasures and advantages, and with-

holds from others many a social benefit, which he might confer. But the latter plan of deportment is no less faulty. It is weak, undignified, obtrusive, and, to all delicate minds, extremely revolting. Be invariably polite, and ready to accommodate every fellow-traveller ; but never obtrude your acquaintance or conversation on strangers. Rather wait to be drawn out, than run the risk of being repelled as unduly forward. Those who, in travelling, thrust themselves into every circle, and meddle in every conversation, seldom, I believe, get through a long journey without placing themselves in circumstances, which, if they were persons of delicate sensibility (happily for their feelings this is seldom the case) would lead to many an hour of deep mortification. When designing or unprincipled men meet with such persons in public vehicles or places, they are peculiarly apt to single them out as objects of their artful approaches, under the confidence that they shall find them more accessible than others, and more open to imposition.

16. In travelling in public vehicles, and in putting up at public hotels, be ever ready to perform the appropriate offices of religion, but never force them on those who manifest no desire to receive them. It has often been made a question, whether at public tables, in hotels, or steamboats, it is proper for a clergyman to make a practice of asking a blessing and returning thanks. My opinion is, that, if the company be orderly, and a considerable portion of it decidedly respectful to religion and its institutions, such as a minister has frequently the pleasure of meeting in public conveyances, it is expedient for him, in such

circumstances, to approach the table among the first, and reverently to implore the divine blessing. But if the company be large, disorderly, noisy, and apparently indisposed to such exercises, and there be no weighty portion of it ready to act as pioneers, and open the way for him, he ought not, in my judgment, to force his services upon such an assemblage. If after you become a minister, you are ever thrown into such a situation, withdraw to a quiet end of the table, with the little group who may be like-minded with yourself, if there be any such present, and there, in a low voice, only to be heard by yourselves, and the few who sit next to you, implore the blessing of heaven on the comforts of which you partake. When you fall into such turbulent companies, this course, if my observation has not greatly deceived me, is best adapted to make the desired impression.

I have known some clergymen, who, in travelling, thought it their duty, and laid it down as a rule, at every public house at which they put up, whether crowded with company or not, without exception, to call the family together to morning and evening prayers. That this may often be done, very acceptably, and to great advantage, in the private, or family room, where the keeper of the house and his family are respectful to religion, I am well persuaded. And, therefore, a clergyman in travelling ought ever to be on the watch to perceive, and ready to seize, favourable occasions to introduce the worship of God. But to insist on doing it in the face of manifest aversion, and even in the midst of a noisy and profane throng, as I have sometimes known to be the fact, is, verily, in my opinion, "casting pearls before swine," and adapted to dishonour rather than recommend religion.

17. In travelling, be not ready to entangle yourself with obtrusive or troublesome strangers. In almost every crowded public conveyance that you enter, there are passengers who answer this description; persons who, from vulgarity, from officiousness, or from some sinister motive, will be disposed to fasten themselves upon you, and endeavour to make you subservient to their convenience. They will, perhaps, oppress you with their conversation, pester you with their plans, and even lay a snare for your politeness, which may give much trouble afterwards. Be on your guard against such persons. Give no encouragement to their intimacy or their schemes, especially until you know something about them. The exercise of common civility to them may entangle you to a most inconvenient degree. To this class of travellers females are sometimes found to belong. Travelling without a protector, they may feel desirous of engaging a clergyman to act the part of one; whom, though a stranger to them, they consider as furnishing, in his profession, a pledge of fidelity and benevolence. Often have I known females travelling in these circumstances, impose themselves on clergymen travelling in the same direction, and form an incumbrance and impediment of the most serious kind. I have known ministers, young and old, on journeys for their health, really oppressed, and their movements most unhappily and injuriously trammelled, by these self-created charges. Guard against every such imposition. If you do not, you will never be without incumbrance. In travelling, be polite, accommodating and benevolent

to every body, especially to females, and, above all, to unprotected females of decent appearance and character. But do not allow them, in ordinary cases, to identify themselves with you; to consider you as their humble servant; and to expect you to regulate your motions by their convenience. Perhaps no class of men have so much reason to be on their guard against this species of imposition as ministers of the gospel.

18. In travelling, guard against giving unnecessary trouble, and making unnecessary complaints. I have often observed clergymen and theological students to act indiscreetly in this respect. They have given so much trouble, and addressed themselves so offensively to stage-drivers, boatmen, innkeepers, and servants at public houses, as really to be regarded, after a while, as a nuisance wherever they appeared. Guard against this mistake. Speak to persons in such humble stations mildly but respectfully. Be sparing in your demands on their time and services; and when they are civil to you, manifest a thankful spirit. Be not ready to complain when your accommodations are not such as could be wished, and even when they are shamefully bad. What good will your complaints do? You are always completely in the power of those persons in whose vehicles you travel, or in whose houses you put up; and, in most cases, loud complaints will only make the matter worse. Besides, ministers ought to exhibit, every where, a patient spirit, and contentment with such things as they may chance to have. Be easily satisfied, backward to complain, and respectful to every body; and the impression made on the minds

of all you fall in with, will operate more strongly in your favour than you can easily imagine.

19. Whenever you travel out of your own immediate neighbourhood, be careful to seek and treasure up all the information which you may have an opportunity of gaining. It is wonderful to observe under what a lethargy of mind many intelligent men labour, as to this point, in their most interesting excursions. They travel, perhaps, hundreds of miles through the finest regions of country, without making a single inquiry, or treasuring up a single fact, adapted to solid use afterwards.

This is a fault, really as criminal as it is disreputable. I advise you to consider every journey that you take as "a price put into your hands for getting wisdom." Try to return from every excursion laden with knowledge, concerning the agricultural, the commercial, and the manufacturing state of the districts through which you pass; their various internal improvements, their literary, moral, and religious condition; the numbers, prospects, wants, &c., of the different ecclesiastical denominations; and particularly any institutions or practices which may be worthy of imitation. In travelling, always keep a diary. If it be as minute in recording what you see, as well as what you do, and as rich as it ought to be, it may be to you a document of great value as long as you live.

20. Learn the happy art of turning every thing into the channel of religion, and making every thing subservient to it. You remember that Dr. Johnson, in his life of Dr. Watts, remarks, that "whatever he took in his hand, was, by his incessant solicitude for souls, converted to theology." This is, indeed, exalted

praise for a minister of the gospel. May you be enabled to merit the same eulogium! If you should live to be invested with the sacred office, never, for a moment, lose sight of that office nor the duties which it infers. Let all your reading, conversation, plans, journeys and recreations, point directly to the advancement of the Redeemer's kingdom, and the temporal and eternal welfare of men, as their grand centre. Whatever others may do, consider yourself as a man consecrated to the great work of doing good, to your latest breath. To this let every pursuit and acquirement be subservient; to this make every thing bend. Wherever you sojourn or reside, be ever on the watch for opportunities of promoting the moral and spiritual benefit of yourself and others. Recollect that you have but one object to pursue,—the extending and building up that "kingdom which is not meat and drink, but righteousness and peace, and joy in the Holy Ghost." Let the last words, emphatically repeated, of the old English prelate,—PRO ECCLESIA DEI—PRO ECCLESIA DEI—be visibly inscribed upon every thing you possess and do. This is the real art of "turning every thing to gold," in the best sense; the art of being, in the highest degree that this world admits, useful and happy.

And now, my dear young friend, I must bring to a close this collection of counsels; which I fear my desire to omit nothing important has led me too much to extend. A wish, also, that nothing might escape your notice, has led me to present the same thought more than once in different connections. For this I make no apology. The truth is, there is so intimate a relation between different parts of truth and duty;

they so run into one another, that occasional repetition is unavoidable. Nor is it, for various reasons, undesirable. The impression is thereby reiterated, and perhaps deepened.

In reviewing the various details to which your attention has been called, I trust you will often be ready to exclaim—"Who is sufficient for these things?" Who can hope, in the diversified situations and duties of a minister of the gospel, in public and private, to avoid the numberless faults to which he is exposed on every side, and to exhibit in regard to all the points which have been specified, a blameless example?—I answer, truly no one who is not favoured with that divine wisdom and aid, which are promised to those who unceasingly ask for them. The sentiments, therefore, which I should wish to see reigning in your mind in reference to this whole subject, are those which recognize your own weakness, the number and power of the temptations which surround you; the extreme arduousness of the task of doing well; your need of continual help; and the obligation which you are under to "watch and pray," that you may be enabled, in any tolerable degree, to observe the rules enjoined.

But, while I wish these sentiments to be deeply impressed on your mind, I am, at the same time, persuaded that the substance of all that I have recommended may be considered, with that divine aid which is promised to all who faithfully seek it, as fairly within the reach of every candidate for the holy ministry, who has decent talents, and genuine piety. Do not, therefore, by any means imagine, that the manners and habits which I have described, are such as very few, and those only who have special endowments and advantages, can attain. There is not a student in our Institution who might not make the attainment, if he had the piety and the perseverance to use the proper means for the purpose. In this opinion, I am happy in being fortified by the venerable President of our Board of Directors,* with whose declaration, delivered to a body of your predecessors in the seminary, I shall take my leave of you.

"In this matter we are under no necessity of contemplating an impossibility.—I maintain that there is a point in good manners, which every theological student, without exception, may and ought to reach; and which whoever reaches, will be acceptable and agreeable to persons of every rank and condition in life. The attainment requires little more in order to make it, than the meekness, and gentleness, and benevolence, and courtesy, which the gospel itself explicitly recommends and enjoins; and a failure in which must, of course, be reckoned a real defect in Christian character. The man who has reached the point I have in view, is as free from all that boorish roughness, all that reserved haughtiness or sullenness, all that clownish rudeness, and all those disgusting habits and actions, which are so generally and justly offensive, as the courtier himself. This man is neither forward nor sheepishly bashful; he is self-possessed, but modest and retiring; he is kind and civil; he is social and pleasant; he is desirous to please, and willing to be pleased; he is respectful to age and station; he is never intrusive or officious; he is on all occasions accommodating and ready to do

* Rev. Dr. Green.

every good office in his power; and he never arrogates precedency of rank, nor demands an undue attention to himself. Now I affirm, that every minister of the gospel, and every theological student, may possess this character; and that, if he possess it, he will be offensive to no one in point of manners. Aim at the attainment which I have here described: aim at it constantly: consider it as a Christian duty to do so. It is, in the strictest sense, a Christian duty; for believe me, your usefulness, your ability to do good, will greatly depend on your visible demeanour."

That you, my dear sir, may have grace given you to attain this character, and thus to adorn the sacred office, and become an eminent blessing to the church of God, is the unfeigned prayer of

Your sincere friend,

SAMUEL MILLER.

PRINCETON, April 10, 1827.

www.ingramcontent.com/pod-product-compliance
Lightning Source LLC
LaVergne TN
LVHW020123110826
845151LV00001B/255

* 9 7 8 1 4 2 5 5 4 0 9 4 4 *